FIRE, PESTILENCE, AND DEATH: ST. LOUIS 1849

By Christopher Alan Gordon

Missouri Historical Society Press

St. Louis

Distributed by University of Chicago Press

Library of Congress Cataloging-in-Publication Data
Names: Gordon, Christopher Alan, 1967- author.
Title: Fire, pestilence, and death : St. Louis, 1849 / by Christopher Alan
    Gordon.
Description: St. Louis : Missouri History Museum Press, 2018. | Includes
    bibliographical references and index.
Identifiers: LCCN 2017044607 | ISBN 9781883982935 (pbk. : alk. paper)
Subjects: LCSH: Saint Louis (Mo.)--History--19th century. | Saint Louis
    (Mo.)--Social conditions--19th century.
Classification: LCC F474.S257 G67 2018 | DDC 977.8/66--dc23
LC record available at https://lccn.loc.gov/2017044607

Cover design: Wade Howell
Text design: Lauren Mitchell

Printed and bound in the United States by Integrated Books
International
Distributed by University of Chicago Press

TABLE OF CONTENTS

Introduction   5

Chapter One: Fearful Visitation   12

Chapter Two: '49ers Coming Through!   68

Chapter Three: Great Conflagration   88

Chapter Four: Where Were the Watchmen?   126

Chapter Five: No Rights and Few Freedoms   152

Chapter Six: The Strange Case of Nathaniel Childs Jr.   192

Chapter Seven: The Montesquiou Brothers Murders   222

Chapter Eight: The Lasting Legacies of 1849   248

Acknowledgments   252

Notes   254

Bibliography   272

Index   276

About the Author   280

INTRODUCTION

Although St. Louis has faced a multitude of challenges and disasters in the years since 1849—division spurred by the Civil War, devastating heat waves, the Great Cyclone of 1896, and a variety of floods—no local tragedies receive as much attention in the reminiscences, recollections, and histories of the city's past residents as those of 1849.[1]

Even as the dramatic events of that fateful year were unfolding around them, the citizens of St. Louis seemed to realize that what they were enduring was destined to become embedded in the city's collective memory. Judge James B. Colt noted as much in a statement to a grand jury in July of that year: "The summer of '49, so full of every thing calculated to dishearten the most courageous, will long be remembered by the citizens of St. Louis. . . . We shall rise above it, phoenix-like; nevertheless we cannot forget. It will afford the darkest and brightest page in the history of our city."[2]

Colt wasn't alone in believing that through the daily miseries they suffered, St. Louisans would ultimately emerge stronger and more prosperous when their ordeal was finished. This belief resonates through the surviving accounts of many witnesses, and considering what the city experienced during that tumultuous year, they must be commended for never letting go of a sense of optimism.

Certainly when a population collectively experiences the same trials and tribulations, a rich set of stories emerges. This book seeks to tell those stories through the voices of the people who lived them so that we can gain a more meaningful sense of place and time, and a greater respect for the daily challenges our ancestors faced.

Thankfully, within the collections of the Missouri Historical Society and other repositories, journals, diaries, letters, court records, newspaper accounts, and reminiscences have been preserved for us to examine and contemplate. Only by reading the words of the eyewitnesses and reliving their emotions can one get a true sense of the crises of the day. These men and women seemed to possess an inner strength and an ability to rebound from tremendous personal and collective stress, characteristics that can't be viewed without some degree of awe. It makes one question how well modern society, with all its comforts, might endure similar hardships. Conversely, one can't help but feel grateful—and relieved—that we've made so much progress in a mere 170 years.

Of course, that progress was as much a part of the problem as it was a part of the solution in 1849. To live back then was to be swept up in a society undergoing incredible change. St. Louis may have sat on the edge of the American frontier, but it wasn't isolated from the transitions occurring throughout the country and the world. If anything, St. Louis experienced them to a greater degree, because the opening of the West drew so many different groups to the city, each with its own set of aims and expectations.

One of the primary reasons why St. Louis experienced the level of crisis and shock that it did in 1849 was because it was ill prepared to deal with the westward-bound settlers, ambitious East Coast merchants, opportunists of all stripes, and thousands of immigrants who'd set their sights on St. Louis as either a home or a launching-off point. City authorities and the basic infrastructure in place more closely resembled what one would expect from a small frontier town than a functioning urban center.

Despite this, the incoming steamboats provided a nearly steady flow of new arrivals each week. Between 1835 and 1840 the city's population practically doubled, growing from 8,300 to 16,400. Within the next five years it had just about doubled again. By 1849, St. Louis was home to 77,800 individuals. The town's old footprint, which essentially encompassed the area on which the Gateway Arch stands today, was no longer adequate to contain the masses. In 1841 the Missouri General Assembly allowed the city to expand its limits from a mere three-quarters of a mile to 4.78 miles. The old common fields of the early French colonial days disappeared, replaced by streets, row houses, businesses, and factories.[3]

All the growth was a good sign for a city that had managed to successfully transition itself from the dying fur trade to the developing economy of manufacturing and merchandising. St. Louis had been founded as a trading post to collect the much-demanded furs of North America's wild creatures, which were all the rage in Europe, but tastes

Julius Hutawa created this map of the growing city of St. Louis in 1846. Back then the city was bordered by the Mississippi River to the east, Dock Street to the north, the U.S. Arsenal to the south, and the present-day Union Station area to the west. Map by Julius Hutawa, 1846. Missouri Historical Society Collections.

in fashion changed, important fur-bearing animal populations became depleted, and trade with Native American peoples grew less important to the emerging industrial nation. Yet St. Louis still had an advantage: Situated at the crossroads of the continent, it truly was the Gateway to the West. Here the Mississippi and Ohio rivers channeled people and merchandise from the East Coast toward St. Louis, where they were redirected westward either by the great flowing highway known as the Missouri River or by overland routes such as the Santa Fe Trail.

Throughout the 1830s and 1840s, businessmen arrived in St. Louis, eager to take advantage of its prime location. New industry emerged, and goods were produced in the city itself instead of being shipped from points back east. Local resources such as good-quality clay deposits, iron ore, and oak timber made the city synonymous with bricks, ironware, stoves, and wagons. Likewise, the city became a center of information as multiple newspapers—printed in both English and German and appealing to different political, religious, and trade interests—sprang up to satisfy a society eager to know what was happening at home and beyond the horizon.

Culturally the city was changing too. St. Louis's original inhabitants had been Frenchmen who journeyed down from Canada and up from New Orleans to dominate the fur trade. They were later joined by Kentuckians and Virginians seeking new land for farming and cultivation. These groups, the Creoles and the Southerners, had lived side by side for several generations. They shared some commonalities, such as a steadfast belief in the principles of personal independence, rural perspectives on life and politics, and the acceptance of slavery. But by the 1830s these were no longer the only interests in town. Northeasterners had begun to arrive in the city as the steamboat economy took hold, followed by Irish and German immigrants. These groups brought their own perspectives, which sometimes challenged the locals' long-held beliefs. For example, St. Louis's Protestants had lived alongside their Catholic Creole counterparts for generations, but with the arrival of thousands of Irish Catholic immigrants, they were becoming vastly outnumbered. Old-stock Kentuckians, such as Dr. Joseph Nash McDowell, reviled the Roman Catholics, declaring that they were disloyal Americans and puppets of the Pope.

Likewise, the arrival of significant numbers of Northerners and Germans challenged firmly held beliefs regarding the institution of slavery. Connecticut Yankees such as Giles Franklin Filley, who established Excelsior Stove Works in St. Louis in 1849, were disgusted by the notion of slavery—but not because of the immorality of owning human property or the inhumanity of enslaving Africans. They hated the idea that, through the use of free slave labor, slave owners were taking jobs from hardworking white laborers and farmers and accumulating great amounts of wealth in the process. The arriving German immigrants shared the same beliefs, although their opposition to slavery was grounded in the political struggles disrupting European society at the time, namely issues of class and wealth redistribution and attempts to replace long-established monarchies with more democratic systems of government.

These diametrically opposed beliefs naturally led to tension. Fortunately, most fights took the form of fiery speeches, sharply worded letters to newspaper editors, or hotly contested political races. Nevertheless, these tensions did produce a certain degree of distrust and open resentment within the communities, which sometimes spilled over into actual violence. In 1849 mob actions occurred between nativist and immigrant communities, and even within immigrant communities divided by differing religious beliefs. It was all to be expected in a city that was in flux and not yet accustomed to handling diversity.

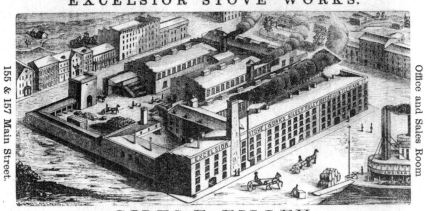

Yankees streamed into St. Louis in the 1840s. One, Giles Filley, founded Excelsior Stove Works in 1849. Years later Filley's company was one of the country's most successful manufacturers of cast-iron stoves. Engraving, maker, and date unknown. Missouri Historical Society Collections.

Adding to the pressures of the internal forces at work within St. Louis were the external forces that brought both opportunities and problems. In the late 1840s, America was literally pushing the boundaries of the country with its sights on controlling the better part of the interior of the North American continent. Attempts to bring Canada into the Union had been unsuccessful, but Mexico was still within grasp. In 1848 the Mexican War concluded with the United States conquering its neighbor to the south and taking California, Texas, Nevada, New Mexico, and parts of Arizona and Colorado as its permanent possessions. Much of this war had been staged from nearby Jefferson Barracks, the nation's largest military installation and home to the infantry, cavalry, and artillery companies that marched westward along the Santa Fe Trail and steamed southward by boat to the Gulf of Mexico or down the Red River to Texas. Ultimately the fight against Mexico had lasting implications for St. Louis, both good and bad.

Additional territory gave promise to those who saw chances for expanding the city's economic empire. This was a likely result given that most trade flowed through St. Louis, but it came with a price. In the years following the war, crime increased significantly. Violent assaults, robberies, and murder, as well as social ills such as alcoholism and prostitution, became commonplace problems for which the authorities had little to no ability to keep in check. Change was happening faster than the city could keep up with, both in terms of municipal structure and the law.

The outcome of the Mexican War also brought political turmoil to St. Louis. The controversy over the westward expansion of slavery aggravated sectional politics in Missouri. Thomas Hart Benton had represented the state in the U.S. Senate ever since it had been admitted to the Union. Now differing opinions over the necessity of spreading slavery into new territories divided citizens and politicians alike, threatening to end Benton's career. Divisions over the concept of slavery as a whole deepened as well. Caught in the middle were the people most directly affected by it all: St. Louis's African American residents, both enslaved and free. A combination of the fear of slave reprisals and resentment at what was seen as meddling by abolitionists led proslavery elements in Missouri to crack down on the state's African American population. However, the growing abolitionist movement must have also given hope to some blacks who longed for the end of slavery in America. In St. Louis, free persons of color and the enslaved could see it all play out.

A final product of the war that greatly influenced St. Louis's development was an event that occurred far to the west in the newly acquired territory. In January 1848 two men who worked for Swiss immigrant and former St. Louisan John Sutter found gold on Sutter's California property. As news of the discovery spread, gold fever swept the world. Troops of gold seekers, mostly single young men, dropped everything and made plans to go west. Just like the throngs of families heading westward to the Oregon Country, these bands of men flowed through St. Louis. They arrived by the hundreds, sometimes passing through immediately, sometimes staying to find work until they could gather enough money to purchase supplies or save up for the continued journey overland. The phenomenon of gold fever created a spectacle never again seen in the city.

Introduction

Against this backdrop, St. Louis faced a unique set of challenges as the calendar rolled over from 1848 to 1849. Residents relied on every bit of strength they had as the year progressed. It was a trial by fire and pestilence, and those who survived had amazing stories to tell.

CHAPTER ONE: FEARFUL VISITATION

Meditation of the Sexton
My trade is brisk and gay
What profits I shall win!
For I'm digging gold the livelong day,
As I take the coffins in.
Delve and shovel, and fling
From morn til midnight's gloom
Death's angels all are on the wing
'Tis the triumph of the tomb!
And joyously I'll work and sing
For the cry is—"still they come!"
—Richard S. Elliot, St. Louis, 1849

n June 1849, St. Charles County resident R. B. Frayser received a letter from his friend and political ally, Edward Bates. Bates, a prominent St. Louis attorney and rising political figure, concluded his letter by mentioning this bit of family news: "I forget whether or not I mentioned in any former letter the death of Peter, my mother's freed-man. He came to our house last Saturday night a little unwell, and died of cholera before sunrise."[1]

At first glance, Bates's words seem rather matter of fact and lacking in sentiment, but when you consider that St. Louis was in the midst of the worst cholera epidemic the city would ever endure, Bates's words seem much more profound. It's almost as if they're calling attention to the fact that life is fragile—you may be here one instant, then gone the next. Indeed, this was the reality of life in St. Louis in 1849, when nearly 10 percent of the city's population perished from cholera. Death took people with minimal warning and often within hours. In a time when there was little to no understanding of the causes of disease and its transmission, the city could only pray for relief and bury its dead.

The tragedy of Peter's fate was unfortunately one that many families would come to share during the long months of the cholera epidemic. Officially, 4,547 men, women, and children succumbed to the disease, but most historians agree that the actual number is probably much higher. From the moment people first became aware of cholera within the city, in late 1848, until its final departure the following autumn, St. Louis was seized with fear. Residents watched endless processions of funeral wagons pass through the streets as church bells tolled, desperately hoping that they or their loved ones wouldn't be the wagon's next occupants.

It wasn't until the 1850s that physicians and scientists began to slowly chip away at the mysteries of contagious diseases. For centuries when epidemics such as cholera or the bubonic plague struck, people could only speculate as to their causes. The most common belief held by the medical community since the time of the ancient Greeks was that communicable diseases were caused by *miasma*, or bad air. Foul odors drifting off of rotting vegetation or piles of refuse were most often identified as the source of disease—medical science had yet to connect the concept of germs with contagion. But in 1855, Dr. John Snow, a London physician who had practiced medicine during two of the world's most devastating cholera pandemics, published a report on the findings of his cholera investigations. That paper had a profound effect on the understanding of how cholera is transmitted.

Snow had been a longtime critic of the miasma theory. His observations in several neighborhoods of London, a city that had lost tens of thousands of residents to cholera, curiously appeared to show that those individuals who took their water from sources near known deposits of human waste and sewage were more likely to contract cholera. In 1849, Snow published *On the Mode of Communication of Cholera*, in which he first proposed a link between contaminated water and the disease. He stated, though could not prove, that "the views here explained opened up to consideration a most important way in which the cholera may be widely disseminated, viz., by the emptying of sewers into the drinking water of the community."

As a second cholera epidemic swept London in the early 1850s, Snow continued his observations. This time he plotted cases of cholera on a map as they appeared in London's SoHo district and discovered that most of the victims had received their water from a single community pump. When Snow asked that the pump's handle be removed, thereby eliminating it as a water source, cholera cases began to diminish. Snow theorized that the pump's water supply was taken from a section of the Thames River that was particularly contaminated by raw sewage. He therefore concluded that fecal contamination, not bad air, was the source of cholera. Further weight was added to Snow's theory later on when excavations of the pump site revealed that it lay only three feet from an old privy.[2]

Although Snow had made a major discovery, many clung to old beliefs and questioned the role of water in the transmission of diseases. The great nineteenth-century debate that divided the medical community was the question of contagionism versus anticontagionism—in other words, whether diseases were communicable. It wasn't until eminent German physician Dr. Robert Koch was able to isolate the bacteria *Vibrio cholerae* by taking samples from the intestines of deceased cholera victims that the role of bacterial infection gained much-needed proof and supporters of contagionism won a major victory. Koch's finding eventually eliminated doubt within the medical field about the cause of cholera and contributed to an acceptance of what modern society has long known—that bacteria cause various diseases.[3]

But in 1849, the causes and nature of cholera were still a matter of speculation.

Cholera Strikes St. Louis for the First Time

For as long as humans have existed, plagues and epidemics have punctuated our historical landscape. The Black Death changed the entire course of western civilization during the fourteenth century, and serious outbreaks of smallpox meander in and out of the timelines of many countries. Yet few maladies have affected humanity as widely as cholera.

The disease is thought to have emerged on the Indian subcontinent thousands of years ago and spread east and west as traders and explorers ventured out. Accounts written by the ancient Greeks describe symptoms that largely match those suffered by cholera victims; the texts of the ancient Chinese and medieval European chroniclers do too. As connections between civilizations strengthened across the globe, cholera seems to have followed. By the early nineteenth century, its deadly presence was felt on every continent. From the Arctic Circle to the equatorial tropics and beyond, millions succumbed to a disease that had no visible cause and seemingly no cure. To quote the Bible's Book of Psalms, cholera was truly "the pestilence that walketh in darkness."

Medical science has recognized six cholera pandemics since 1817, with the most deadly occurring between 1829 and 1879. It was during the second of these pandemics that cholera first arrived in the heart of the North American continent. St. Louis may have lain on the edge of civilization in the first decades of the nineteenth century, but the constant crossings of humans across the Mississippi River made the arrival of cholera in the city inevitable. The 1849 epidemic is by far the most well-known occurrence of the disease in the city, but St. Louis's first encounter with cholera actually occurred seventeen years earlier, in the autumn of 1832.

In the summer of 1832, St. Louisans began to hear stories about the devastating effects of cholera on the populations of New York and other port cities on the East Coast. Immigrant ships from Ireland are generally thought to have brought the disease to Canada, where it crept slowly southward across the continent. Rumors soon began to circulate about the presence of cholera in the Mississippi River valley. On September 4 the concerned editors of the *Daily Missouri Republican* noted that publications in other American cities were printing news of numerous cholera deaths in St. Louis. They assured their readers that the stories were completely baseless because not a single case had been reported. The editors promised that should the disease arrive, they wouldn't fail to print an announcement of its presence. In the meantime, they confidently declared that "the city may be visited with perfect safety."[4]

Seven days later the same editors once again purported St. Louis's sound health, but they chided officials for the city's filthy conditions: "On every side, our senses are saluted with the most offensive odours, which are mainly indebted to an inactive and inefficient police. . . . If the Corporation have power to change this state of things, they should speedily be invested with it. . . . If we do escape the visitation of the Pestilence, it may be attributed entirely to the natural salubrity of the town, and not to the measures of the authorities."

Although the lion's share of the editors' disgust was clearly pointed at the town fathers for their lack of diligence in keeping the streets tidy, the public wasn't spared its share of the blame. The *Republican*'s editors went on to write, "We have also remarked in most all of our citizens a shameful inattention to every thing like cleanliness."[5]

Cleanliness was becoming a serious issue as the city's population expanded. Adventurous settlers arriving from the East and a growing number of immigrants were starting to call St. Louis home. The growth of the river trade and the town's position as a center of commerce were just beginning to build momentum. St. Louis was the largest urban center on the American frontier in 1832, but it still remained small by most standards, with around 8,300 residents. Much of the town lacked any serious infrastructure, and city services were nearly nonexistent because city officials didn't have a sound tax base from which they could secure the necessary funds. This lack of adequate city services and an ever-growing number of people inhabiting a relatively small area of land created a suitable environment for contagious disease.

The same issue of the *Republican* that chided the city included a smaller article noting that a suspected case of cholera was being treated at Jefferson Barracks, a military post just south of town. A soldier had arrived at the base from Rock Island, Illinois, displaying symptoms of the disease. Unease spread as word of his condition leaked out into the community, but the editors expressed that this was "much unnecessary excitement" because it was an isolated case.[6]

Yet as September progressed, so did the spread of cholera through St. Louis. Physicians found that they faced an all-out public health emergency like none the city had seen before. Newspapers urged citizens to stay calm and remain home, but as the disease spread, St. Louisans' level of anxiety grew to near-panic proportions. Writing to her cousin Dr. Dennis Delany in Maryland, city resident Ann Biddle summarized the feelings of many by noting, "I intended to written to you long since—but my thoughts were so completely engrossed with that idea of that deadly plague that I could not attend to anything else."[7]

The swift nature of the disease upon a population ignorant of its causes created a sense of looming doom. Biddle noted that so many were falling victim as the weeks passed that it was estimated that at least half the town would perish before the epidemic ended. This, of course, was a highly inflated perception of the reality of the situation. Many were dying, but the numbers never reached such a critical level. Fear was far more widespread than cholera. However, in the final days of October, just when the disease seemed out of control, it suddenly subsided and all but disappeared. On November 13 the *Republican* declared that the cholera epidemic had run its course and "no apprehensions need be entertained of any serious return of the pestilence."[8]

The winter passed with no alarm, but in May 1833 the pestilence did indeed return. Towns up and down the Mississippi River from St. Louis were once again suffering as the weeks of summer passed. William Carr Lane, a physician and former mayor of St. Louis, noted that about a dozen cases a week were reported in the city over the course of the summer. Particularly hard hit were the single young men who worked on the city's levee and the steamboat workers who plied the river on the boats, but they certainly weren't the only victims. The disease struck people from all walks of life. The *Republican*'s editors pointed out that "cholera proves itself, in its progress every where, to have no respect for persons or situations. It is a 'genuine Republican' disease, and attacks everybody." At no time was this more apparent than when news arrived from Ste. Genevieve that Alexander Buckner, one of the state's U.S. senators, had fallen to the disease in that city.[9]

In August cholera again began to disappear, much to everyone's relief. There are no reliable records to tell us exactly how many people were lost during the 1832–1833 outbreak, however, from existing historical sources, we can surmise that approximately 140 succumbed to the disease in the autumn of 1832. Based on William Carr Lane's estimates, the number of deaths in 1833 was in the range of 150 to 200. Some claim the numbers were as high as 300, but the relatively small size of St. Louis's population and the fact that its residents weren't as tightly packed as their counterparts in urban centers such as New York or Philadelphia kept the numbers low. Weather conditions may also have been a factor in confining the disease. Contemporary accounts mention that 1833 was a dry year with little or no extended rainfall during the summer. This dry weather may have slowed the transmission of the water-based contagion.[10]

Across the globe, cholera also began to disappear, bringing an end to the second pandemic. Normalcy reigned supreme for more than a decade—until reports of cholera's return began to surface in 1848. Europe was on alert as cases became known in many of the continent's port cities, but the disease wasn't to remain confined. As thousands of Europeans boarded ships bound for North America in hopes of leaving behind political unrest in their home countries, cholera once again hitched a ride.

A Hero Is Called Back into Battle

On New Year's Day 1849, the people of St. Louis awoke to a mild winter morning with bright sun melting the snow that had blanketed the city since Christmas. At his residence on Locust Street, Dr. Hardage Lane received his copy of the daily newspaper. Its tightly packed columns spoke of the tribulations of the '49ers heading to California (described in chapter 2) and of the latest reports received from military expeditions on the plains. A small announcement noted that Mayor Krum's home would be open to all who wished to come by. (It was a longtime tradition in St. Louis for the city's inhabitants to use the holiday to visit friends and express best wishes for the year ahead.) But Lane also read something that surely caused him unease and brought back a rush of memories: The scourge of cholera was terrorizing New Orleans, which meant the dreaded disease had returned to North America.

Seventeen years earlier, Lane had been a tireless warrior against the ravaging menace of cholera in St. Louis. His actions had earned him the respect of the community and made him a leader among his medical comrades. Although he never achieved the lasting notoriety of his politically successful cousin, William Carr Lane, he nevertheless did well for himself. After graduating from the University of Pennsylvania's medical program in 1819, he returned to Missouri; married Anne Rebecca Carroll, descendant of a distinguished family from the Chesapeake region of Maryland; and established a private medical practice in St. Louis. He also became a land speculator, purchasing and developing property in both St. Louis and Illinois.[11]

In 1832, Lane's skills as a physician were put to the test. As it became clear that cholera was taking the town's citizens, he fought to ebb the tide of the disease. He even developed his own cure based on personal observations and the accepted practices of the day—and it worked. Lane successfully treated members of St. Louis's prominent Mullanphy and Biddle families who had displayed cholera symptoms. He so impressed Ann Biddle with his drive and stamina in the face of the pestilence that she revered him as the real hero of the epidemic. After cholera had subsided in St. Louis, she wrote to her cousin, a physician in Maryland, gushing over Lane's work: "Dr. Hardage Lane has earned great praise for his great exertions during the prevalence of the cholera. He was remarkably successful in the treatment & he attended upwards of two hundred in two weeks 4 days of which he was confined at home with the disease."[12]

Lane's star continued to rise. When Saint Louis University established its medical college, he was appointed to the teaching faculty. He later opened a practice with a partner, Dr. Edmund McCabe, on Seventeenth Street and bought a home on Fifth Street, near Locust. Then in 1844, things took a turn for the worse when his beloved wife was diagnosed with an incurable disease. The historical record doesn't specify what she suffered from, but based on the language of the day it was probably either cancer or tuberculosis.[13]

The couple's oldest child, Elizabeth, was nearing adulthood at the time, but their son Hardage Jr. was only four years old. Anne suffered through two years of sickness before dying in the summer of 1846. In a time when newspapers reserved detailed obituaries for only the most prominent of citizens, the *Republican*'s editors published a heartfelt piece that extolled Anne's virtues and praised her strength: "More than heroic—the Christian fortitude with which, for more than two years, she sustained the ravages of a cruel disease—the cheerful resignation with which she learned, at an early period, its fatal character—the unshaken courage with which, though deprived of hope from human skill, she met the approach of the King of Terrors."[14]

Now in 1849, at the age of sixty and a widower, Dr. Hardage Lane was once again called upon to assist in the fight against cholera. Little knowledge had been gained in the years since the last epidemic, so the medical community was still very much at the mercy of trial and error. Lane, however, did hold the advantage of experience that many of his fellow physicians did not.

The Outbreak Begins

As the year 1848 drew to a close, newspapers were filled with alarming reports of cholera, noting the deaths of scores of passengers aboard steamboats headed up the Mississippi River from New Orleans. Near the end of December 1848, one victim was said to have died only minutes before the steamboat docked at the St. Louis levee. It was apparent from the daily thread of newspaper stories that public anxiety was building. The question in everyone's mind was not *if* but *when* the first local victim would fall—the answer was soon to come.

Around four o'clock in the afternoon on January 5, 1849, a "stout, healthy, laboring man" suffering from diarrhea, vomiting, and cramps entered St. Louis Hospital. Dr. William McPheeters was called to treat him. The man told McPheeters that he had eaten a hearty dinner of sauerkraut before falling into his present condition. Now he showed all the signs of a fully manifested case of cholera. He was overtaken with frequent vomiting and uncontrollable diarrhea until he reached the point where his stools were completely devoid of substance, a condition known as rice water. Well aware of the fact that the public was highly fearful of the presence of cholera and not wanting to misdiagnose the case, McPheeters summoned several other doctors whom he trusted so they could observe the patient as well. Each agreed that it was "a well-marked case of cholera."[15]

All through the night, the man's condition deteriorated despite treatments "of the most vigorous character," to quote McPheeters. Unfortunately, McPheeters, like all other doctors of the period, didn't understand what was truly happening. As the water drained from the man's body, he began having violent cramps, his heart rate slowed, and his eyes sank into his skull. Eventually his skin turned blue, and his tongue and extremities grew cold with lack of circulation. By 2 a.m. the end had come.

In questioning the patient and his family, McPheeters was told that the man had no contact with anyone who was known to have had cholera. He worked a distance from the river, where most of the steamboat-related cholera cases were understood to have occurred or were expected to occur. How then, wondered McPheeters, did this man contract the disease? The usual suspects of warm weather and bad air were ruled out because it was winter and too cold for cholera. McPheeters could only conclude that the cause of the disease was already present in the patient's system and that what had allowed it to become fully manifested was the sauerkraut he'd eaten for dinner.[16]

Like Hardage Lane, McPheeters was a graduate of the University of Pennsylvania's medical program. He was an experienced physician and served as the professor of clinical medicine and pathological anatomy at Saint Louis University. But as well trained as he was by nineteenth-century standards, he had as much understanding of cholera as the most respected medical practitioners in the world—which was next to nothing. Without a clue about the existence of bacteria, knowledge of how diseases are transmitted, or an understanding of the effects of dehydration, all treatments were essentially futile. Given the extent of medical science at the time, truly only the strongest would survive.[17]

The death of McPheeters's patient doesn't appear to have been immediately reported to the public, perhaps in an attempt to maintain calm. However, McPheeters encountered another certain case two days later. This time, though, the patient, an Irish riverboat worker, recovered.

Over the next few days, the number of cases began to build. By January 11 a small article in the *Republican* quietly proclaimed that seven fatal cases of cholera had been reported in the city, but only two of those cases had originated there. The other cases were steamboat passengers who had disembarked on the levee and died soon afterward. No further details were provided, so it's unclear whether one of the two local cases alluded to was Dr. McPheeters's deceased patient or whether there were already additional patients.

Three days later, the *St. Louis Daily Union* supplied readers with more detailed reports of cholera's presence in the city. An enslaved person belonging to Richmond Curle allegedly had died of the disease, along with another city resident named only as Mr. Fyler. It was now clear that all manner of citizens were at risk.[18]

Steamboat Perils and a Worthwhile Gamble

Even though cholera was not yet a serious problem in St. Louis, businessmen and steamboat operators throughout the Mississippi River valley were already experiencing disruption due to its very presence. In fact, it was affecting operations in the most disturbing ways. Each day passengers and crewmen were dying on voyages, turning deckhands into gravediggers. The banks of the Mississippi were becoming a cemetery as boats stopped to bury their dead whenever or wherever they could. As a result, crewmen began to desert their boats, fearing they would become the next reason for an unscheduled stop.

The seriousness of this problem made headlines in St. Louis when the captain of the steamboat *Constitution* found himself nearly abandoned. At Vicksburg, Mississippi, the *Constitution*'s pilot decided he didn't want to risk contracting cholera either on board the boat or upon arriving in New Orleans. Many of the deckhands shared the pilot's sentiments, so when the boat docked, they all abandoned ship. But the *Constitution* was fully loaded with a valuable cargo that had to reach the Crescent City without delay, or else her captain would be financially ruined. Captain Tyler, like many of his fellow steamboat owners and operators, was a merchant, not a pilot. He most likely had no clue how to navigate his vessel, so he appeared to be left high and dry.

When all seemed consigned to doom, the boat's apprentice pilot, Barton Bowen, confidently approached Captain Tyler with the proposition that he pilot the vessel the rest of the way to New Orleans. With its winding channels, swift currents, frequently shifting sandbars, and other obstacles, the Mississippi River was a challenge even for experienced pilots. Not only was Bowen an apprentice who had a mere six months of experience on the river but he was also just seventeen years old. Captain Tyler was between a rock and a hard place for sure, but he decided trusting Bowen was worth the gamble, given the circumstances.

Two days later the *Constitution* docked safely in New Orleans, with Bowen at the helm. It then returned home with the young St. Louisan still at the wheel. "The *Constitution* came in on Friday," reported the *Daily Union*, "with Barton Bowen as first pilot, a stripling of seventeen years, who brought her through without accident or detention."[19]

Setting the Stage

Although cholera was certainly present, so far the number of deaths was hardly worthy of panic. As a result, the city's newspapers weren't quite sure how to proceed. Feeding panic was irresponsible, but downplaying the seriousness of the matter too much could backfire as well and encourage a general incautious attitude. Editors were pulled in both directions and used the occasion to criticize rival papers.

The *Weekly Reveille* printed a satirical column written under the name Dr. Peter Khaustif, M.D., which sarcastically implied that all the panic was foolish and unnecessary. The column launched a thinly veiled attack on the *Republican* and the city's physicians for spreading fear without real evidence of a crisis: "You must know, friend Reveille, that on the first announcement that the cholera was approaching, I, in common with the rest of the medical fraternity, experienced the most intense delight. The whole profession, sir, myself among the number, has left no means untried to create a panic, and we have been aided, too, by one of the city newspapers, but to no purpose. Now, my dear sir, tell me, are we doomed to disappointment?"[20]

The *Reveille*'s caustic piece was primarily in response to an open letter to the community—printed in its own pages—submitted by Dr. Joseph Nash McDowell, a man known as much for his eccentricities as his understanding of medicine. McDowell had arrived in St. Louis from Cincinnati in 1840 to find a town with great potential as a regional health center. Saint Louis University was just beginning its foray into teaching medicine, but it was alone in the wilderness. The population of the city and the West was growing by leaps and bounds, without a sufficient number of trained physicians to accommodate it. In this, McDowell realized that a medical school could be both beneficial and lucrative. Furthermore, McDowell's sense of competition and bigotry fueled his desire to develop an alternative school of medicine to counter Saint Louis University, an institution he considered an evil papist training ground. Viewing Catholics and immigrants as the greatest threat to the American nation, the ardent Protestant Kentuckian never once masked his sentiments or his intentions.[21]

But for all his faults, McDowell was held in high regard as a physician, and his medical opinions carried a considerable amount of weight. Like Hardage Lane, McDowell had practiced medicine during the 1832–1833 cholera epidemic and understood that St. Louisans' fears were grounded in historical precedents. In his letter to the community, McDowell urged residents to brace themselves for what might lie ahead. Cholera, he stated, was a disease whose origins are found in the hot, wet climates of India. New Orleans, muggy and surrounded by swamps, was naturally disposed to attacks of this kind of disease because it shared so many of the same climatic conditions as India. Using the same logic, McDowell proposed that the hot and humid St. Louis summer would be the perfect environment for a visitation of cholera to become an epidemic. But although he may have seemed like the voice of doom, he sought to ease fears by offering good advice and reassurance.

Based on his own experience, McDowell swore by a treatment, formulated by doctors during the earlier epidemic, that could be administered when patients first exhibited symptoms. Recipes for the cure were offered to the community with the hope that everyone would gather a stock of the necessary ingredients. "The medicine can be obtained in every store, and the poor can get them as well as the rich," wrote McDowell. His advice for anyone confronted by cholera was to "keep cool, have confidence, and send for the family physician."[22]

With the disease now known to be in the city, the weather toyed with residents' emotions. Many feared McDowell's predictions about warm, balmy days, particularly if that weather came early. Sunshine in the first week of January melted the snow and turned the streets into a mire of mud, manure, and puddles. The editor of the *Reveille* described the scene: "Our streets are anything but agreeable for pedestrians, at present. . . . Heavy boots and over shoes are necessary articles of wear for old and young, who desire to preserve health. We expect in a few days to greet those same old streets again, with all their caverns, hollows, sink holes, &c."[23]

But the sun retreated soon afterward, to the relief of many who feared that a mild winter would allow cholera to run rampant. As the *Reveille* noted: "A cold piercing wind is now sweeping through our streets, and over the surface of the river. It may be that we are, in mercy, visited with a continued frost to keep us free from the fatal and dreaded cholera."[24]

Many St. Louisans who felt that the city was generally filthy and unhealthy questioned the state of its streets and its overall cleanliness. Contemporary sources provide plenty of evidence to suggest that their concerns were justified.

The city's streets had a longtime reputation for not meeting the demands of the region's widely contrasting seasonal weather. In summer the muddy thoroughfares of spring gave way to dry stretches when heavy traffic ground the dirt into fine particles. A young lieutenant with the Corps of Engineers who was stationed in the city as part of an 1837 river-improvement project—one Robert E. Lee, of Civil War fame—complained in a letter to his wife, Mary, that you could find yourself "ankle deep" in dust just by walking in the street. He went on to lament the great clouds of dust that were "put in motion by the slightest wind." Some main streets in St. Louis were paved with stone and even included gutters, but most didn't have this luxury. There was also little governmental investment in road maintenance; officials generally preferred to put the cost of repairs on the property owners who fronted the streets.[25]

Besides the dust and dirt, residents had to contend with ever-present mounds of manure. Hundreds of horses, mules, and oxen flooded the streets during the busiest times of day as they traveled to and from the levee. The resulting street traffic could be just as congested as it is now in any modern city, but instead of producing air-clogging exhaust as modern vehicles do, these animals produced gallons of urine and pounds of excrement *daily*, all of which fell into the already muddy streets. And it wasn't just the work animals that contributed. When Reverend Charles Peabody visited St. Louis in 1846, he noted in his journal that "lounging about at the corners of Front St. thick around are scores of swine ready to pounce upon any offal that may be thrown out, or claim as their appropriate property the contents of any unlucky sack of wheat that may have broken open in the hurry of removal." The daily contributions made by pigs, horses, mules, and oxen—along with the refuse often cast into the streets by St. Louis's human residents—must have made for a pungent and sickly soup in times of heavy rain.[26]

Additionally, drainage problems after showers, thunderstorms, or snowmelt were a constant source of irritation for residents. In May

Most streets in 1849 St. Louis were choked with dust in the summer and a muddy quagmire in the spring and winter. Photograph by unknown photographer, 1852. Missouri Historical Society Collections.

1848, Mayor John Krum declared in a message to the city council that improvements to the streets and drainage system could no longer be ignored. He told the gathered council members that "the demand for street improvements is very great" and "in my judgement the time is not far distant when a different method will be adopted for the drainage of the city." A system of sewers to empty the streets of runoff soon began, but constructing such a system was slow business.[27]

Another issue was the fact that St. Louis's multitude of sinkholes and caverns allowed water to accumulate in basements and low areas throughout the city. The largest of these nuisances was a sinkhole near Biddle and Tenth streets. With the hope that it could be used to drain off much of the standing water from the streets, city officials diverted water into the hole, but this only created more problems. Sometimes the water remained for long stretches of time and became just another stagnant pool of sewage and scum. Locals soon came to know the stinking landmark as Kayser's Lake, in honor of Henry Kayser, the city engineer who had developed this failed remedy.[28]

The mystery of the spread of contagious disease may not have been generally understood, but many people did believe that cholera had something to do with unsanitary conditions. So when the first reports of the disease arrived in late 1848, the city council made some effort to appease those who called for St. Louis to clean up its act. It passed an ordinance that allocated $2,000 "for the purpose of effectually cleansing the city, the cellars, sink holes, et cetera" and pledged to employ two physicians to "devise such sanitary measures as to them shall seem proper and necessary for the complete cleansing of the city, in anticipation of the scourge known as the *cholera*."[29]

Yet in the weeks that followed, little was done to carry out the plan. Arguments over governmental spending and general delays kept improvements from progressing at any sufficient speed. Critics, however, bemoaned the lack of action and lashed out. The *Reveille*, for one, declared: "It is really time to make a movement towards the cleansing of our streets and alleys which are in a shocking situation. . . . Three days of warm weather, coming on suddenly would render [the city] unsafe, even if the chance of an epidemic were out of the question. The authorities should certainly give attention to this point, and citizens, generally, should be aware of the importance of leaving nothing to chance."[30]

Despite the outcries, and even after cholera was clearly present, city leaders put minimal effort into reversing unsanitary conditions throughout the winter months. By the time winter cold had receded and spring had arrived, little had changed in terms of cleanup or preparation. In most ways, it was back to business as usual. Residents knew that they would have to endure the usual mired streets and backed-up cellars. They also knew they had to prepare for the other realities of life in a city whose infrastructure and services were still more in line with that of a small village.

As the temperature warmed, it brought to life the vapors emitted from places where residents and business owners stashed their garbage, for lack of any organized public sanitation efforts. Vacant lots and alleys were filled with trash. A force of street inspectors was employed to police the city for sanitation violations, but there were few options for disposal other than finding a convenient dumping ground. In early March one man found himself hauled before the St. Louis Recorder's Court for depositing filth in the street. He was ordered to pay a ten-dollar fine, but cases like this were rare. Overall, city officials appeared to take a rather lackadaisical view of the whole matter.[31]

Residents weren't the only ones looking for a place to dump their refuse; factories were too. Some of the most blatant sources of noxious fumes and rancid waste were the city's tallow factories and slaughterhouses. At the former, great loads of animal fat were boiled and rendered down to produce tallow for candle wax or consumption, and the pungent smell of hot fat filled the streets for blocks. Likewise, gallons of livestock blood, feces, and offal exited from the slaughterhouses.

Numerous artists chose Chouteau's Pond as the subject of their paintings. It was a prominent feature and a favorite recreation site, but in later years it became a dangerous reservoir of industrial waste. The city drained it in 1851 in the wake of the cholera epidemic. Painting by Emile Herzinger, ca. 1859–1876. Missouri Historical Society Collections.

Much of the waste generated by these industries was released into the once-clear waters of Chouteau's Pond, an early man-made lake located just west of the city, near the present site of Union Station. Its pleasantly still waters frequently provided local artists with subject matter for oil paintings and landscape drawings. Since its creation in the late eighteenth century, the pond had provided countless hours of relaxation for fishermen and recreation for local swimmers. On Sundays many newly baptized Christians even washed away their sins under the spreading sycamores and cottonwoods that lined its banks. Chouteau's Pond was a fixture of the community, but with the arrival of new industry, many naturally saw it as a reservoir capable of containing the great quantities of runoff and waste produced by the city's factories. By 1849 the tranquil pond had transformed into a cesspool—and the perfect breeding ground for dysentery, cholera, and other water-borne diseases.[32]

The Disease Spreads and the Public Reacts

From February 1849 through April 1849, the number of cholera cases in St. Louis remained fairly low, but their occurrence was steady. The initial panic seemed to subside, however, given that the disease hadn't overrun the city as originally feared. The newspapers continued to make a point of mentioning that most cholera victims were recent arrivals who had contracted cholera elsewhere. For example, during the last week of March, the *Republican* reported seventy-nine deaths in the city, twenty-four of which were the result of cholera, but they assured readers that "the majority of those whose deaths are reported from cholera arrived in this city but recently from New Orleans, and evidently were affected when they reached this point."[33]

Most residents were likely left unrelieved by such arguments. Just the fact that cholera was in their midst was enough to place them on edge, as exemplified by the story of a local landlord identified only as Lynch, a resident of Battle Row. He was made the target of scorn when, upon learning that one of his tenants was in the throes of the disease, he "seized the sick man and threw him into the street notwithstanding there was a heavy rain falling at the time." The afflicted man was found by two St. Louis City Guard officers who took him to the Sisters of Charity Hospital, where he died the next day. "It does not often fill in our lot to record a more inhuman act than that of which this landlord was guilty," proclaimed the *Daily Union* editor.[34]

As the spring progressed, the weather remained cool and damp. Mentions of weather conditions in diaries and other contemporary sources written during this period show evidence of a wet and unusually cold season in the Midwest. In the areas just west of Independence, Missouri, snowstorms continued on the plains well into April, which delayed the departure of wagon trains heading west. These delays had less to do with the hazards of moving wagons through the snow or enduring icy winds than with the fact that the snow slowed grass growth, denying precious sources of food needed to nourish the oxen, mules, cattle, and horses so critical to a cross-country journey. Although this was a problem in itself, no one realized that the delayed wagon trains would also allow cholera to more easily take hold within the groups of waiting travelers. Just as the ships had carried cholera across the Atlantic, the covered wagons would transport the disease efficiently across the plains and throughout the West.[35]

Back in St. Louis, the Mississippi River was rising as snow from the upper Midwest region slowly melted and made its way down the Missouri River, through the confluence, and onward down the Mississippi. It didn't help that St. Louis was also getting its share of rain: A clerk at Jefferson Barracks recorded in the post's Meteorological Register that it rained eleven days in March. In April heavy storms arrived as warm and cold air battled for dominance. Thunderstorms were frequent in the early weeks of the month, but just like their brethren on the plains, St. Louisans experienced a cold snap in late April that brought snow to the city. Whether the precipitation came down as snow or rain, the end result was the same—the Mississippi River remained high, and the city stayed wet.[36]

In May the rain continued to fall, and the death toll continued to rise. The *St. Louis Daily New Era* even featured a report on the city's health as its top story in the May 15, 1849, edition: "It appears that from Monday morning the 7th to Sunday evening the 13th instant inclusive, there were 273 deaths in the city, 181 of which were from cholera. . . . This morning the Register received from the sextons of all the cemetery's their daily reports, from which it appears there were 36 deaths yesterday, 21 of which were from cholera."[37]

Because measures to fight cholera's presence in the city were weak, if not nonexistent, the public's level of concern quickly climbed toward panic stage once more. As public officials failed to control the spread of the pestilence, some believed the intervention of a higher power was needed. During the 1832 epidemic, mayors and governors had declared public days of fasting and humiliation as a way of appealing to God's mercy; now many felt it was again time to spend days praying for God's assistance.

At the Fourth Street Methodist Church, Reverend J. A. Henning scheduled a religious service for May 17 and joined with other city churches to declare that day one of prayer, fasting, and humiliation. Henning's plan was announced on May 16. However, on the following evening, St. Louisans were praying for relief from a more immediate threat as the Great Fire of 1849 consumed a sizable portion of the city's center. With first a plague and then a fire, many St. Louisans began wondering why their city was subjected to such trials.[38]

The Reverend William Stephen Potts, minister of the Second Presbyterian Church, whose congregation was one of the largest and most prominent in the city, had no doubts as to why St. Louis was suffering—it was divine retribution. On the Sunday following the Great Fire, Potts told his congregation that just as the Israelites had to suffer for their sins against God before entering the Promised Land, so too must St. Louisans be chastised by the Almighty for their wicked ways. Others echoed Potts's pronouncements. "All things considered the City is a bad location for one who is aiming to get to Heaven," wrote I. H. Headlee to a family member in out-state Missouri soon after Potts's sermon. "Truly if the 'wicked are turned into Hell' at least St. Louis will be strongly represented there."[39]

Potts and concerned Christians such as Headlee pointed to all manner of sins in the city as evidence of God's wrath. Growing crime, prostitution, alcoholism, and greed were daily problems, but one of the most outrageous sins, according to Potts, was residents' failure to observe the Sabbath. For Potts, this was simply a manifestation of wickedness among those who didn't properly revere God, but in truth, it had its origins in both the evolution of secular political thought in America and St. Louis's cultural transformation.

Those who adhered to strict Jacksonian political beliefs held firm views on the separation of church and state. Traditional religious observances, ardent Jacksonians argued, should not detract from individual freedoms within the secular world. Consequently, local saloons, merchants, and other businesses were increasingly open for business on Sundays, despite criticism from local ministers. A year earlier, many of the devout were shocked when the *Republican* went so far as to begin printing a Sunday edition. To regular church-going Protestants, it seemed as if the world were turning upside down.[40]

On the cultural front, German-speaking immigrants from throughout central Europe had congregated in St. Louis. For them, Sundays in the New World were to be celebrated as they had been in the Old Country—by visiting one of the city's many new beer gardens. This infuriated many local nativists, who saw this practice as a direct threat to Protestant American ideals and the cause of temperance. A culture war of sorts played out as each side struggled to cope with the other.

In the case of cholera transmission, the Protestants may have unwittingly had a point: The threat of communal drinking may not have endangered residents' souls, but it could have threatened their health. Large crowds consuming food and drink together, especially given the lax sanitary conditions of the day, would have allowed cholera to spread more easily between individuals. The consequences of too much partying on Sunday therefore had less to do with divine judgment than with the realities of epidemiology.

A Fiery Reprieve

In the spring of 1849, St. Louisans searched for silver linings wherever they might find them—however flawed they might be.

After the Great Fire, those who still held to the belief that cholera was caused by miasma noted that all the smoke most likely killed much of the cholera. The changing number of victims seemed to support this theory. In the two weeks preceding the fire, the number of people claimed by cholera increased from 78 to 193, but in the two weeks following the fire, the death toll fell to 128, dropping down to 118 by the end of May.

Dr. William McPheeters noted that the decline was attributed by some "to the influence of the fire in purifying the atmosphere, and it was confidently believed by many that the disease would thenceforward decline." McPheeters rightly viewed this as wishful thinking. He believed that the fire's only influence was to temporarily divert the public's attention away from cholera.[41]

A Change in Leadership

May ultimately saw a grand total of 517 deaths from cholera, a number that was far too high for many St. Louisans. Those who had the means responded by fleeing the city for the country. Some contemporary accounts placed the number of residents who abandoned St. Louis in the tens of thousands, but this was certainly an exaggeration. However, several chroniclers noted how the city streets became empty and commerce all but dried up. "The city looks like a desert compared to its usual animated appearance," commented merchant Joseph Mersman in a letter to a friend.[42]

Among those who left were numerous St. Louis City Council members who had chosen to abandon their posts at a time when municipal guidance was crucial and most expected. A turnover in a number of governmental offices following the April municipal elections didn't change the overall spirit of civic leadership much, but it did provide the city with a new mayor, James Barry, who proved himself worthy of praise. Years later, another St. Louis mayor, John Darby, remembered Barry's willingness to lead the city while others had "left the desolating hand of pestilence to sweep over the devoted city."

Despite Barry's act of courage, the selfish lack of concern shown by St. Louis's other officeholders left the general public with no alternative but to take matters into their own hands. Darby attributed the continued survival of the city during the worst of the epidemic to the efforts of a handful of private citizens who stepped forward to fill the leadership vacuum. In his memoir he wrote, "In the hour of anguish and desolation, when death was claiming its victims every day by the hundred, noble, generous-hearted private citizens of the great city met in public meeting and strongly censured the neglect thus shown by the city government."[43]

James Barry was elected mayor of St. Louis in April 1849. He was praised for his leadership during the cholera epidemic, in part because many of the city's other leaders fled to avoid falling ill. Photograph by unknown photographer, ca. 1860s–1870s. Missouri Historical Society Collections.

Prominent citizens gathered at the Old Courthouse to voice their concerns over the lack of leadership from the city council. When the newspapers published the proceedings of the meetings, the self-exiled city councilmen read the accounts and returned—before quickly leaving town once more. Darby wrote, "These fugitives very soon came sneaking in, and privately, hurriedly, and hastily met and passed, in advance, an ordinance to transfer to the members of the committee of citizens all the power of the Council respecting the health of the city, and made an appropriation of ten thousand dollars to carry out the objects contemplated by said ordinance."[44]

Handing over municipal power to an unelected body of men was unprecedented. At a time when party politics and democratic ideals were held in the foremost regard, this action surely would have met with raucous criticism, but perhaps the public had more faith in this group of civic leaders than in those who had waited so long to face the reality of cholera's presence. If so, they could hardly be blamed for having little confidence in their elected officials when the council members had been so hasty to hand over power that they hadn't even taken the time to properly notify those directly affected by the transfer of authority.

When the citizens group finally learned of the power bestowed on it, it promptly formed an official Committee of Public Health, with prominent local attorney Thomas T. Gantt at the helm. Serving with him were J. M. Fields, secretary pro tem; R. S. Blennerhasset; Trusten Polk; William G. Clark; L. M. Kennett; Lewis Bach; George Collier; James Clemens Jr.; A. B. Chambers; Isaac Hedges; Thomas Gray, and Uriah Wright. Each man represented a different ward within the city.

Upon convening for the first time on June 27, the committee declared an all-out war on cholera and its determination to see the fight through, as evidenced in meeting minutes, which note, "We will meet again this morning, and every day during the continuance of the cholera among us, as an epidemic, and will endeavor to do our duty in preventing or relieving the evils which it brings in its train." The committee quickly passed four critical resolutions aimed at "arresting the progress of the cholera amongst us." The first resolution was an agreement with the St. Louis Public Schools and the sisters of St. Vincent's Catholic School to use the schoolhouses located in the Fourth, Fifth, and Sixth wards as temporary cholera hospitals, thereby addressing the public's call for better health facilities. The second resolution appointed two physicians to provide services at each hospital and empowered them with the ability to obtain necessary supplies and assistance. The third and fourth resolutions formally appointed representatives from each ward to sit on the committee and charged them with carrying out the committee's directives, including appointing district or ward inspectors to police the neighborhoods for health-code violations.[45]

Making Do in the Time of Cholera

Although many residents may have wanted to seek the healthier environments of the rural countryside, most didn't have that luxury. Working men, small-business owners, and the like had little choice but to go about their lives in the best way they could. Merchant Joseph Mersman noted that "people parting for a day bid farewell to each other," because they knew there was a very real chance they wouldn't see each other again. For his part, Mersman and his business partner, Clemens Nulsen, took to sleeping in the same bed so as "to be within groaning distance" if one of them should suddenly become ill. It was a practical solution for a problem that could strike quickly and often left little time for good-byes.[46]

Others simply prepared for the worst and hoped for the best. The sobering reality of the epidemic forced some to see that practical matters were squared away. Gustavus Wulfing decided that the best course of action was to get his affairs in order, writing, "We have prepared ourselves for all eventualities." He dictated his will and "talked the matter over thoroughly as to what should be done in case of a sudden death in our family."[47]

Cleansing the City

Speculation as to the causes of cholera continued both within the medical community and among laypersons. Theories that the origins of the disease could be found in everything from atmospheric disturbances to intemperate lifestyles continued to find their way into local newspapers, but most physicians seemed to agreed that sanitation— or the lack of thereof—was either a cause of the disease or a means for its transmission. Given this train of thought, the Committee of Public Health set its sights on cleansing the city.

One of its first actions in this effort was to order regularly scheduled visits by "scavenger and slop carts" to all areas of the city for the purpose of removing accumulated trash and waste. Backed by the enforcement powers of the street inspectors and under the threat of a five-dollar fine for noncompliance, residents were ordered to remove any potentially harmful debris from their property. Responsibility for transporting the collected debris fell to the municipality's first sanitation worker, the city scavenger, who carted away both solid matter and liquid waste. Unfortunately, few details remain about the daily labors of this individual, but given the contemporary complaints about the state of the city, he certainly had his work cut out for him.

The next step was to clear the air in case the disease was being caused by miasma. However, the committee's method for cleansing the atmosphere—purification fires—was in direct contradiction with the goal of cleansing the air. In the mid-1800s, people assumed that to kill airborne agents they needed to fill the air with smoke and fumes.

So, on June 29, committee member A. B. Chambers set forth a motion to order the block inspectors to "cause at least five bushels of stone coal, with at least one gallon of resinous tar & two pounds of Sulphur, to be burned" in areas of the city that were suffering the most. The fires were to burn slowly and be maintained until all the fuel was spent. This was ordered to begin each night at 8:00 p.m. and continue for a week. Clouds of smoke thus enveloped St. Louis each evening as the purification fires were lit.[48]

Furthermore, with the hope that additional smoke would give the committee's efforts an added boost, the city's carpenters, cabinetmakers, and other woodworkers were asked to burn whatever wood chips, scrap wood, and lumber they might have at the end of each day. Individual residents were even encouraged to light small tar fires within their homes as an additional preventive measure. Obviously the smoke did nothing to stop the spread of cholera, but it did keep the local fire companies busy as home fires became an increasing problem.

Finally, although it didn't fully understand the role of contaminated water at the time, the committee nevertheless suspected tainted water was somehow contributing to the spread of the disease. In the months before the 1849 outbreak began, the city had been creating new reservoirs and water mains in response to the demands of massive population growth. While this was happening, many of the city's residents were still dependent on water sources that were no doubt contaminated by industrial runoff and human waste. Add in the fact that most nineteenth-century individuals paid little attention to good personal hygiene, and you have all the ingredients for effective contagion.

In order to provide immediate clean water to neighborhood residents in several areas of the city, the committee had municipal water hydrants opened for free use by "indigent citizens." Providing this clean water was ultimately the most critical and effective tactic in all of the committee's efforts to defeat cholera.[49]

Adding to the misery was the weather, which continued to be rainy even as the cool of spring gave way to the heat of summer. The rain caused boats on the levee to ride high on the Mississippi's banks; it also led to flooded cellars and sinkholes. The officer in charge of recording the daily weather readings at Jefferson Barracks counted twelve days of rain in June with notations such as "heavy showers with thunder and lightning."[50]

The frequent showers were joined by temperatures that created a stifling humidity. On June 4 the *Republican* printed that "yesterday the heat was far more oppressive than at any time before this season." Temperatures rose into the high eighties each day as the month progressed, essentially turning the city's tightly packed, poorly ventilated homes into ovens. Furthermore, the standing water in the streets, alleys, and lots became warm kettles of bacteria-rich soup with little chance of drying up as new rainfall frequently replenished them.[51]

Persistent water problems tended to occur in areas considered undesirable by St. Louis's more fortunate residents. These leftover properties were largely settled by the Irish and German immigrants who had been flooding into St. Louis since the early 1830s. City residents had long viewed these immigrants, particularly the Irish, as prone to living in filthy hovels and crowded tenements, and had therefore paid little attention to them prior to the outbreak. However, after cholera began spreading throughout the city, these neighborhoods soon attracted a great deal of attention and ridicule. Reports submitted to the Committee of Public Health often specifically stated the nationality of subjects who were approached by street inspectors for sanitary issues and violations, like this one shared during a July 2 meeting: "At a house on the corner of Plum and Main, I found two Irish families lately arrived—one a family of 7 & the other of 11 persons—there was a foot of water in one of the rooms & about half an inch in the other—I requested them to move which they have promised to do within 10 hours."[52]

As the epidemic raged on, an area of considerable concern was Shepherd's Graveyard, a Third Ward neighborhood located between Ninth and Tenth streets and Market and Walnut. On July 3 the Third Ward submitted a report to the leaders of the Committee of Public Health that included a plea for help cleaning up a neighborhood that "was the most filthy place in the city if not the world." It was a conglomeration of shanties and shacks that sat near the swampy drainage area at the foot of Chouteau's Pond. The ward inspectors held nothing back when describing the neighborhood as a place occupied by "hovels of the most wretched description, each one of them a receptacle for utter destitution." Inhabited primarily by the city's poorest immigrants, Shepherd's Graveyard was hit hard by cholera. In the weeks since the start of the epidemic, two-thirds of the neighborhood's inhabitants had succumbed to the disease, including twenty-one victims living in one house. Third Ward officials wanted the committee to burn or remove the shanties of the deceased as a precaution.[53]

The low ground on which the Third Ward was situated made it particularly vulnerable to standing water and flooded basements. Case in point: When block inspectors visited a property owned by landlord Dr. Reuben Knox, they discovered eight families, including fourteen children, all living in a building whose cellar and first floor below the street level were half full of stagnant water. Committee members understood that identifying these types of properties was crucial to the fight against cholera, but they also recognized that block inspections were only a portion of the solution. In an effort to make the public more aware of the committee's focus and reach, five hundred copies of the regulations of the Committee of Public Health were printed in English and German for distribution.[54]

Gaining Insight on Tragedy

Although the Committee of Public Health was engaged in the battle in the streets, the real fighting took place among the families and individuals who were enduring the ravages of the disease. Just as in the 1832–1833 epidemic, all citizens were at risk for contracting cholera, but certainly the majority of the victims were children and the poor.

Early on, the pestilence began to take the city's youngest residents. A report on St. Louis's health published in a March edition of the *Republican* pointed out that of the seventy-nine deaths that had occurred during that week, twenty-four of the victims were children under the age of five. As the sickness evolved into an epidemic, the age of the victims climbed upward as older children and teenagers began to die as well.[55]

Women also suffered higher mortality rates; this was a trait of cholera epidemics worldwide. As medical experts began to understand cholera as a fecal-oral transmitted disease, they speculated that the high mortality rate among women was due to the duties of child-rearing. Mothers who were changing diapers and bathing infants logically would have had a greater risk of exposure.[56]

Yet single young men were also likely to contract and die from the disease, particularly those who worked within the typically wet and muddy conditions of the levee. Young men who didn't live at home with their parents also usually lived in boarding houses in some of the areas with the highest incidents of contamination. Lifestyle may have played a part as well. The often-intemperate nature of this group, which was known to frequent the saloons near the wharf, was seen by many as proof that hard drinking and bad personal habits were certainly causes.[57]

Although demographic breakdowns and statistics provide perspectives on the seriousness of St. Louis's cholera epidemic, individuals' personal stories give us the truest insight into this tragedy that swept over the city and its people. The voices of both sufferers and survivors reflect the weight that fell upon St. Louis's inhabitants as they were surrounded by the dead and the dying.

In the first days of July, when the epidemic was still gaining ground, Eliza Keesacker Howard wrote to her sister in Delaware to describe the conditions in which she was living.

> It is undescribable, nothing but death, you may see a person well and hearty and the next day hear of their death, everyday is dull and gloomy no one goes to church, no one to the stores, no one in the streets, but funerals passing all the time, a great many of the citizens have left the city, all the courts have adjourned, they have turned the public school houses into hospitals, to which they take all those who have no one to take care of them, which are a good many. Lime is strewn through every street in the city and large bonfires of tar and sulphur are burned every night, the physicians are worn out, have to hide to get rest.[58]

Howard was fortunate in that no one in her family perished, but others weren't so lucky, including John Grigg. He and his wife, Margaret, were Irish immigrants who lived in the Fourth Ward. They had come to St. Louis around 1840 with their son, Thomas. By June 1849, Margaret was thirty-eight years old and tending to the couple's five children. In their crowded Irish neighborhood near the wharf, the family operated a boarding house on Green Street. This street, as noted by Dr. William McPheeters in his 1850 article in *The St. Louis Medical and Surgical Journal,* "became celebrated for its mortality."

Such was the situation for the Grigg household. On June 19 the couple watched as eldest son Thomas became the first of their children to fall. William, age nine; Richard, age seven; Benjamin, age five; and Mary, age four, joined their brother in a matter of days. Then on June 24, Margaret became the last victim. Of the family of seven, only John seems to have survived. The duration of each Grigg family member's illness was, according to the record, a single day, a fact that shows just how fast and brutal cholera was. Perhaps McPheeters was recalling the Grigg family when he later wrote that "scarce a family" along Green Street "escaped without one or more deaths, and some were almost entirely swept off."[59]

Obituaries Shared Near and Far

Death notices weren't a daily occurrence in St. Louis newspapers in the 1840s. They were expensive and typically reserved only for prominent individuals. Yet by the summer of 1849, death notices appeared each day in the *Republican* and sometimes contained a list of ten individuals. These notices were simple, though sometimes accompanied by a heartfelt testimonial to a victim's good character. From these few words the wrenching heartbreak experienced by so many grieving families is clearly discernable.

On June 27 readers were presented with the notice of the death of thirty-nine-year-old Judge C. W. Schaumbourg, who died of cholera on the same evening as his two-year-old son. On July 1, Helen Shoemaker, wife of William Shoemaker, passed away along with their twenty-one-day-old daughter, Fannie Jane. Hannah Burroughs, wife of James Burroughs Jr., passed due to the "prevailing epidemic" on July 5, with her obituary noting that "the devoted wife, the kind mother, the exemplary Christian, the lovely and heroic woman—she sleeps well."[60]

One of the most moving entries announced the death of twenty-eight-year-old Mary Elizabeth Cook, wife of George Freeman Cook. It reads:

She was one who carried the sunshine of happiness with her wherever she went. Trouble never came within her doors, for she met it with a smile and disarmed it of its power. Her disposition was naturally gentle, and it was more so by the benign influence of faith. She was so happily constituted that it was easy for her to look upon the bright side of everything, but it was her habitual trust in God which gave to her cheerfulness the spiritual beauty by which it was converted into a Christian grace. She was kind to the poor, affectionate to her friends, devoted to her family—they unite to mourn her loss.[61]

News of the seriousness of the cholera epidemic in St. Louis soon spread far and wide. Reprinted stories from the local dailies and telegraphic reports of the pestilence's devastating presence were circulated in newspapers throughout the country. Word even reached across the Atlantic, where British newspapers busy printing stories of their own country's cholera epidemic also included information on the scourge in St. Louis.

The death notices in the *North Wales Chronicle* of Bangor, Wales, informed readers of the death of the family of John McHurick, formerly of Manchester, England. Although thousands of Brits were taken to the grave by cholera, even the editors of this British newspaper seemed amazed by the merciless spread of the contagion throughout the St. Louis community.

On the 4th of May, at St. Louis, Missouri, age 31, Mary, wife of John McHurick, formerly of Manchester. On the same day, age 6 years, Jane, daughter of the above. On Saturday, the 6th, aged 35, Mr. John McHurick himself, and on Sunday, the 7th, aged 8 months, his only surviving child—all of cholera. The minister who read the funeral service at the grave of Mrs. McHurick, the nurse who took charge of the infant after the decease of the mother, and a neighbor who kindly attended on Mr. McHurick in his illness, also fell victims to this dreadful scourge. The household furniture, wearing apparel, and stock in trade of Mr. McHurick, which were taken in charge by the authorities, there being no representatives of the deceased in the locality, were all destroyed in the great fire which recently occurred at St. Louis.[62]

Perspectives on Morale

As the epidemic worsened, the members of the Committee of Public Health became concerned about public morale. It was impossible to escape the constant reminders of cholera's presence; it dominated the sights and sounds of the city. Tradition in the nineteenth century dictated that church bells toll at the conclusion of a funeral. Likewise, local fire companies rang a fire bell when they lost a member of their company. During the summer of 1849, bells were ringing so often that there was little silence from morning until dark. But, printed *The People's Organ*, "The church and fire bells will not ring out their mournful tell tale notes in the future." The committee ordered the practice curtailed out of concern for the effects of the constant ringing upon both the sick and the healthy.[63]

Just as unnerving was the seemingly endless parade of funeral hearses that now dominated St. Louis's streets. "Hearses may be seen moving to the different graveyards, at every hour of the day, and even in the night," wrote attorney Edward Bates in his diary. But Bates believed conditions in the city were having little effect on the minds of residents. He also wrote: "The public spirit is kept up with wonderful vigor. I hardly see a man with anything on his countenance like blank despondency."

Most chroniclers didn't share Bates's rosy assessment of the city's spirits. I. H. Headlee wrote to his friend during the epidemic and gave a much different sense of the public's demeanor, noting that "the streets are the almost constant scene of funeral trains, while the long solemn tolling of funeral bells, announcing that the destroyer is still doing his fatal work, altogether has imparted a feeling of gloom among the citizens, that is a great many of them."

These different takes on the population's prevailing attitudes may have been molded by the men's stations in life. Bates, a prominent and wealthy attorney who lived in a country estate, most likely didn't mingle with the same crowd as Headlee. Nor was he likely to tarry long in the city each day. On the contrary, residents who lived along St. Louis's narrow streets and witnessed the deaths of their neighbors daily probably often did display "blank despondency."[64]

A Gravedigger's Reminiscences

Whatever the overall spirit may have been, the gruesome scenes witnessed by many created lasting memories in the minds of those who survived to tell the tales years later. Albertina Glyckherr Loring was only a child when she arrived in St. Louis with her family after a long journey to the New World from their home in Germany. In an autobiography published in 1907, Loring recalls that "from the windows of the Planter's House I saw bodies thrown into wagons, several feet high to be carried away."[65]

One of the most vivid and emotional accounts of the summer of cholera was written by Michael McEnnis. He was the son of the superintendent for the Catholic graveyard, which at that time sat near the junction of Franklin (now Dr. Martin Luther King Drive) and Jefferson avenues. While McEnnis was serving in the army during the Mexican War, his father passed away; the archbishop of St. Louis then appointed McEnnis's mother as superintendent. Unable to dig graves herself, the work became the responsibility of McEnnis's younger brother.

McEnnis returned home from the war in 1846 and resumed life in St. Louis. All was well until the outbreak. One evening, McEnnis received a note from his mother stating that his brother was very ill. He was so weak from an attack of cholera that he was taken home on a litter. Four men whom he had employed as gravediggers had died the night before. Without anyone to dig graves, the bodies began to pile up at the cemetery. With the help of a group of friends, McEnnis took over the task of digging graves for the victims, recalling, "We kept the place clear, but the number dying filled up the graveyard so fast that there was hardly any more room left." Because of this, the archbishop granted McEnnis permission to start digging graves in a wooded area west of the city, in what later became Rock Springs Cemetery.

The daunting work of burying the dead fell to McEnnis and a force of six to eight teenage boys who received about four dollars a day for their toil. This was more than a week's wages for a non-farm laborer during this period, which means despite the gruesome task, the boys were handsomely compensated. For his part, McEnnis was lucky to find a crew: Laborers had become scarce due to the disease, and many people were leaving town.

As the epidemic worsened, McEnnis recalled, the economic strain on the city's poor became much more evident. Those who were sick needed treatment and medicine, which placed a heavy burden on those who were scraping by. Burying the dead was also expensive. McEnnis noted that "the immense number who died or were sick made the mass of the people so poor they could hardly buy food or bury their dead." Soon the archbishop stepped in and offered free burials to those who couldn't pay.

Few others witnessed the epidemic like McEnnis, who wrote, "The scenes of sorrow, grief and distress of that year will never be effaced from the writer's mind." One memory in particular stayed with him forever, and it can be told only in his own words.

> On a very hot day, near the close of the cholera, I was standing at the graveyard gate, coming up the road was a woman carrying a large bundle. I stepped out, seeing she was staggering under the load, and invited her to come into the shade of a tree and rest. She walked in, laid the bundle on the grass and laid down beside it, exhausted. I ran and brought a bucket of ice water. She revived slightly, and I walked away, keeping my eye on her. After some time she rose, and I went over to tell her to stay longer, but her answer was she had to get back to town. She then handed the writer a "Poor Ticket", for the grave for a child twelve years old. I told her that was all right and asked when the remains would be brought. She answered by pointing to the bundle, "it is here." She told me her husband and one child had died with the cholera, and now this child was the last, and she felt she would follow soon. She did not have a friend or one cent to bury the child, so she went to the archbishop for a free grave. I am certain he never knew how poor she was. She then went home, wrapped her darling in a quilt and carried her in her arms to the graveyard.

McEnnis was heartbroken by the woman's story. He took it upon himself to construct a simple coffin for the child and lay her inside it, along with some flowers, before lowering her into the ground. So as not to disturb the woman with the noise of the hard earth landing on top of the box, he covered it with leaves to soften the sound. McEnnis then fashioned a board to act as a grave marker and walked the woman back to the gate. As he later recalled: "She held out her hand with tears in her eyes [and] thanked me for the comfort I had given her, walked away, and I never heard of her since. . . . I can almost see that poor mother now as she looked, staggering down the road alone, holding up her hand as if she was praying for comfort or a happy death with those she loved. I can feel the tears running down my cheeks now, fifty-eight years after."[66]

New Families for the Orphaned

Cholera was victimizing St. Louis's children by taking them to the grave, but it was also victimizing them by making them orphans. Because nothing like our modern system of child protective services existed in 1849, dealing with orphaned children typically fell either to a religious organization or, when that wasn't available, to the mayor. As the number of orphaned children swelled in the face of the epidemic, Mayor Barry found himself securing homes for parentless children, appointing individuals to distribute the orphans to capable families whenever possible. One of these appointees was Peter Wegman, whose story is found within the records of the local registrar.

Among other incidences, Wegman was charged with investigating the deaths of two unknown adults who left behind two very young children, a boy about five years old and a girl around six months old. Such a situation was complicated enough even when dealing with the deaths of city residents, but it was another matter entirely when transient individuals with no known ties to St. Louis became victims as they passed through the city on their way to points westward. Wegman arranged for the siblings to be given to two worthy, but separate, families; he also had the deceased parents' belongings distributed between the two families as compensation. The boy was given to the family of Christian Lowenstein, while his sister was placed in the care of "a man named Joseph Schneider." Each recipient provided a signed affidavit attesting to their responsibilities as adoptive parents. Lowenstein stated that he would "keep in my family, and bring up the same giving it the necessary schooling, and to learn him the profession or trade of wagon making, which I am carrying on." In order to cover the expenses of his new charge, Lowenstein was given a cooking stove and a rifle whose total estimated value was thirteen dollars. Schneider was given a horse and cart along with old clothing, all of which was valued at around fifty dollars.[67]

As the epidemic progressed, the task of finding homes for orphaned children began to overwhelm the mayor's office, so the Committee of Public Health stepped in to help. It appointed three men from each ward to canvas their respective neighborhoods "to collect contributions and distribute the same for the relief of children made destitute by the prevailing epidemic." Like Lowenstein and Schneider, the families who chose to take in the orphans received relief funds to cover necessary expenses. The number of eventual adoptions isn't recorded, but it's safe to assume that there are many families today with little knowledge of the effect the 1849 cholera epidemic had on their family tree.[68]

Hospitals Helping and Physicians Falling

With each day in early July, the number of victims increased. Physicians in the city struggled to keep up with the demand of those needing medical attention. The temporary ward hospitals opened in late June by the Committee of Public Health filled up quickly. Conveniently located hospitals were a blessing to those families who had sickness among them, but in at least one case the hospital's neighbors weren't grateful for its presence.

A group of people living in the city's First Ward filed a complaint with the committee on the grounds that the hospital's presence was causing families to be "exceedingly alarmed." It wasn't that they felt threatened by disease itself, believing as they did that cholera wasn't contagious, but rather that the "conveyance of the sick & dead, their groans, etc" was unnerving, especially "upon the female portions of the families." One resident, Mr. Tesson, had already moved his family "to save them from the injurious effects produced by the groans of the dying." The First Ward residents further contended that although no one in their area, which included the modern Soulard neighborhood, had contracted cholera, the anxiety produced by the hospital's very presence was sure to make someone ill. Despite being signed by forty-five heads of household in the ward, the complaint had little effect, and the hospital remained open.

Cholera was later reported in the area, but First Ward residents suffered very few cases, likely due to the ward's location on higher ground and its population of mostly middle-class residents. Additionally, the ward's streets were well maintained, and water supplies had little chance of contamination from runoff.[69]

Ultimately the temporary ward hospitals proved critical in easing the spread of cholera by providing physician care to those who might not otherwise have had access to treatment. The committee acted fast to provide at least two doctors per ward hospital, but keeping the doctors at their posts was sometimes challenging. For example, Dr. J. M. Wilson was called in to replace doctors Campbell and Gemp when they failed to report for their shifts at the First Ward Hospital. Wilson, with the help of three nuns from the Sisters of Charity, managed to stabilize the situation and reportedly saved some patients from the grave who would otherwise have been neglected.

There's no doubt that the hospitals were less than ideal and may have, on some occasions, proved more harmful than good, especially among the physicians. Dealing with any contagious disease requires strict attention to protocol so as not to spread or acquire the illness. But because the medical community didn't yet comprehend this, naturally doctors began to be counted among the dead. This was also true of those in general practice.

The hero of the 1832–1833 epidemic, Dr. Hardage Lane, resumed his fight against cholera when the pestilence reappeared in St. Louis. Using the remedies he felt he'd perfected previously, he treated patients and shared his knowledge with his fellow practitioners. Lane's famous recipe, which was preserved in a leaf of his family Bible, called for a concoction of asafetida, an herb used in medicine since antiquity; opium; and black pepper. Whether the recipe produced any real effects is questionable, but modern research has proven that asafetida does have some antimicrobial qualities. What was probably more effective for patients was Lane's insistence that they be given quantities of water to reduce "the thirst which is great." The main fatal component of cholera isn't blood infection but a rapidly induced dehydration by means of nearly uncontrollable vomiting, diarrhea, and sweating that causes the victim's organs to shut down. By giving patients regularly administered amounts of fluids, severe dehydration could be prevented, making recovery possible.[70]

During the 1849 outbreak the sixty-four-year-old physician found himself pushed to the limits of exhaustion until it finally caught up with him. Lane suffered through illness for two weeks before passing away in the early days of July, when the epidemic was at its worst. Local newspapers, including the *Republican*, informed readers of Lane's passing and praised him as one of the most accomplished physicians in the state, noting, "During the prevalence of the epidemic, until he was forced to his bed by physical exhaustion, he was employed night and day, in his professional duties, and it may be said of him, with great propriety, that he died 'with his harness on.'"[71]

Lane was joined in short order by others in his profession who had contracted cholera, no doubt during the course of their duties. Doctors James Wisehart and George McCullough died in early July as well. At the Sixth Ward Hospital, the staff was shocked by the death of its attending physician, William C. Hull, who was still a student at one of the local medical colleges. The young Tennessee-born physician had been seen as an up-and-comer in the community who, despite his young age, had been elected to the Board of Delegates soon after arriving in St. Louis. (The Board of Delegates was one of the two elected bodies that formed the early St. Louis City Council.) He had enthusiastically accepted the appointment of Sixth Ward physician by the Committee of Public Health, "a post he filled with credit to himself and the profession up to the time of his sickness."[72]

Crude Care in Nineteenth-Century Hospitals

Although hospitals provided a source of medical care that might otherwise not have been available to the less advantaged of the city, they weren't exactly models of sanitation. They can only be described as crude by modern standards and probably benefited the community the most by isolating patients from the general population.

The City Hospital was established by an act of the St. Louis City Council in 1845, and the care that patients received there was primitive at best. For example, patients typically lay on straw mattresses on the floor rather than in beds, and aside from the resident physician, there was nothing that resembled professional staff. Nursing was provided by local women who were often recruited, it was said, by local policemen who recommended women whom they knew from their daily beats. In the evening, the nursing staff went home, and a night watchman was left to provide care, if necessary. (During the cholera epidemic, the temporary ward hospitals had an advantage in that nursing care was provided by volunteers, including nuns, members of the local fire companies, and other good-hearted citizens.)

Overall, St. Louis's hospitals in 1849 would have appeared as warehouses of the sick rather than health care facilities. Consequently it isn't hard to understand why reformers such as Dorothea Dix sought to improve conditions in America's health and welfare institutions during this period.

The Creation of Quarantine Island

The Committee of Public Health knew it wouldn't be possible to stabilize St. Louis's cholera situation without slowing or stopping the influx of new cases that arrived via steamboat each day in the form of travelers and immigrants. Many of them were fresh from the immigrant ships arriving in New Orleans directly from Europe, where cholera had been raging for more than a year. Contamination was easy on these vessels due to the tightly packed conditions, and passengers fell ill by the dozens as they steamed northward up the Mississippi River.

After the pestilence found its way to St. Louis, the public viewed every new boat that landed on the levee with extreme suspicion, as demonstrated in this excerpt from the *Republican*: "[Immigrants] bring much wealth to the city, improving their condition, and enhancing the value of everything around them. Within the last few months, however, a greatly increased number of foreigners have arrived, and thus they have, unfortunately, brought diseases with them, to such an extent as to carry alarm whenever an arrival is announced."[73]

The committee passed a resolution creating a temporary floating quarantine hospital—a steamboat moored ten miles south of the city. The *St. Louis* was contracted from McAlister and Company to serve as a temporary administrative and patient clinic until more permanent structures could be built. This proved to be a lucrative deal for the McAlister agents, who received $35 for each day of the steamboat's service—the equivalent of nearly $1,000 today. The *St. Louis's* captain, D. D. Moore, and a crew of eight men served as the support team for the boat's operations, including sailing the yawl that transported quarantine officers to and from the incoming vessels.[74]

Because an old steamboat was hardly adequate to service all the sick passengers arriving each day, the committee actively sought out a spot where a more permanent, fully equipped quarantine station could be established. On July 3, Dr. Richard Barrett and two companions, committee members A. B. Chambers and R. S. Blennerhasset, stepped from a ferry boat onto the sandy bank of Arsenal Island, a large expanse of land that emerged from the muddy waters of the Mississippi River along its western bank, about five miles south of the levee. The three men were there as part of a tour of local sites that had the potential to serve as suitable quarantine grounds.

Arsenal Island showed promise compared to the other options. Unlike Bloody Island, which was located just north of the city's wharf and far too close to the city's center, Arsenal Island was situated well above the river line and dry. A sizable portion of the island had been cleared for pasturing cattle, yet a stand of trees provided plenty of shade and wide-open spaces for outdoor recreation. The waters surrounding it were deep enough to handle all sizes of steamboats, and legally it was thought to be within Missouri's jurisdiction—a situation that wasn't always clear when dealing with the river's ever-shifting sandbar islands. (Arsenal Island was later determined to be in Illinois and exists today as part of the eastern bank of the Mississippi.)[75]

Just seven days after the Committee of Public Health had taken charge of St. Louis, it accepted the recommendation of Dr. Barrett and the quarantine committee to establish a quarantine station on Arsenal Island. Barrett was appointed superintendent and physician in charge of the facility and provided with "a carpenter with a sufficient gang of men," plus a generous supply of lumber with which to begin construction of the quarantine wards. The committee also resolved to outfit the station with all the necessary medicines and disinfectants the physicians and staff might need.[76]

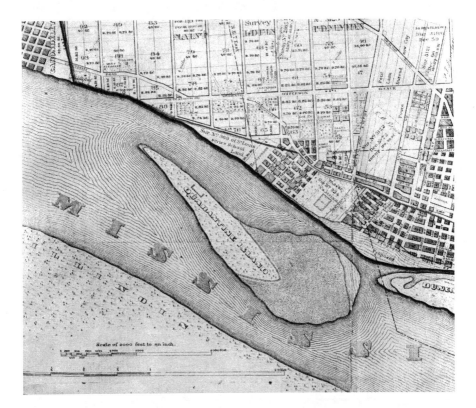

Quarantine Island, also known as Arsenal Island, as pictured in an 1853 map of St. Louis. The complex of hospital buildings can be seen just above the letters *Q* and *U*. Quarantine Island Collection, Missouri Historical Society Collections.

The next step was to ensure the dozens of steamboats arriving in St. Louis each week would actually stop at the checkpoint, a potential challenge considering some steamboat captains might be eager to stay on schedule and reluctant to stop. The committee appointed quarantine officers who were required to board and inspect every steamboat approaching the city from the south. Both day and night, a yawl tied up near the Montesano House, a local resort south of the city, was to be at the ready for the officers in charge of boarding the boats. The approaching steamboats were alerted to the quarantine situation by a system of conspicuously placed "yellow flags as an indication that a quarantine is established." The flags were flown from the moored *St. Louis* at Arsenal Island, an old shot tower that stood near the Montesano House, and the yawls used by the quarantine officers. Lights indicated the same at night.

If the flags were ignored or unseen, the committee had a more direct method of communicating with the boats: It called on the St. Louis Arsenal to outfit "a cannon of proper calibre supplied with cartridges" and place it on the bluff overlooking the river near the Montesano House. Officially, the plan was to fire the cannon if a boat failed to stop for inspection, thereby alerting officials upriver in the city that a potentially contagious load of passengers might be headed to the wharf, but certainly no one failed to see the significance of a loaded cannon pointed toward the river. After all, intimidation is often an effective tool. Regulations called for ten rounds to be fired from the cannon as the errant steamboat powered by, clearly making the point that the city meant business.

If the boat still failed to stop, a man on horseback was to be dispatched at top speed to race into the city and alert the mayor and committee officials. Minutes from the July 5 committee meeting show that, "On receipt of such notice, the fire bells will ring an alarm, and the firemen, police, and citizens [will] turn out to prevent the boat infringing the Quarantine from landing in the city, and to arrest the person or persons in charge of the same."[77]

Everything was in place, and the quarantine was in effect. The incoming boats stopped, and the sick, who arrived without pause, were taken from them to the floating clinic. On shore at Arsenal Island, soon to become Quarantine Island, the carpenters worked furiously to construct the hospital wards. No one was at a loss for work.

Unexpected Efforts to Slow the Spread in the City

Meanwhile, in the city, the challenges of cleansing the streets, treating the sick, and eliminating filth continued night and day despite the frequent rain. The newspapers continued to run daily tallies of burials as submitted by the sextons of the area cemeteries, and the number of dead rose higher and higher as July progressed. There was little anyone could do but press on and pray that relief would soon arrive.

Despite nature's continual resistance, the disinfecting and cleansing of St. Louis continued. In addition to the constant burning of tar and sulphur to "purify" the air, great quantities of lime were spread on the muddy streets. Lime or calcium-oxide treatment is an effective measure for eliminating some bacterial threats and is still used to treat livestock pens and barnyards; although spreading the lime wasn't harmful, it probably did little to reverse the contagion. No one, however, can fault them for trying. They were fighting an enemy that seemed to have no reason, cause, or cure.

Grappling with the cause of cholera did occupy the minds of some of the city's physicians, who provided their best advice to the Committee of Public Health. Many of these "experts" drew conclusions based on casual observation and deeply held nineteenth-century middle-class values. Because cholera victims were most often immigrants, mainly from Germany and Ireland, there was a tendency to link cholera with the consumption of alcoholic beverages, specifically beer. Within days of the committee's takeover, Alderman Luther Kennett proposed a ban on the consumption of malt beverages, particularly those known as beer, so long as cholera was present. By stating that the proposal was based on the advice of physicians who declared that the intake of such was injurious and likely to be the cause of cholera, he gained the support of the committee, which passed his resolution.

Vegetables and fruits as a cause of cholera was a theory met with more controversy. Back in January, one of the first local victims was thought to have succumbed from consuming too much sauerkraut. Such pickled foods, and fruits and vegetables in general, were considered "excitable" to the human digestive system; many physicians of the day declared them a hazard. Given our knowledge of the nutritional benefits of vegetables, this seems absurd. However, there may have been some basis in this theory if vegetables were washed in contaminated water and eaten raw. Without an understanding of the presence of bacteria, it would have been difficult to judge which vegetables were safe to consume. Therefore, the city council banned all vegetable sales in the early days of the epidemic, which meant people caught selling them could be arrested and fined.

One of the physicians who adamantly opposed the vegetable ban was Dr. Simon Pollak. It was, in his words, "a stupid ordinance." His autobiography provides one of the few accounts of the cholera epidemic as told by someone who was both a physician battling the pestilence and a survivor of the disease. On July 5, Pollak found himself immobilized by cholera. Discovered unconscious by his office boy, he was later transported to the Sisters of Charity Hospital at his own request. He spent eleven days under the care of doctors Englemann and Pope, two of the city's most respected physicians, who both ascribed to the antivegetable argument. After many days of being denied vegetables by the hospital staff, Pollak arranged an illicit transaction to acquire his favorite fruit, fresh tomatoes, because his craving for them had become "intolerable." Pollak employed the help of his office boy to secure some of the contraband: "This intelligent and faithful friend carried out my orders to the letter. I quickly consumed one tomato with great relish, and waited experimentally but impatiently to learn its effect. After one hour I ate another and again another."

When the doctors arrived for the evening rounds, Pollak made a full confession of his crime. The doctors, he said, were incredulous, but "to prevent my overdoing it they ate up all that were on hand themselves." After indulging in his forbidden fruit, Pollak "recovered rapidly without another dose of medicine." Pollak's intake of the nutrient- and vitamin-rich fruit no doubt did help aid his recovery, and he later lamented, "I am persuaded that many lives were lost in consequence of this insane ordinance."[78]

Pollak wasn't the only one secreting the illicit food. It seems that anytime something is declared forbidden, there are those who wish to circumvent the law. One frustrated block inspector reported that "vegetables are now brought clandestinely into the city & used to the great injury of health." Soon afterward, potato vendor Henry Horns was caught and hauled before the St. Louis Recorder's Court, which hit him with a hefty twenty-dollar fine.[79]

It was most likely a concern over the economic impact on produce sellers, along with a change in heart about vegetables' contribution to cholera's spread, that caused the Committee of Public Health to ask city authorities to relax the vegetable ban. The committee agreed to advocate for the allowance of ripe tomatoes, potatoes, and okra on July 14, which happened to coincide with some of the worst days of the epidemic. Unripe vegetables, however, were still prohibited.[80]

Standing water and unsanitary conditions, although not completely understood as a cause, were luckily still the prime suspects, so the war on filth battled on in neighborhoods such as Shepherd's Graveyard. Yet inspectors from the Third, Fourth, Fifth, and Sixth wards repeatedly brought bad news to the evening committee meetings. The Third Ward inspector once reported that upon morning inspection of his neighborhood he found "10 to 12 persons lying dead—two in one house—making 24 already buried from that & the adjoining house." He was later forced to hire a guard whose sole job was to keep new immigrants from occupying houses left vacant by the dead. It was requested that all the dilapidated shanties be completely removed in order to keep new inhabitants from entering the area.

Slow Quarantine Progress Meets System Failure

Back on Quarantine Island, business was brisk as the steamboats complied with their required inspections each day. Yet by the second week of July, the island was still in a primitive condition. The constant heavy rain delayed the erection of permanent buildings, which meant the old steamboat *St. Louis* was the only structure available to house the inspection crews, waiting passengers, and the suffering.

By July 7 the boat was crowded, but nevertheless Dr. Barrett felt it could hold up to two hundred additional individuals, if needed. Accordingly, every inch of the *St. Louis* was in use as the captain ordered all the baggage collected from those in quarantine be stored on the island's shore, leaving it at the mercy of the elements. Inside was little better, with the boat's roof leaking steadily on those awaiting examination.

> Dr. Barrett in his reports referred to, state that he visited Quarantine yesterday & found some 50 additional foreigners who had been taken the night before from 3 Ohio river boats, most of whom had been residents of the United States for some months or years, & were on their way to the Upper Missouri, Illinois, & Iowa, & that therefore some 40, who were clean and healthy, had been allowed to proceed. Some hundred odd still remained on the island—the quarters were uncomfortable, & would engender disease,

unless shanties were erected speedily. 3 or 4 sick persons had been taken from the Ohio boats, in addition to the 4 last reported. 2 or 3 whom had died.[81]

Heavy steamboat traffic on the river naturally resulted in long wait times as the inspectors searched each ship and evaluated each passenger. The process ran night and day, and the nerves of the waiting boats' officers wore thin as things bogged down. The steamboat *Robert Morrison* arrived at Quarantine Island at 11:00 p.m. on July 6 only to find a line of ships ahead of her. "The captain received me & my quarantine authority with very unbecoming language," noted the inspector assigned to that ship.[82]

Although tensions were running high, committee members were confident that the system of checks and warnings put in place would work and that any errant steamboats would be easily stopped. This was true to a point, but the system was put to the test on July 8 when the *Buena Vista* arrived at Quarantine Island. The boat's chief officer, Captain Johnston, stopped as required, and inspectors went aboard. Prior to arriving in St. Louis the *Buena Vista* had carried nearly 400 passengers up from New Orleans, but by the time she reached Quarantine Island, only 175 remained on board. The majority of the other passengers had disembarked at other landings below the city. When Dr. Carrow, the attending physician, examined the passengers, he found them all free of cholera—but he also discovered one with smallpox.

The boat was deemed unclean due to its previously crowded state and the fact that it had made the long voyage up from New Orleans. Captain Johnston was served with an order from the physician, backed by the authority of the Committee of Public Health, to keep the *Buena Vista* at the island for forty-eight hours so she could be thoroughly disinfected. Johnston "acquiesced" to the order and tied up. Meanwhile, plans to erect a separate smallpox quarantine shed were ordered so as not to risk spreading yet another deadly disease among St. Louis's population.[83]

It all seemed routine until the *Buena Vista*, loaded with a large number of immigrants, suddenly shoved off from the island and headed toward the wharf. No doubt irritated by the wait and the fact that the boat was without cholera victims (only smallpox!), someone clearly decided to take matters into his own hands and ignore the docking order. City officials rushed to the levee and were shocked to find the boat moored there, unloading its cargo as if nothing were awry. They were further angered because their warning systems had failed. There were no ringing bells or racing horse messengers to alert the city of the boat's arrival. The *Buena Vista* had docked quietly amid the bustling din of daily commerce.

After Mayor Barry learned of the *Buena Vista*'s defiance, he immediately sent word that the boat was to return to Quarantine Island or face stiff consequences. Captain Johnston, who had apparently left the *Buena Vista* while it was docked at the island so he could travel into the city, immediately cast the blame on his chief clerk, whom he claimed had ordered the boat to leave the island. As for the alarm, Captain Moore, who was in charge of enforcing the quarantine regulations among the boats, also quickly denied any responsibility for the matter by claiming he didn't sound the alarm because he assumed the *Buena Vista* had been authorized to leave. All of these claims seem thin given that written orders freezing the boat's movement had been distributed to all parties.

Soon the *Buena Vista* was en route back to Quarantine Island, courtesy of a tow from the *Governor Biggs*. Hoping to avoid another incident, Mayor Barry ordered that two police officers from the city be posted to the quarantine station at all times. Johnston, on his claim of innocence, asked for mercy from the committee, which decided that as long as the *Buena Vista* could be completely cleaned and declared safe, he wouldn't be charged with violating the quarantine regulations. Johnston complied, and his ship was released.[84]

The rain let up in the days after the *Buena Vista* incident, allowing greater progress toward building construction. This opportunity to establish a more efficient and effective quarantine presence was strengthened by two additional actions. A new regulation ordered all quarantined patients to remain on the island for no less than ten days. This kept passengers from leaving the island too soon, before they could be truly isolated and examined. Two nuns from the Sisters of Charity then offered to care for the sick on the island, which came as a relief to the overworked quarantine crew. With the addition of the more-permanent hospital structures and the arrival of the nun-nurses, conditions on the island were slowly improving.

The Pestilence Peaks and Violence Erupts

Back in St. Louis, block inspectors were also reporting victories in the war to clean up troubled neighborhoods. Conditions in places such as Shepherd's Graveyard were improving as the city gave these areas its full attention. Yet as July progressed, the death toll continued to rise, and the real graveyards received a steady stream of new occupants. Englishman John Martin, a Mormon immigrant, arrived in St. Louis in April just in time to see the disease bloom into a full-blown epidemic. He had originally intended to find gainful employment in New Orleans so he could save enough money to complete his journey to Salt Lake City. A friendly fellow Mormon traveler, however, persuaded him to continue on to St. Louis. As the steamboat carried them up the Mississippi, Martin got a taste of things to come: His friend contracted cholera and died before reaching St. Louis. As luck would have it, Martin found an old acquaintance from his hometown of Liverpool, and the two at first tried to go into business together. When this didn't work out, he sought other opportunities and soon found one develop out of the extreme nature of the epidemic itself.

When cholera was in full force, Martin and three other men agreed to become wagon drivers for one of the ward hospitals. They were handsomely compensated fifteen dollars a week at a time when a good job paid on average twelve dollars, but the work was extremely unpleasant. Instead of taking new patients to the hospital, Martin and his co-workers spent most of their time transporting deceased individuals from the hospital to the cemetery. Because most people of means hired undertakers to bring their dearly departed loved ones to graveyards, Martin and his crew were responsible for burying those who were deemed paupers. Martin later wrote about the experience in his autobiography: "Three of us were kept busy running light wagons and we took two loads a day each and four dead bodies on each wagon at a time. The average paupers we buried each day was 24." Before the pestilence subsided, one of Martin's co-workers also joined the ranks of the dead; another became ill but survived. For his part, Martin remained healthy and was on his way to Utah by the end of summer.[85]

Hundreds of others didn't experience such a happy ending. For them the seven days leading up to July 15 saw the last breath of life leave their bodies as the cholera outbreak finally peaked. As they had since the first weeks in May, sextons around the city sent their daily burial counts to the local newspapers, which then published the figures for each local cemetery. The sextons' count, as reported in the *Republican*, totaled 709; the official numbers for the week as supplied by the City Register's office reflected a staggering 722 persons dying from cholera out of 937 total deaths recorded. Of those deaths, more than a quarter of the victims were children under the age of five. Dr. William McPheeters later wrote that July 9 "will long be remembered by the citizens of St. Louis" as the most tragic day of the epidemic, when 145 residents died in the span of twenty-four hours.[86]

With the spectre of death seemingly lingering on everyone's doorstep, fear and anxiety within the most vulnerable populations began to man-

During the height of the cholera epidemic in July 1849, the *Daily Missouri Republican* regularly reported the number of deaths due to the disease and interments in local cemeteries. Newspaper clipping, July 1849. Missouri Historical Society Collections.

THE REPUBLICAN.

ST. LOUIS:
WEDNESDAY MORNING, JULY 11, 1849.

CITY MORTALITY.—The reports for Monday, as far as received at the Register's office yesterday, show an increase in the mortality of the city, compared with the day previous. Since the epidemic, which is now sorely afflicting our city, first commenced its ravages, it has been a fact worthy of notice that the mortality for Monday, and during the first of the week, largely exceeds that of the previous three or four days. This may be accounted for from the fact that during Sunday dissipation or irregular habits are indulged in to an excessive extent by a large class of citizens, upon whom, if their systems are the least predisposed, the disease is fatal in its consequences. For the general increase upon these days, we can ascribe no other cause, most especially when the weather as been as pleasant and clear as that which has prevailed the past two days. The interments for Sunday were 107 in all, and eighty of cholera. The interments for Monday were as follows:

		of Cholera
Catholic, (old,)	27 in all	22
" (new,)	10 "	10
St. Vincent,	20 "	16
City,	17 "	13
Holy Ghost,	16 "	12
German Protestant,	14 "	10
Christ Church,	8 "	8
Wesleyan,	8 "	7
Methodist,	4 "	2
Baptist,	1 "	1
Lutheran,		
Presbyterian,	} Not reported.	
United Hebrew,		
Total,	125	101

THE MORTALITY FOR YESTERDAY.—We have the painful duty to announce to our citizens that the returns for yesterday, show a fearful and mournful increase of the epidemic. Arrangements were made yesterday, by which the interments of each day, could be reported the succeeding morning.

There is nothing in the reports of yesterday to congratulate our citizens upon. We all know that the tide of foreign emigration has been stayed by the Quarantine, and many of our residents have fled from the city, our population is now reduced many thousands, and yet with all this the bills of mortality are swelled to an alarming extent.

The following are the returns for yesterday up to 10 o'clock. They do not include the Baptist, and we may add, that there were five corpses in the City Cemetery, the causes of death the Sexton had not the time to ascertain. The total number of interments we set down at 189.

		of cholera
City Cemetery,	33 in all.	28
German Protestant,	19 "	15
Lutheran,	3 "	1
Holy Ghost,	18 "	14
St. Vincent,	27 "	20
Catholic old,	35 "	28
" new,	8 "	6
Methodist,	13 "	9
Wesleyan,	13 "	13
Presbyterian,	4 "	3
Christ Church,	10 "	7
United Hebrew,	1 "	1
Baptist,	not reported.	
Total,	184	145

Without intending to excite any improper alarm we are compelled to call upon our citizens to greater exertion and prudence in their habits and modes of living. The existence of this disease has seemed to give a latitude to dissipation and indulgence which are as fatal as absolute abstemiousness. It is high time that every one candidly considered the course of life he ought to preserve and the prudent restraints he should impose upon his appetites and his pleasures. In the bills of to-day we see many who are the victims of fear, of over indulgence, and all more or less the result of an indifference to the regularity of their bodies.

BANK ATTORNEY.—The office of Attorney to the

ifest itself in violence. In the midst of the worst weeks of the outbreak, business on the levee also deteriorated. Dozens of steamboats laden with goods were stranded in port, unable to move their cargo. As a result, hundreds of Irish deckhands were laid off. Now with little to do but wait around the levee hoping for job prospects, these men found themselves with plenty of time on their hands.

Just as in the Old Country, tensions existed between the city's Protestant and Catholic Irish communities. Although these differences rarely erupted in violence, the one-two punch of cholera and unemployment changed the situation. A quarrel between Northern and Southern Irishmen on the levee one Friday afternoon in mid-July resulted in a running melee as one gang overran the steamer *Governor Briggs* and forced its crew to abandon ship. Things weren't much better on the steamboat *Iowa*, where a laborer was severely beaten and stabbed. Police broke up that fight, but more skirmishes erupted periodically over the next several days. The *Republican* noted one possible reason why on July 22, reporting, "It was currently rumored yesterday that near two hundred men from the North of Ireland had taken an oath to their leaders to whip the Southern Irishmen whenever and wherever they may find them." A heavy police presence on the levee seemed to keep the peace for a while, but problems persisted.[87]

The Beginning of the End

What the city couldn't realize at the time was that the darkest days of the outbreak were past. Soon the reported numbers of daily burials began to drop. Not wanting city residents to abandon the practices that appeared to be slowing cholera's spread, the newspapers approached the improving situation with cautious optimism. Within the column featuring the daily number of interments in city cemeteries, the *Republican* wrote: "We congratulate our citizens upon this evidence of the rapid decline of the epidemic. . . . In doing so, we would urge upon the propriety of continuing to observe prudence in their diets and habits."[88]

The number of daily interments reported certainly provided some proof that things might be improving. As soon as July 10—one day

Wood-and-ivory piccolo of Otto Wocher, one of the first musicians to perform in the St. Louis Philharmonic Orchestra, founded in 1845. Wocher fell victim to cholera during the worst days of the epidemic in July 1849. Piccolo, ca. 1845. Missouri Historical Society Collections.

after the highest recorded amount of daily deaths—124 persons were buried in city cemeteries, a decrease of 21 victims. Each subsequent day showed a marked decrease in interments. By July 20 the number had fallen to 36; by July 25 it was down to 19. Although the weekly totals still remained disturbingly high compared to the city's normal mortality rates, it was becoming clear that an end was in sight.

The situation was also improving over on Quarantine Island. The number of sick confined to the station was declining. Members of the Committee of Public Health inspected the facility in the days after the epidemic had peaked in the city and found that the island had only eighty residents awaiting permission to leave. Few of these individuals were actually sick, and those who were ill did not, by the conclusions of the physicians examining them, suffer from cholera. City officials were pleased with the quarantine experiment and felt that had it not been imposed, mortality rates might have been even higher in the city. Based on this assumption, the committee recommended that Quarantine Island become a permanent fixture of city operations.[89]

Over the course of the cholera outbreak and the development of the quarantine station, the facility at Quarantine Island took on a life of its own. The physicians and staff who worked there witnessed countless heartbreaking stories of death and survival. Thousands of scared and confused immigrants passed through, many of whom felt they were being unduly confined. The *Republican*'s editors were quick to point out that despite the fact that mortality on the island was much lower than in the city, "no power of argument will convince a person in quarantine that he is not a great deal better off in the city."

Often angry with their predicament, the "mass regard it as imprisonment, and, with tears and threats, implore and demand liberation."

The staff found themselves caring for all manner of situations, including orphaned children. In one instance, a German woman and her two young daughters were traveling upriver on their way to Galena, Illinois, to join her husband who had immigrated earlier. Upon arriving at the quarantine station, the mother passed away, leaving Captain Moore, the station's administrator, and the resident Sister of Charity to care for the girls' well-being.[90]

An even greater challenge was the case of a mentally ill woman who identified herself as Catherine Weber. Her predicament intrigued some who found her both pitiful and mysterious. A *Republican* reporter wrote: "She is a harmless creature, and might be said to be more idiotic than crazy. She roams all over the grounds visiting every bed, especially the sick, and seems to have a very correct idea of those who are going to die. A few minutes before death occurs, she is there, standing by them, and when they die she is very officious in closing their eyes, laying their bodies out, and fixing their limbs in proper position." Weber went to great lengths to see that her fellow patients received a proper burial by making wreaths for the graves and singing hymns upon their interment. When she wasn't engaged in her funeral rituals, she was up "nearly all hours of the night and day," waiting for the arrival of the next boat and standing by the river bank chanting "her songs." The reporter also noted, "We are not much given to the melting mood but when we see a female exposed to the pitiless jests, annoyance, and even insults of the unthinking crowd, we are more afflicted than with death in all its haggard forms."[91]

Tensions Explode

As July progressed, the number of victims in the city continued to decline until, by the final days of the month, the end of the epidemic was apparent. For weary residents and exhausted city officials, the most horrific summer ever witnessed in St. Louis finally seemed to be coming to an end. But just when things looked up, July supplied one more ugly surprise: The tensions between the Irish gangs, which had simmered for days, at long last came to a boil in the wee hours of July 29.

That morning the fire companies responded to an alarm on the levee that threatened to repeat the disaster of the Great Fire in May. Aboard the steamer *Algona*, a fire had started in the engine room. It quickly engulfed the boat and spread to the four steamboats nearby. According to some reports, the firemen asked some local Irish boat-men to assist them with working the engine only to be rebuked. Un-deterred, the firemen contained the fire to the boats, preventing it from spreading inland as the Great Fire had two months earlier. Everything was under control, at least for a while.

After the fire was extinguished, several of the firefighters lingered on the levee, supposedly watching a dogfight at one of the area's saloons. A member of the Franklin Fire Company approached one of the dogs and reportedly patted him on the head. As he did so, for reasons that are lost to history, a member of the city's Irish Catholic community stepped forward and slammed him in the back and head with "a heavy piece of iron." The perpetrators fled immediately, with the angry firemen in hot pursuit. A policeman in the vicinity man-aged to arrest the guilty Irishman, but soon his friends arrived. They threatened to demolish the Franklin Fire Company's fire engine. Soon the engine and its crew were being bombarded with stones and mis-siles. According to an account later provided by the fire company, its members then took cover and awaited calm.

When the crowd of assailants dispersed, the firemen returned to their engine and prepared to take it home. Another wave of men sud-denly arrived with firearms and began shooting at the firemen. In the ensuing gunfire, Captain Grant of the Franklin Company was hit, but his wound wasn't serious.

Under fire, the firemen, who were also apparently armed, found themselves in a running battle through the streets of St. Louis's Irish neighborhoods. When the Irish Catholics retreated to James O'Brien's coffeehouse on Morgan Street, the firemen responded by shooting into the building. Fleeing up Morgan, the Irishmen moved from building to building; the angry firemen followed behind, leav-ing demolished structures in their wake. The sounds of shattering glass, whizzing bullets, and the crashing of kicked-in doors rever-berated along Morgan and Green streets in the city's Battle Row neighborhood.

Finally, the police arrived and managed to restore some calm. Men on both sides were arrested and taken to the calaboose (jail), but this was only a temporary reprieve. Crowds of furious Irishmen soon gathered outside the fire stations and paraded up and down the streets in "threatening squads." Fearing that they were outgunned, the firemen organized a raid on an old steamboat moored in the boatyards of Gaty, McCune, and Glasby, north of the levee. There they seized an old six-inch howitzer from the steamboat *Missouri*. They took the cannon, which was loaded with iron slugs and boiler-iron punchings, to the levee and positioned it in such a way that it would "rake Battle Row," where many of the Irish boatmen lived in boarding houses.

The St. Louis Greys, a local militia unit, was mobilized along with a group of volunteer citizens to restore the peace. Violence continued well into the night, but the police ultimately were able to seize the cannon and make arrests. Although scores of men were involved, only twenty-seven rioters were arrested on both sides. Over the next few days, the St. Louis Recorder's Court was the scene of many trials for those who were charged with rioting and assault. The court handed out numerous guilty verdicts, but no one was sentenced to anything more than fines ranging from five dollars to twenty-five dollars, despite the fact that thousands of dollars in property damage and countless injuries had occurred.[92]

The Epidemic Finally Ends

On August 1, 1849, St. Louis could finally say with confidence that the worst of the cholera epidemic was behind it. As the city cleaned up from the July 29 riot and the death toll from cholera subsided, the Committee of Public Health prepared to disband. The newspapers announced the following day that the epidemic was officially concluded and that the business of monitoring the city's health would return to those in charge at city hall.[93]

Many St. Louisans viewed the committee members as heroes. Dr. William McPheeters, the physician who encountered the first local case of cholera back in January, believed that although the benefits of the committee's efforts couldn't be truly quantified given the mysterious nature of cholera, the group deserved commendation. In an essay for *The St. Louis Medical and Surgical Journal* he wrote that "too much praise cannot be awarded to the Committee of Health, for the prompt and efficient manner in which they discharged the duties assigned them."[94]

There will never be an accurate count of those who fell victim to the pestilence in 1849 St. Louis. Officially, according to McPheeters, the total number was 4,547, but he admitted that the true number was impossible to calculate. During the epidemic, 8,603 individuals died in the city, but because the medical community didn't truly understand all aspects of the disease, many more of that number may have died from cholera than the official 4,547. "As frightful as this array of figures may seem," noted McPheeters, "they do not tell the whole story, as it is well known that scores, even hundreds, were taken to the country, and across the river, or otherwise secretly buried, without having reported to the Register."[95]

Furthermore, the number couldn't account for the thousands who simply passed through the city heading westward. The deaths of slaves and other marginal community members likely weren't recorded accurately either.

Although cholera didn't disappear completely from this corner of the world— occasional deaths from the disease occurred well into 1850—it would never again inflict the same amount of damage on the people of St. Louis. In the year following the Civil War, cholera returned, but it was met with a more immediate response. Casualties were high but didn't match those of 1849. As the nineteenth century progressed, medical science finally caught up with its bacterial enemy, and cholera became far less of a threat. However, the disease continues to take its share of victims today, mostly in countries with inadequate supplies of clean drinking water.

Though we tend to give cholera little thought now, those who faced it deserve to be remembered. So too do the medical scientists, such as Dr. John Snow, who fought to ease cholera victims' suffering—they paved the way for our modern understanding of medicine and saved countless lives in the process.

CHAPTER TWO: '49ERS COMING THROUGH!

Anyone familiar with the history of the American West will certainly recognize the name John Sutter. It was his California property where the first flecks of gold were seen glittering through the silt deposited by the waters at his mill. The resulting gold fever spread across the world and transformed northern California from what had been a quiet Spanish backwater to the most bustling point on the planet in 1849.

Tens of thousands of men from Europe, Asia, and South America joined equally excited Americans in a frenzy to become rich in the gold fields. Many of the gold seekers arrived in California by sea, sailing from ports in New York, Boston, and New Orleans. Some endured the slow, treacherous journey around South America's Cape Horn. Others took the faster, yet no less risky, Central American route across the Isthmus of Panama via the yellow-fever–infested, bandit-ridden Chagres River. The remainder took the third option: the overland route up the Missouri River to Independence, Missouri; across the Great Plains; and over the Rockies and Sierra Nevadas. This path took them straight through St. Louis, the Gateway to the West. For the city's merchants, manufacturers, public officials, and con men, the gold rush was truly a golden opportunity—one each group sought to exploit in any way it could.

The Gold Rush Begins

In August 1848, Richard Barnes Mason, a general in the U.S. Army, forwarded an official report to Washington from his post in California, dramatically changing the history of America and altering the lives of hundreds of thousands of people around the world. The report was compiled to confirm for President James K. Polk the existence of gold deposits in upper California. Speculation and rumors about the nature of the gold finds in California had filtered back east, but Mason's report put to rest any ideas that it was all an exaggeration. Gold fever, the descriptive term given to the obsession people developed with striking it rich in the gold fields, immediately seized populations worldwide, especially young, single men. Those afflicted with gold fever dropped everything to head for California.

On the West Coast, everyone from San Francisco to Oregon seemed to abandon their homes and livelihoods to try their luck at panning for gold along the Feather and American rivers in the foothills of the Sierra Nevada Mountains. In St. Louis the local newspapers expressed more concern for the approaching threat of cholera, the 1848 presidential elections, and William Smith O'Brien's failed rebellion in Ireland than for rumors of gold. A few scattered reports of Sutter's discovery made the papers through the spring and summer of 1848, but the "California gold question"—as it was referred to in the *Daily Missouri Republican*—only began to receive more generous coverage near the end of the year.

In November it was reported that General Mason had come across a company of army deserters who had gone AWOL in order to try their luck in the gold fields. The general had them arrested and hauled off to a military jail to await a court-martial. The story seemed to give a bit more credence to the seriousness of gold fever. Then in December an article mentioned that a group of men returning from California had reached St. Joseph, Missouri. They brought back gold dust with them from the Feather River, which seemed to better satisfy skeptical Show-Me State residents. The *Republican* also noted that two nuggets had reached a St. Louis jeweler, who declared them genuine. With these reports, excitement began to build. Finally, samples of gold reached the War Department in Washington via courier from Mason. The American press sounded the alarm, and the gold rush was on.[1]

In his diary, Reverend Charles Peabody recorded his thoughts and observations about the gold mania from his new permanent home in St. Louis. He noted, "Various rumors have been afloat during the past three months that gold had been found there but nothing in a definite or tangible shape till within a few days past when the official statement of Col. Mason, Gov. of California, has been published." Confirmation of the rumors, Peabody declared, was "wonderful news." He rightly predicted that "there are hundreds in this city who as soon as spring opens will start for California." But he also speculated, in his puritanical way, that the discovery would lead to years of banditry and moral erosion throughout society.[2]

A slow trickle of gold seekers began to join the growing number of westward pioneers passing through St. Louis by late 1848, but winter kept most people from attempting an overland crossing. Snow and ice may have forced them to stay put for the moment, but neither kept them from planning and dreaming. The editor of the *Weekly Reveille* told readers a story about his friend, a local shopkeeper who displayed all the signs of gold fever. The lure of adventure and the possibility of achieving spectacular wealth tormented him while his rational side tried to keep him firmly planted in reality. After a snowstorm had dumped several inches on the ground in early December, the shopkeeper shoveled his front walkway and used the time to ponder his choices. "He labored away, every motion in the wet, cold snow relieving him of a portion of the fever, until the hard work, the unpleasantness of digging with a sure enough iron spade, out in the disagreeable atmosphere of December, almost worked a perfect cure." Then, nearly

Newspaper editors and others enjoyed poking fun at those who dropped everything to join the Gold Rush. This caricature shows a well-outfitted '49er on his way to California. Hand-colored lithograph by N. Currier, ca. 1849. Missouri Historical Society Collections.

done with his labors and mostly convinced that a trek across the continent to California would be a waste of time, "his eye caught a hillock of snow, which he had neglected, and seizing his spade, he made a vigorous dash at the obstruction." He thrust the spade into the pile and turned over the cake of snow and "there lay, snuggling embedded in the ice, a two-and-a-half-dollar gold piece!" With the discovery, his fate was sealed. "He set about taking an inventory, with a view of making an instant journey to the Pacific *El Dorado*."[3]

Impatient as those stricken with gold fever may have been, they had to wait for Mother Nature to give the all clear. Heavy ice on the Mississippi River kept the steamboats on the levee until late January, when temperatures began to warm and the ice broke up. No sooner had the river cleared than the afflicted began to move. The first to leave town was a local group of seven young men who boarded a New Orleans–bound steamboat on January 20 and set off for glory. The *Republican* reported that "all, or nearly all of them, have thrown up good situations, and leave behind them friends, comfort, and all the luxuries of civilized life, for the prospect of reaping a few hardships and a rich harvest of the glittering dust."[4]

Because winter made taking the overland route difficult, the St. Louis men were bound for the tropics and the Isthmus of Panama, where they could cross to the Pacific. This shortcut across Central America, which basically followed the route that would one day be transformed into the Panama Canal, potentially shaved weeks off the journey, making it the fastest way to California from the Midwest. Each day ships left New Orleans with passengers determined to cut through the jungles to reach the blue waters of the Pacific. With hundreds arriving daily, the Panamanians soon realized there was plenty of money to be had at this popular jumping-off point. Tales of overcrowded ports and slow-to-arrive steamers bound for San Francisco became commonplace in the letters sent back to St. Louis from the isthmus. One correspondent reported that an American, likely recognizing he could make as much money in the Panamanian port as in the gold fields, had opened a restaurant for travelers in a grass hut.

Crime along the route became increasingly problematic as the number of travelers grew, and the Isthmus of Panama became known for bandits who preyed on gold seekers. Others were victims of petty criminals and opportunists. As one traveler wrote in a letter to home, "I bargained with two or three natives to carry my 'plunder,' only I have arrived before them, and they may possibly not [have] troubled themselves to follow me at all."[5]

Making Money Off the Miners

Back in St. Louis, like their Panamanian counterparts, all manner of businessmen realized they had to appeal to miners' needs in order to cash in. Stories of large companies of men forming gold-mining collectives in the East and purchasing their supplies and equipment from suppliers in eastern cities pushed St. Louis businessmen to appeal to miners' sense of efficiency. According to the *St. Louis Daily New Era*, "A single concern in Pittsburgh are building one hundred and twenty-five wagons, all of which have been contracted by emigrants and adventurers to California. Persons east of this should not attempt to fit out until reaching St. Louis. Here, and in the vicinity, everything necessary can be procured upon at short notice and [at] more reasonable terms than in any other city west of the Alleghenies."[6]

Merchants and manufacturers readied for the flood of travelers by going into high production. Ads in the classified sections of the newspapers began to fill with notices targeting the westward-bound consumers. One merchant on Broadway announced he had surplus army tents, bridles, holsters, mule harnesses, and other essential items needed for the trip west. For those seeking a better bargain, he also promoted that he was due to receive tents salvaged from the wrecked steamboat *Andrew Fulton*, to be sold at half price.

Another business owner, George Getzendenner on Fourth Street, decided that a raffle was a good scheme for cashing in on desperate travelers. For the cost of a two-dollar ticket, gold seekers had the chance to win a team of oxen and a wagon. The drawing was scheduled to take place on St. Patrick's Day. For the lucky winner, it would have been a good investment because a yoke of oxen typically cost forty dollars and mules cost fifty to sixty dollars each. But buying a two-dollar ticket wasn't a small purchase considering this was the modern equivalent of nearly fifty dollars. Whether the raffle pro-

CALIFORNIA BEDS.

Be wise, and on your way to wealth,
Seek comfort, and preserve your health.

THE subscribers offer for sale and make to order, portable folding bed and bedstead, (for which they exclusively have a patent right,) which for the camp, or extra steamboat berths, are beyond comparison, superior to any before known in this country. They weigh only eighteen pounds, fold into a very small space, easily carried on a mule, and without matress or pillow make a substantial and comfortable bed, and may in a moment be converted into a table or sofa.

a4   SCARRIT & MASON.

ARMS FOR CALIFORNIA EMIGRANTS.

PERSONS desirous of procuring arms, ammunition &c., from the United States Arsenal in this city, under the recent act of Congress, can have the necessary papers prepared by calling on the undersigned. By this process they will make a considerable saving.

B. F. STOUT,
a2 tf   north-west corner of Market and Third streets.

CALIFORNIA RISKS.

THE NAUTILUS MUTUAL LIFE INSURANCE COMPANY, are insuring the lives of persons going to California. Those wishing insurance will apply to

JAMES M. FRANCISCUS, Agent,
mh29   corner Main and Vine sts.

CALIFORNIA PROVISIONS.

WE are prepared to furnish emigrants with flour in bags, kiln dried meal, dried beef, dried venison clear bacon sides, rice and beans in bags, the best sugar cured hams, &c., &c.

a16 1m   KING & FISHER, 40 Water st., up stairs.

FOR CALIFORNIA.

FITZGERALD'S PATENT PORTABLE FRONTIER FRENCH BURR MILLS, will grind from four to eight bushels of wheat or corn per hour; are very simple in construction, and not liable to get out of repair. They can be propelled by hand, horse, water or steam power. They are packed (all complete) in a box 2½ feet square and will weigh (including box) three hundred pounds. Persons going to Mexico, will find these mills profitable and they will do well to call and examine them, at the Clothing Store of   [feb7]   KING & CO., 62 Main st.

St. Louis merchants hoped to make a killing by supplying California-bound miners with provisions. All manner of products from beds and mining equipment to maps and travel guides could be purchased from the city's stores. Newspaper ads from the *Daily Missouri Republican*, April 9, 1849. Missouri Historical Society Collections.

ceeded or was successful for Getzendenner isn't recorded, but if it did happen, he likely pulled in a generous profit.[7]

A full range of products was soon available to those seeking to outfit themselves for the journey west. By March the *Republican* featured a full column in the classifieds section to announce the sale of goods and services just for California-bound travelers. Tools, rifles, mules, tents, gold washers, pumps, and an array of other useful products were advertised each day. St. Louis bookseller John Halsall also advertised his assortment of California maps and guides, including Edwin Bryant's *What I Saw in California*, a memoir describing the best routes across the Rockies and the Great Desert Basin.[8]

Merchants understood the gold-rush traveler's need to have useful products that were not only lightweight and easily stowed but also simple to assemble. From its furniture factory on Second Street, the firm of Scarritt & Mason sold a California bedstead of its own invention. It claimed the hinged bed "shuts up and occupies but little space, and is very light." When not used for sleeping, the bed doubled as a table, bench, or settee. Each end of the folding bed also contained pockets for storing clothing.[9]

The overland journey westward also required the use of a good, sturdy wagon. A number of wagonmakers had established themselves in St. Louis by the 1840s to take advantage of the needs of Santa Fe traders and emerging pioneers. Among them were Louis and Henry Espenscheid, who owned a factory that was located conveniently close to the levee. Now the gold seekers were their targeted consumers.

New wagonmakers got in on the game too. Henry Linsoth and his partner, Carl Keune, started Linsoth and Keune Wagon Company, which would later become one of the biggest wagonmakers in the West. Others sought to appeal to travelers' desires for comfort and multipurpose utility. One example is the merchant Taylor & Ferguson, which licensed out the right to manufacture and sell Bruff's Emigrant Wagon. This wagon contained a number of conveniences designed to make the overland trip easier. Much like a modern pop-up camper, Bruff's Emigrant Wagon provided an extended sleeping space for when the wagon train came to a halt at the end of a long, dusty day on the Oregon-California Trail. From the ridge pole of the wagon, an extension allowed for the attachment of a tent, which formed from the wagon's rear. On each side of the wagon, hooks and chains were attached to create instant corrals for livestock. Whether the wagon worked well isn't apparent, but it was just the kind of product that appealed to gold-rush consumers.[10]

Realizing that getting the would-be miners to their destination had the potential to be just as profitable as outfitting them, St. Louis's steamboat owners prepared for the coming travel season by remodeling and upgrading their investments. In February and March 1849, owners of the Missouri River steamers *St. Joseph, Julia, Borea No. 3,* and *Mandan* spruced up their ships with new paint and fancy molded decorations. Next, they refitted the boats with new mechanical systems in anticipation of the fierce competition for westward-bound passengers. Ready to join the others was the *Highland Mary*, commanded by a popular and well-known Missouri riverboat captain, Joseph Atchison. She was barely a year old, having been built in St. Louis the previous season. Despite being touted as "safe and fast," the *Highland Mary* would literally "hit a snag" in April and sink in eighteen feet of water, depriving her of a successful early run on the river. Luckily for Captain Atchison, she was able to be raised and repaired.[11]

The Next Wave Arrives—and Departs

By late February and early March, the westward emigrants were ready to set out, despite the fact that winter was far from over on the plains. One of the first to depart the levee was the steamboat *St. Joseph*, laden with "several wagons, a number of mules, and a large amount of baggage destined for California." Her destination was Independence, Missouri, where the company was forced to wait until the appropriate time to depart. Unfortunately for the eager travelers, it was a long wait, because the spring weather wouldn't cooperate. Snow was still falling in late April throughout the upper reaches of the Missouri River and Platte River valleys, delaying the growth of the prairie grasses that were crucial in feeding wagon companies' mules, oxen, and livestock. Nevertheless, back in St. Louis the arriving troops of '49ers continued rolling in.

By April 15 more than one thousand California-bound migrants had passed through the city in just two months, with more arriving by the hundreds each week. On April 18 the *Belle of the West* arrived with 150 men bound for St. Joseph; two days later the *Grand Turk* pulled in, its decks lined with another 400. Even for a town that was used to seeing hundreds of travelers on the levee, this was an impressive sight.

It was also an entirely different type of newcomer. Unlike the usual groups of families heading west to Oregon and the open territories, these cadres of gold seekers were typically informal groups of young men who had decided to travel together for safety and support. Many of them were friends from the same small farming towns in Ohio or Pennsylvania; others were groups of acquaintances from factories or trade associations in the East. Still others were better organized com-

> MORE GOLD DIGGERS.—The steamer Pontiac, ar-
> rived last night from Cincinnati. She brought around
> 229 passengers; of these about one hundred and
> twenty are bound for the gold region of California.

Local newspapers reported on the arrival of gold seekers almost daily. These groups were often large, such as this company of 120 men that arrived on April 16, 1849. Newspaper clipping from the *Daily Missouri Republican*, April 16, 1849. Missouri Historical Society Collections.

panies of men who pooled resources and money to outfit their journey. For example, a group of fifty men from St. Clair County, Illinois, came together in March to travel overland to the Feather River region of California, where they planned on constructing a "dike across the eastern half of Feather river, in order to form bars, whose sands will, it is supposed, abound with gold dust!"[12]

The Washington City and California Mining Association

One can sense the level of excitement and degree of determination in the stories of gold-rush travelers. They had big dreams and were ready to fulfill them. Such was the tale of the Washington City and California Mining Association, a company of sixty-six men led by J. Gainsborough Bruff, an adventurer, artist, and thrill seeker. Back in Washington, DC, Bruff had read Mason's report on the gold fields and was instantly seized with the need to pack up everything and head west. A dedicated Freemason, Bruff pulled together a party of his friends and Masonic brothers to create an extravagant, fully equipped, and military-inspired company complete with designated officers. Wearing specially made uniforms and decked out with their gear, the men gathered in Lafayette Park across from the White House on April 2 for a send-off ceremony. In a grand display of patriotism, style, and bravado, the men bid farewell to their wives, families, and sweethearts before marching past the White House as a band played them out of town.

77

On April 16 the *Republican* reported, "Yesterday morning the steamer *Robert Fulton* reached this port with one of the best organized and equipped companies we have seen." Bruff and his men impressed St. Louisans with their uniforms "consisting of gray cassimere pants and coats, glazed caps, white shoulder straps and belts, cartridge belts, canteens, &c." Everyone was taken with how well planned it all seemed. "They are also amply furnished, having every thing from comfortable subsistence, and the implements, tools, & c. deemed necessary for digging, smelting, and refining gold."[13]

The group spent just two nights in St. Louis, despite the fact that it was still waiting for some supplies and the company surgeon to arrive. The men were too anxious not to continue on to St. Joseph immediately. They boarded the large Missouri River trader *Belle Creole* on the afternoon of April 17. Bruff recorded the scene, writing, "We were on board amid such a dense medley of Hoosiers, Wolverines, Buckeyes, Yankees, and Yorkers, including black legs and swindlers of every grade of proficiency and celebrity, as is seldom found together." He was amazed at the amount of provisions, equipment, and supplies all packed on one boat. Every square inch from the decks to the holds was crammed full, and every stateroom "was an arsenal of rifles, fowling-pieces, bowie-knives, hatchets, pouches, powder horns and belts."

Despite being hampered along the way by falling water levels, the group eventually reached St. Joseph—only to find long lines of wagons stretching for miles, waiting to cross the Missouri River via a single ferryboat. Unwilling to wait the days or weeks it might take, Bruff and his compatriots followed a trail along the east side of the river into Nebraska before finally crossing the river and heading west. They arrived in the gold fields seven months later, a little worn from wear and less impressive than when they left the U.S. capital. In the end, Bruff returned east in 1851 with nothing to show for his efforts but a full diary and a portfolio of sketches—California's gold had eluded him.[14]

Matilda and the Con Man

Groups such as the Washington City and California Mining Association were full of excitement and optimism, but they were primarily composed of the greenest of men. They were inexperienced, naïve, and unworldly to say the least, and many of them were taking their first real trip far from home. The journey across the Great Plains and the Rockies would be the ultimate test for many of them—if they were lucky enough to make it that far. Thousands died of cholera and other diseases on the trails, while others suffered accidents or became victims of violence. One veteran '49er commented years later that the gold rush broke more hearts and claimed more victims than many of the country's battles.[15]

In St. Louis some of these greenhorns fell victim to the schemers and con men who were laying in wait for the next easy mark. In one case, a young man appeared at the police office "under great excitement," demanding that an officer go with him to arrest a man who had robbed him of the $150 he had brought with him to pay his way to California. When the police questioned the man, they determined that "the loser had engaged in a game of monte, by which he was fleeced." With a smirking tone, the *Republican* summed up the young man's story by stating, "His golden dreams were all thwarted by this affair; and, for want of funds to proceed farther on his journey, 'he supposed he would have to return home again and go to plowing.'"[16]

Laugh as they might about the misfortunes of naïve yokels, St. Louis investors soon came to find that one didn't have to be a clueless hick to get fleeced. The near-endless stream of westward travelers brought visions of incredible wealth to many who believed they just needed to discover the right means of tapping into the wellspring to make their dreams come true. This line of thinking certainly had the potential to cloud the judgment of even the most savvy businessmen, which is exactly what some people were hoping for. All it took to turn a dream into a nightmare was a believable story and a good game face.

Preying on the dreams of the vulnerable was the modus operandi of Parker H. French, an enigmatic but ethically challenged character whose real identity remains shrouded in mystery. The only things we know for sure are that he was a first-rate con man and that St. Louis has the dubious honor of being the location of his first successful scam.

In 1848, French was living in St. Louis with his young wife and seemingly making his living as one of the city's many merchants. It must have been a boring existence for someone who had spent his previous years serving in the Royal Navy as a powder monkey aboard one of Her Majesty's warships during the Opium War in China—not that he was an Englishman. Depending on which source you wish to believe, French was born in either Kentucky or Illinois, or maybe even in Boston. According to him, he was orphaned as a small boy and taken in by the family of a kindly Kentucky judge who raised him to be a proper young man. French never supplied much in the way of details, ambiguity being a better strategy for him, but he did generate magnificent tales and promises. Certainly claiming to have amassed a small fortune in the service of the Royal Navy in Asia was more interesting than reality.[17]

He happened to be in the right place at the right time by 1849. When word reached St. Louis that there was gold in the California hills, French wanted a piece of the action, but he didn't propose the conventional tack of becoming of a miner. Like most good con men, French didn't bore people with simple plans that seemed tried and true. He had something much grander and awe inspiring in mind. It was a plan that seized the imagination while offering the promise of sizable returns: French told local businessmen that he wanted to be the first to construct a fully rigged sailing ship in St. Louis and then sail it to California. Would-be miners could purchase a ticket in St. Louis, outfit themselves with everything they needed, and hop aboard the seagoing vessel without worrying about wasting the valuable time it took to make a transfer by land.

French had the plan all laid out. His ship would sail down the Mississippi to the Gulf of Mexico, past the east coast of South America, around Cape Horn, and then up the west coast of South and North America to San Francisco Bay. It was just the kind of scheme that appealed to those who had visions of St. Louis becoming the trading capital of the West. After all, why as a port city did they need to limit themselves to relying on inland waterways when they had a direct route to the sea?

Along with his partner, Peter Driskell, French expanded his mercantile business to become French and Company. Now the men needed the funding to cash in on their venture. They found that opportunity in the form of a relative newcomer to St. Louis, an Ohio-born wholesale grocery and commission merchant by the name of Winthrop S. Gilman. With Gilman's financial backing, French and

Company obtained the resources to fund construction of the *Matilda*. In late February, for what was probably the first infusion of cash to pay the workmen and obtain the needed materials, Gilman endorsed bills of exchange drawn from Hamlet Davis of New Orleans.[18]

Although St. Louis didn't possess a workforce of skilled shipbuilders, no one seemed to find fault in French's plan. For his part, French most certainly assured his backers that everything was under control. Victims of his later schemes noted that his most lethal quality was a combination of disarming charm and unquestioning confidence that seemed to make anything he proposed seem not only possible but also extraordinarily necessary.[19]

As the cold winds blew across the icy Mississippi River, construction began. Local ship carpenters Primus Emerson and John Thomas, who normally worked on steamboats, were contracted to build French's envisioned masterpiece, the unsurpassable and majestic *Matilda*. She would be made of the finest materials and include accommodations worthy of a first-class vessel. Designed by New York engineer E. Lufton, whom the *Republican* described as "a gentleman who as a mechanic and draftsman stands perhaps unequaled in his profession," everything about the *Matilda* sounded impressive. She was to be built entirely of oak and her hull secured with copper. She would have a 121-foot-long keel and a width of 28 feet, plus a hold that was 16½ feet deep. Her two decks would have the capacity to store the bulk of six thousand barrels.[20]

For passenger accommodations, the *Matilda* would have a 40-foot-long cabin divided into seven staterooms, each containing four berths. A main hall would stretch the length of the cabin and could be transformed into two apartments for ladies and gentlemen by means of folding doors. Even a portion of the ship's cargo was extraordinary: It was reported that aboard the *Matilda* would be forty prefabricated houses bound for the gold fields, valued at between $130 and $200 each, as well as a pre-assembled warehouse.[21]

The excitement of building an oceangoing vessel so far from the sea delighted and enchanted the city's boosters, including the *Republican*'s editors, who proclaimed that "the sailing of the *Matilda* from St. Louis for California affords an excellent opportunity for emigrants who intend going by way of Cape Horn." With all the excitement, it's easy to picture citizens gathered at the foot of Cherry Street, where Emerson and Thomas had established their shipyard, watching the workmen hammer away at a hull that was gradually taking shape.[22]

French promised that with good weather the whole thing would be ready to launch and sail by March 15. Passage aboard the ship was filling up as promoters advertised that the *Matilda* was the safest and most reliable means of reaching California. What the investors didn't realize was that French was also planning to sail away on the *Matilda*, with no plans of either paying for the ship's construction or providing any investor with a return on his seed money. However, because French was likely almost as clueless about the intricacies of shipbuilding as the average St. Louisan, he didn't count on certain basic problems that began to plague the project. First was the difficulty of finding skilled workmen who knew the ins and outs of constructing a quality ship in an inland city. Second, building anything outdoors during the coldest parts of the year isn't easy. These two factors com-

The *Matilda*, the only fully rigged sailing ship ever constructed in St. Louis, was touted as an easy way for '49ers to get to California, but she may not have ever made it there. Photograph by unknown photographer, 1849. Missouri Historical Society Collections.

bined to slow the project considerably, ultimately delaying the *Matilda*'s mid-March departure.

As the weeks wore on, French must have grown more and more nervous that his victims would eventually discover he had no plans to repay the money entrusted to him. As the construction limped along, he was forced to borrow more money. Gilman lent him another $2,400 by means of a thirty-day promissory note, and David T. Wheeler gave him a note for $600 in April. The debts were piling up, and soon the notes came due. Gilman had no choice but to notify the sheriff that French hadn't made good on his loans. As proscribed in the promissory agreement, if the borrowers didn't pay back the amount of the loans, which now totaled more than $6,000, the ship could be sold at auction to the highest bidder. In the meantime, construction continued, and a definite launch date was set.[23]

When news of the *Matilda*'s completion was finally announced, newspapers as far away as New York City heralded her anticipated launch. Between three and four thousand curious and excited residents crowded the shipyard on May 4 with "every shed and stand in the neighborhood . . . occupied with spectators" to watch what many believed to be the first of several sailing ships to soon launch from the St. Louis riverfront. Whether French was there to witness the *Matilda*'s launch isn't recorded, but given his uneasy position, he was probably far from St. Louis by this point. It can be assumed, however, that Gilman was there to see what his signatures had financed.

Reporters from the various city newspapers were on hand to witness the *Matilda*'s "introduction to her destined element." A *Republican* reporter captured the scene for readers as follows:

> Agreeable to the previous notice, a multitude of our citizens assembled last evening at the shipyard of Messrs. French & Co. to witness the launching of the first ship ever put upon the ways in this city. We arrived at the ground rather late, and found no little difficulty in getting an eligible position to see, so dense was the throng, including a large number of ladies. Some difficulty was experienced at first, in getting the ways ready, but at a few minutes before 6 o'clock, she glided off in majestic style into her native element, with colors flying, without any accident to mar the scene. As she struck the water the force of the current caused her to

careen to starboard, to the terror of a number of persons on board not acquainted with the cause, who rushed to the opposite side of the deck to the infinite delight of those on shore; but as soon as her full length reached the water she righted, with her bow upstream, and sat upon the river as graceful as a swan. The starting from the ways was hailed by the multitude on the shore with a prolonged shout, and long after she reached the element where she is destined to float, loud and repeated applause told too plainly how heartily our citizens greeted this new era in the growth, prosperity and mechanical improvement of our city.[24]

The *Reveille*'s editors were no less optimistic about St. Louis's future as a shipbuilding center, contending that "the launching of this vessel may be regarded as an event in the history, not of our city's growth, but of our city's unprecedented prosperity." St. Louis's position in the center of an area covered with fine timber, rich with mineral resources, and in possession of a growing manufacturing base surely meant that "we may see the launching of a ship become an everyday occurrence." Romantically reflecting on the progress of man over nature in the West, the *Reveille* proudly professed that "it produces a strange association of ideas when we reflect that not a century has elapsed since the children of the forest wandered over a territory where now education, science, and the arts have transformed the wilderness into a cultivated and civilized State; and that we shall soon see launched into the Mississippi ships whose sails are destined to whiten the most distant seas."[25]

What disappointment they would all come to know! Instead of traversing the rushing waters of the Mississippi, the *Matilda* sat moored to the river's bank as creditors sorted out her fate—St. Louis's future in shipbuilding had sprung a leak. Trustees' notices printed in the local papers advertised an auction to take place on the levee on May 28. Hoping to recoup his losses, Gilman apparently decided that he would buy the ship and pay off what was owed to the other creditors. As he waited for the day of the auction, the levee suffered its own losses when the Great Fire consumed twenty-three steamboats and barges on May 18. Fortunately for Gilman, the *Matilda* was far enough from the flames that she escaped injury.

On the day of the auction, Gilman succeeded in purchasing the ship. He took possession of it and made plans to take her south to the Port of New Orleans. For all the hoopla about the benefits and practicality of an inland-constructed sailing ship, the *Matilda*'s eventual departure received hardly any coverage. A small, nearly hidden mention in the *New Era* noted that the steamboat *Iowa* was contracted for $700 to tow the *Matilda* downriver. She quietly slipped out of port on July 21, bound for her new home where "she will be sold for the benefit of the present owners." The editors conceded that "her construction has been a losing business to all who engaged in it."[26]

The ultimate fate of the *Matilda* is difficult to ascertain, but the most reliable sources suggest she never realized her purpose of becoming a California-bound vessel. She was instead sold upon arrival in New Orleans to Johnathan O. Woodruff & Company, which ran an advertisement in an autumn 1949 issue of *The Daily Crescent* announcing that "the new, fast packet ship *Matilda*" would soon be departing for the Port of New York. The last clear mention of the boat in newspapers suggests she encountered some structural problems after leaving New Orleans, returned for repairs, and then finally left for her New York destination.

However, historian Charles van Ravenswaay's research notes mention that eventually the *Matilda* did sail from New Orleans for California with a load of gold seekers on board. Under the command of a well-known captain of the Pacific trade, John Evans, she rounded Cape Horn and sailed up the coast of South America—only to sink upon arriving in San Francisco. Nevertheless, no official record of her journey or verifying account of her demise has been located to substantiate the story. Certainly many ships were abandoned by their crews for the gold fields after they arrived in California, and others were intentionally grounded to convert into floating storage docks. Perhaps the *Matilda* made the long journey only once, but she still maintains the honor of being the only fully rigged sailing ship to be constructed and launched in St. Louis.[27]

As for Parker French, he was on to his next adventure. He turned up in a rented office space in New York's Tammany Hall in 1850, where he persuaded gold seekers bound for California to pay him $250 a piece to guide them to the gold fields. As a measure of good faith, he promised that he would refund them $5 for every month in which their arrival in California might be delayed. He did take them as far as the deserts of Arizona before abandoning them and taking their money to Mexico, leaving a haggard, half-starved group of men to limp their way toward the Pacific.[28]

Reflections on the Gold Rush

As the year 1849 progressed, companies of would-be miners kept rolling through St. Louis. The lucky ones reached their destinations, but for many others, death came to them on the trails before they ever set eyes on the stunning peaks of the Sierra Nevada Mountains. Cholera contracted aboard steamboats and during stopovers in St. Louis claimed thousands of lives, prompting St. Louisan E. G. Simmons to write to a contact in New York that "many of the eastern gold hunters on the way to California have fallen . . . and the river banks are becoming strewn with graves." The journey westward wasn't an easy trip even in healthier times, but the lure of adventure and possible riches continued calling to young men eager to head out on their own and find their fortune.[29]

Of course, the vast majority of them never found it. A large number returned home weary and heartbroken. Others never came back, choosing instead to remain in the Golden State and create new lives. Among them were many Missourians, causing California to be referred to as a colony of Missouri for decades. For a lucky few, like James G. Agnew, whom the *Reveille* announced was on his way home with "a considerable quantity of gold in its original state," the trip produced something beyond simply tales to tell the folks back home. Happy endings did occur, changing lives in many ways. For example, when Robert Lewis went to the gold fields, he took his wife's enslaved man, Jesse Hubbard, to assist him. Upon their return, Lewis rewarded Hubbard by divvying up the $15,000 in gold they had procured. Hubbard purchased a farm with his proceeds—and presumably his freedom too.[30]

Near the year's end, Charles Ramsey, editor of the *New Era*, reflected on the public's fascination with the gold rush, noting that "hardly a single issue of a single newspaper occurs in which is not

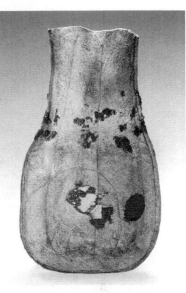

Lucky '49ers who had enough gold to ship used leather bank bags like this one to carry their fortunes back east. Gold rush buckskin bag, ca. 1849. Missouri Historical Society Collections.

seen some mention of the untold, indescribable and inexhaustible treasures of that golden land." Many of these articles, he observed, made terrific claims, but the real stories were those contained in the letters arriving from California, which had become so numerous that they "fall as thickly around us as do Autumnal leaves." Ramsey further observed that within these accounts were the stories of those who had endured deplorable conditions and painful suffering, describing "the personal moral and social condition of the multitudes who have sought that land of promise." Although it was true that those who returned had proof that the gold was present, they also testified that extracting it was a far more difficult task than what many newspapers and promoters had led people to believe.

Ramsey's verbiage was aimed at that species of individual who had been observed so many times over the course of the year passing through the streets of St. Louis and disembarking from the levee, who seemed determined to reach El Dorado without truly knowing what it might take to get there. He ended his comments with these words: "There seems considerable significance in the following sentence, which, from among many others equally emphatic, we clip from a California letter—'Any man in the States who has got employment enough to keep soul and body together had better stay there!'"[31]

CHAPTER THREE: GREAT CONFLAGRATION

From inside her home on Third Street late on the night of May 17, 1849, Sally Smith Flagg heard the clanging of the alarm bell at the local fire station, but because it was such a common occurrence, she gave it only scant attention. She crawled into her bed around 10:00 p.m. and was nearly asleep when suddenly the two other occupants of the house, Mr. and Mrs. Cavendar, burst into her room. The Cavendars, owners of a local mercantile store, had heard reports of a fire on the levee and wished to look out Flagg's upper-story window to see what was really going on. When they peered out the window, the three witnessed what so many others in the city were watching in the same instant—an inferno of burning warehouses and steamboats stretching the length of the St. Louis riverfront.

Flagg watched as two of the boats "completely wrapped in flames" swirled and crashed their way down the brightly lit river while another ship docked near their residence burned where it sat. As the wind grew stronger, the fire began to move with it, spreading the destruction inland toward the heart of the city's business district. Flagg and her companions watched and worried as the fire grew. She later observed in her diary that "many would call it a splendid sight, but to me it was nothing but pain."[1]

That pain was certainly justified given that such a tremendous calamity as the fire could have destroyed the city both physically and economically for a very long time, but fortunately it proved that the St. Louisans of 1849 were a resilient lot. This sense of strength is visible in the accounts left by those who witnessed the incredible destruction. Fifty years after the fire, many could still vividly recall the sights, smells, and emotions of that night. Merchants, city officials, doctors, and firefighters never forgot what it was like to live through the most dramatic event in St. Louis's 250-year history. Their firsthand accounts and recollections paint a picture of horror and bravery, heartache and determination.

Daguerreotypist Thomas Easterly created the only known photograph of the ruins of the city after the Great Fire. Daguerreotype by Thomas Easterly, 1849. Missouri Historical Society Collections.

Life on the Levee

The story of the Great Fire begins in the most vital portion of 1849 St. Louis: the levee on the city's wharf. Today, when all that's left of the old wharf are the worn cobblestones that line the river under the shadow of the Gateway Arch, it's difficult to grasp just how important these few blocks of riverfront property were to St. Louis's economic health. But at the height of the steamboat era, the levee was a busy, crowded, and often dangerous place. It was a hive of activity that stood as a point of pride for a city whose survival was tied to the existence of steamboats and the Mississippi River. Modern visitors walk along a mostly quiet riverfront, but in 1849 this slender stretch of land was a place where fortunes were made, incredible journeys were launched, and new beginnings were had.

A crowded and often dangerous place, the levee was also St. Louis's center of commerce and trade. Daguerreotype by Thomas Easterly, 1852. Missouri Historical Society Collections.

A visitor arriving in 1849 St. Louis by way of the river was greeted by the sight of a bustling levee and an impressive line of steamboats that ran for nearly a mile along the riverfront. Sternwheelers, whose enormous paddle wheels were mounted on their rears, sat moored next to side-wheelers, whose large paddle wheels were centered on their flanks. Great New Orleans–bound traders and smaller packet boats that made regular runs to ports such as Peoria, Illinois, and Westport, Missouri, shared the same span of the wharf. Inscribed on the boats' sides were names such as *Louisiana*, *Grand Turk*, and *Prairie State*. From atop each steamboat black smokestacks reached skyward, coughing out smoke and cinders from the churning engines that lay hidden beneath the white-painted decks.

Despite the levee's importance, little had been done to improve it since its creation in the days of the flatboats. It expanded greatly in length over the years, spreading farther north and south of the city's center, but a significant portion of it was still constructed of dirt and gravel. An expanse of the center portion had been paved with stone in 1844, but otherwise the landing was either a dusty tarmac or a muddy mess, depending on the season. No docks or piers were available for the boats to tie alongside, so steamboat pilots jockeyed to find empty space on the paved portion and lower their boats' landing stages so passengers and cargo could disembark. A reporter for the *Weekly Reveille* once noted that "during eight months in the year an average of forty steamers may be seen loading and unloading in front of the paved portion of the causeway." These steamboats and barges were often packed so tightly against one another at the water's edge that a man could easily jump from boat to boat for nearly the entire length of the levee.[2]

After disembarking from the steamboats, new arrivals found themselves in the midst of an army of deckhands, longshoremen, clerks, businessmen, and warehouse workers who populated the levee each day from dawn until sunset (or later). It was an amalgamation of all levels of St. Louis society. As one observer noted, "Our levee may be likened to a patch of many colored stripes in which are a promiscuous assemblage of human threads, ranging from the finest silk to the coarsest tow." Most of these individuals were employed by the warehouses and merchant houses that lined Front Street, which ran right along the riverfront. A virtual wall of three- and four-story brick and stone warehouses filled with merchandise and goods awaiting the next boat out of town separated the city from the river. Signs attached to their façades bore such names as Chouteau, Pratte, and Von Phul—names that many nineteenth-century Americans, not just St. Louisans, easily recognized as successful traders and merchants of the American West.[3]

Every day thousands of tons of freight arrived in St. Louis from great ports such as New Orleans, Louisiana, and Cincinnati, Ohio, as well as from sleepier ports such as St. Croix County, Wisconsin, and Keokuk, Iowa. In all, between two hundred and three hundred thousand tons of cargo entered the warehouses of the St. Louis levee each year, making St. Louis second only to New Orleans in amount of cargo received annually.

Each arriving boat carried either crates and barrels packed with china, glassware, nails, and countless other manufactured items from the East Coast or imported goods from Europe. The hold of a steamer might contain fruit from Cuba and the West Indies, coffee from South America, or tea from China. Stores of agricultural products, such as grains from the fields of north-central Illinois, were delivered by Keokuk packets, and bales of hemp grown in Missouri's Little Dixie region arrived aboard steamers fresh from the western waters of the Missouri River. Massive piles of wood and lumber from the Great Lakes region were stacked high to feed the city's booming construction needs. Barrels of brined pork from Kentucky arrived alongside barrels of whiskey from the same. The scope of merchandise only increased as the years passed, and by 1849 the selection of goods was equal to any in the great ports of the East.[4]

Most of the cargo that arrived each day fit in the warehouses, but bales of hemp, stacks of wood, and other cargo that didn't need to be stored indoors often were stacked neatly along the levee itself and covered with tarps to protect them from the weather. Depending on the time of year, Front Street might appear as some tremendous open-air market with all the goods piled high upon it, just awaiting distribution.

Responsibility for moving all of these goods to the various points in and out of the city fell to a fleet of drays, horse-drawn wagons that served as the equivalent of today's short-haul truckers. These independent shippers formed a constant stream of wagons leading in and out of the riverfront. Then, as now, traffic could be a headache. Consequently, the city posted day-patrol officers to manage the congestion the best that they could. Because the streets weren't laid out in any systematic way for the flow of traffic, keeping everyone moving and orderly was a frustrating job. Horse-drawn buggies and carts, mule wagons, pushcarts, and crowds of people thronged the levee during the day, dodging each other while attempting to maneuver among the ever-shifting piles of cargo.[5]

When the dray and hack drivers left the confines of the levee, they entered the crowded streets of the city. Built over the site of the original French colonial village laid out by Pierre Laclède in 1764, St. Louis in 1849 reflected a mixed bag of accumulated building styles and structures. Consisting primarily of brick-and-wood row houses, townhouses, early flounder houses,* and shanties, as well as a handful of surviving colonial structures from the city's earliest days, it wasn't unusual for a single street block to possess each of these types of construction. Streets running east to west in the heart of the city bore the names of trees, as if to give the impression that they still had some association with nature. Streets running north and south beyond Main Street were named numerically. All the streets were mostly unpaved and suffered the effects of constant traffic and weather.

The sky above the city was punctuated by the steeple of the Cathedral, the pride of St. Louis's sizable Catholic population. The property upon which it stood was the location of the original French Catholic church used by the colonial inhabitants during St. Louis's days as the fur-trade capital of North America, thereby linking the city's past with its present. The Cathedral was venerated as a place of worship and regarded as a symbol of beauty and progress for the expanding western city.

Overall, St. Louis epitomized the stereotype of a Wild West frontier town. It lacked maturity, sound legal structures, social stability, adequate infrastructure, and many basic comforts, but nevertheless, its people had already developed a deep pride in their community. Residents proudly watched as their bustling town spread out and grew more prosperous each year. It was developing a distinct culture—a blend of French, German, and Irish influences—that set it apart from all other American cities, and the visitors who arrived daily by boat surely sensed that uniqueness as they witnessed the comings and goings of life on the levee.

The Reverend Charles Peabody was one of those visitors. A traveling salesman of Bibles and other religious materials, he first arrived in St. Louis in 1846 and recorded his impressions in a diary that has survived to paint a vivid picture of life in the 1840s. Peabody's diary tells of his visits to many of the major cities along the Ohio, Wabash, and Mississippi rivers, but it's clear from his writing that he considered St. Louis a particularly exciting place. He described it as a "great bustling and wicked city" in the most affectionate of ways: "With all

---

* Flounder houses were common sights in nineteenth-century St. Louis. They have a higher front façade, with a roof that slants down to the lower back wall, making them look one-sided like flounder fish.

the noise and tumult about this city, I like St Louis. There is about it among the people an air of independent frankness & generosity which does not exist in Cincinnati."[6]

People-watching was apparently one of Peabody's favorite indulgences. With no lack of literary flair, he described the St. Louis wharf as a place worthy of being a setting in a Dickens novel. It was a hive of activity where all manner of business—legitimate or otherwise—was conducted among all classes of the city's population. When he arrived on November 6, 1846, he recorded the spectacle of daily commerce on the riverfront.

> One of the most prominent things I have noticed in St Louis is the tumult and excitement of the business world. A stroll of an hour along the levee or through Main St. will give a pretty fair exhibition of this peculiar characteristic of this great metropolis of the West. Here one meets a middle aged man with his eyes fixed upon the ground & contracted brow walking with rapid pace along the street. There in the door of his counting room stands another with a look of peculiar satisfaction in his face as he is congratulating himself over the $1,000 he has just cleared by a smart bargain. A third with pale & care worn countenance is walking slowly along with dejected eyes & in his very gait can be read a very heavy loss. Then there will be scores of well-dressed men hurrying this way and that way intent upon some bargain by which they clearly expect to swing a fortune. As they swap along with hurried pace, thin eyes seem vacant with abstraction while thin lips seemed to move as if in calculation of the exact issue of their schemes of gain. Then in the midst of all this hurrying to and fro of business men with rapid feet & eager looks, may be seen hundreds of mules and horses attached to drays, drawing the immense loads of wheat & produce of all kinds—boxes of merchandise— bales of hemp—hogsheads of tobacco & everything else that is ever seen moving in the business world. In the midst of this mixed medley of donkeys & horses are to be seen innumerable loafers or wharf rats as they may with more propriety be called.[7]

Peabody obviously viewed the levee with a certain sense of excitement, which is understandable considering it could be a fascinating place. But it could also be a very dangerous place. As in other parts of the city, crime was a growing problem on the wharf in 1849. More and more unsuspecting individuals found themselves suddenly separated from their money by means of a pickpocket, a fast-talking con man, or some knife-wielding tough.

Yet when it came to danger, crime was far from the only threat. In a time when personal safety was given very little thought, working on the levee held tremendous personal risk. Workers sometimes fell into the swift current of the Mississippi. One such soul was Peter Nicholson, "an intelligent Scotchman" who tumbled overboard from the steamboat *Revenue Cutter* and drowned. Coroner's inquest records of the day and newspaper entries frequently mention the unfortunate cases of bodies found in the river, many of which went unidentified given the high turnover of levee workers and passengers. However, the greatest danger lay in the vessels that arrived and departed from the cobblestone wharf each day.

The Perils of Steamboats

Steamboats may have been the bread and butter of St. Louis's existence, but the cost was high. Even though steamers had been plying America's rivers for several decades, the intricacies of steam-power technology weren't completely understood, which meant these powerful conveyances often turned into floating death traps. Many passengers eventually came to realize that boarding a steamboat and arriving safely at their point of destination was a roll of the dice. Any kind of calamity could strike as you chugged down the Big Muddy or the Mighty Mississippi.

Snags, whole sunken trees embedded upside down in a river's muddy bottom, were one of the most frequent boat killers on the Missouri River. Jagged roots or a broken trunk pointed up, waiting to catch an unsuspecting boat. Upon hitting the snag, the boat's wooden bottom would splinter, quickly sending it—and its passengers and cargo—to the bottom.

Boiler explosions were also common and often killed steamboat crewmen and passengers. In November 1849, St. Louisans were shaken to read newspaper reports of a particularly shocking tragedy that had occurred in New Orleans's French Quarter. The steamboat *Louisiana*, one of the larger New Orleans traders, had pulled back from the levee, ready to disembark for St. Louis. Suddenly tens of thousands of pounds of steam pressure built within the engine's boiler and found a flaw in the boiler's wall. Like a massive bomb, the boiler burst, creating an explosion that shook the streets of New Orleans for blocks.

The immediate release of pressure sent the wooden structure of the *Louisiana* in every direction and the remains of the heavy iron boiler skyward. The boats on either side of the *Louisiana* had their decks sheared off completely. Splinters and shards of wood rained down on the levee, as did iron shrapnel. Houses and buildings facing the levee were pummeled with debris as if shot by cannons. Traveling at tremendous speeds, a flying piece of boiler cut a mule standing on the levee in two while a heavy piece of engine crashed down on a wagon, killing its driver and horse. Newsboys lining the levee, selling the evening papers, were killed by the flying debris. But most tragic of all were the passengers aboard the *Louisiana*, as well as those on the boats around her. The *St. Louis Daily New Era* printed the grisly details taken by telegraph from a reporter for *The Daily Picayune* in New Orleans.

> We saw one man with his head off, his entrails out, and one leg off. A woman, whose long dark hair lay wet and matted by her side, had one leg off above her knee, whilst her body was shockingly mangled. A large man, having his skull crushed in, lay a corpse, his face looking as if it had been painted red. Others, of both sexes, also with legs and arms off, more trunks, lay about in different places. . . . But it is impossible to describe all the revolting sights which met our view.[8]

Sadly, those described were the lucky ones. Many others were trapped in the wreckage, which was quickly sucked under the water's surface by the swirling current. According to eyewitnesses, some were blown as high as two hundred feet into the air before landing in the river, whereas others were sent onto the decks of other boats. It was "one of the most deplorable catastrophes that ever occurred in the history of steamboat explosions," according to the editors of the *New Era*. In total, 150 persons were killed, including three passengers from

St. Louis: Major B. B. Edmondson, grocer Mr. Wilson, and a Mr. King of the firm E. J. Gay and Company.

The following day, the *New Era*'s editors lamented the loss of life and expressed frustration with the lack of concern that seemed to exist among passengers and boat owners alike when it came to the frequency of boiler explosions, writing, "All persons who travel upon a steamer, are hourly exposed, while thus traveling, to a fate similar to that of the unhappy passengers of the *Louisiana*, yet save only when the public mind is, for a moment, awakened by some awful explosion, it seems possessed by an indifference which almost amounts to apathy." As horrible as the *Louisiana* boiler explosion was, St. Louisans may have been more concerned with another steamboat weakness—flammability—after it had threatened their city's very existence earlier in the year.[9]

Steamboats were built almost entirely of wood, which became dangerously dry over the course of a ship's life. Under such conditions, accidental fires were nearly inevitable, as was the case on May 2, 1849. In what now seems an odd foreshadow of things to come, a fire was discovered aboard the steamer *Highland Mary* as she was moored near the foot of Cherry Street. Within five minutes the fire had spread from the *Highland Mary*'s hold to nearly every portion of the boat. The flames moved so fast that the ship's captain was forced to dive into the river to extinguish the fire flaming on his clothing.

Immediately next to the *Highland Mary* was a fellow New Orleans trader, the *General Jesup*. Acting quickly, the *General Jesup*'s crew successfully moved their vessel out of harm's way. Other boats tied nearby also managed to escape, including some whose moorings were cut so they could float away from the burning steamboat. The *Highland Mary*, on the other hand, was a total loss; she burned to the waterline, the flames consuming thousands of dollars of valuable cargo. The quick response of the crews on all the threatened boats had saved the day, but the circumstances would prove eerily similar to what lay ahead.[10]

St. Louis's Volunteer Firefighters

Prior to the establishment of the present St. Louis Fire Department in 1857, the task of extinguishing fires like the one on the *Highland Mary*

Members of Union Fire Company No. 2 pose with Dinky, the engine they acquired a year after the Great Fire. Daguerreotype by Thomas Easterly, 1852. Missouri Historical Society Collections.

was in the hands of ten proud volunteer fire companies. Motivated by civic pride and service to the community, these groups—which were part fire brigade and part fraternal organization—reflected the ideals of an expanding democracy in America. Reading reminiscences of those who served gives you a sense of the devotion and brotherhood that existed among these men throughout their lives.

The various companies were all tightly regimented and consisted of enginemen, hosemen, and pipemen who manned either the fire engine or the four-wheeled hose reel. In addition to the engines and reel, a two-wheeled tender followed along, typically manned by the brigade's junior members. These were young men in training who helped with less-skilled duties, such as hooking up the hoses to the fireplugs (the early name for the fire hydrants that allowed access to the city's water system).

Each company was governed by a captain or president who was elected by its members. These leaders were, or often became, prominent members of the community. Patrick Gorman, president and captain of Union Fire Company No. 2, was one such individual. Born in Kilkenny, Ireland, he arrived in the United States at the age of thirteen and settled with his family in Cape Girardeau, Missouri. Employment with one of St. Louis's merchant firms eventually brought him to the city, where he easily became a respected member of the growing Irish community. Gorman served as president of Union Fire Company for thirteen years, in addition to serving as president of the Hibernian Society and the Millers Association. Among firemen's written reminiscences, Gorman's name is mentioned frequently as one of the outstanding leaders in St. Louis's firefighting history.[11]

The members of Union Fire Company No. 2 standing on the corner of Fourth and Olive streets in front of the Canton Tea Company. The city's ten fire companies were as much social and fraternal clubs as they were units of firefighters. Daguerreotype by Thomas Easterly, 1848. Missouri Historical Society Collections.

The volunteer firemen were as competitive as they were fearless. Companies were in constant competition with each other to determine who had the fastest and most powerful fire engines. At other times they tested the abilities of the junior crews by holding tender races. The outcome of these competitions of strength, quickness, and agility produced bragging rights for winning companies until the next round of games. Although the rivalry may have been good-natured fun, it offered the added benefit of producing fire companies that displayed coordinated teamwork in the face of serious fires.

In 1849, St. Louis's fire companies proved that their dedication to the community went beyond fighting fires. As the cholera epidemic began to take its toll on residents, the firemen became nurses for the sick and otherwise assisted those who couldn't help themselves. These were true acts of compassion and devotion, but few could imagine that an even greater test of bravery and dedication of service was about to arise.

Samuel Hawken and Union Fire Company No. 2

Samuel Hawken, the renowned gunsmith whose namesake rifle is often credited as the gun that settled the West, was a founder of Union Fire Company No. 2. In December 1848, Hawken was riding on the company's engine, the Emperor, as it was speeding toward a fire near the levee when suddenly the driver lost control on an icy street. With little time to react and remove themselves from the racing engine, the men clinging to its sides, including Hawken, soon found themselves beneath the toppled fire wagon. Hawken lost a thumb and crushed several fingers on his right hand, injuries that left the hand permanently disabled. Undeterred, he continued to serve as part of the crew.[12]

And So the Great Fire Begins

On the evening of May 17, fourteen-year-old Rebecca Jenkins stood on the second-story balcony of her home at Seventeenth and Carr streets, near the farthest limits of the city. She watched as the eastern sky grew brighter with the unmistakable glow of a raging fire. Neighbors in the surrounding houses joined her, alerted by the distant clanging of fire bells. Word came quickly that steamboats on the levee were burning. Most of her neighbors must have surmised this sooner because many of them made their living as boatmen and would have immediately understood the nature of the alarms. The burning of the *Highland Mary* only two weeks earlier also would have been fresh in their memories; the intensity of that fire was a reminder that a steamboat's real vulnerability was the fact that it was constructed almost entirely out of wood.

St. Louis historian Tom Lynch noted in his 1880 book *The Volunteer Fire Department of St. Louis* that a western steamboat was "in reality but a tremendous pile of light pine wood and paint, and when once ignited as impossible to save as a pile of shaving under similar circumstances." When fires did happen, there were no safety features on board for putting them out quickly, other than a bucket. If a steamboat were en route from one port to another when it caught fire, it could mean the tragic end of that boat. If it were tied at a wharf, matters could get out of hand quickly.[13]

Jenkins and her neighbors soon realized that what they were seeing that May night wasn't typical: A fire of this intensity wasn't the result of one burning boat. The levee was a mile and a half from their neighborhood, but Jenkins recalled that they "read a newspaper by the light of the fire." Although it was nearly midnight, the sky shone as brightly as if the sun were rising in the East. The young girl viewed it all with an excitement that was hardly shared by the adults, who better understood that in a town whose old narrow streets were tightly packed with wood-framed structures, fire was the greatest enemy.[14]

Before the fire broke out, St. Louisans had enjoyed a warm and pleasant day. It was typical May weather in Missouri: a sunny spring sky, light wind, and temperatures in the low seventies. At the levee, it was business as usual for the most part. Some twenty-three steamboats were moored there that day, among them the *White Cloud*, which was owned by Captain O. M. Adams. She predominantly traversed the Mississippi River between St. Louis and New Orleans, but because she was smaller than most New Orleans traders, she also made occasional runs on the Illinois River.

At around 9:00 p.m., the night watchman of the *White Cloud* was approaching the boat as he prepared for his evening shift. As he began to board, he looked up to see someone coming toward him as if exiting the boat. It was a man he didn't recognize, so he stopped the individual to inquire about his business there. The stranger, whom the night watchman later described as a "raggedly dressed Irishman" explained that he had come onto the *White Cloud* in search of a friend. This was apparently a good enough explanation because the watchman allowed him to pass and leave the ship.

The watchman made his rounds and found nothing amiss. A typical night on the levee commenced, although a strong, steady wind from the northeast had picked up. Taking a seat on the *White Cloud*'s forecastle, the night watchman lingered for about thirty minutes before he smelled the unmistakable scent of smoke. He immediately suspected it was coming from one of the cabins. On the ship's last trip, a small fire had broken out in the ladies' cabin, so his first inclination was to check that space—he found the room fully engulfed in flames. The watchman knew he had only a few short minutes to try to extinguish the fire before it would become uncontrollable, so whether by his actions or his orders, the *White Cloud*'s fire bell loudly began to ring out an alarm.[15]

Three blocks from the levee, at the corner of Third and Olive streets, John S. Beggs, a member of Franklin Fire Company No. 8, was helping members of Missouri Fire Company No. 5 put away their engine after several of the city's fire companies had responded to a small fire near Twelfth and Olive streets earlier in the night. Just as he was preparing to leave his comrades, he heard "a quick, loud alarm given by steamboat bell on the north levee." Beggs and the members of the Missouri Company quickly sprang back into action. He recalled that the men jumped on the tender and "started at break-neck speed east on Olive Street to the river, and north on the Levee to Cherry Street; as we crossed Cherry Street the fire appeared to be bursting out of a state-room on the steamer *White Cloud*."[16]

The Missouri Company was the first to arrive but was soon joined by Liberty Fire Company No. 6. Beggs and the Missouri Company ran hoses to the nearest fireplug, which was attached to a foundry building near the corner of Main and Cherry streets. As the fire grew more intense, the men raced to prepare the fire engine for duty. They attached the hoses to the plug, then ran back to the engine where the remaining hose was unfurled to fight the fire. Beggs and the others carried the hose aboard an adjacent steamboat, the *Edward Bates*, so they could get a better angle for dowsing the fiery *White Cloud*. They stood on the boat's forecastle, pouring gallons of water on the raging flames. The fire "after a time seemed to be under control," remembered Beggs, "but it was not so, as the fire crept along the passage between the pantry and the main cabin, and set fire to the barber shop and pantry."[17]

As feared, the fire rapidly grew more intense. Flames and burning cinders rose from the *White Cloud* as she became fully engulfed. With steady winds fanning the flames, the fire soon spread to the *Edward Bates*. What happened next isn't entirely clear. Eyewitnesses later recalled that members of the *Bates* crew and a group of firemen had, in sheer panic, decided that the best course of action was to get her away from the burning *White Cloud*. Scrambling, the *Bates* crew untied the ship from her moorings in the hope that she would drift gently away from the danger. This tactic had certainly worked two weeks earlier, when the burning *Highland Mary* had threatened the boats around her. Contemporary newspaper accounts, on the other hand, reported that the *Bates*'s moorings had snapped as they were burned through by the fire. Perhaps this was an attempt to release certain parties from blame. Whatever the truth, the release of the *Edward Bates* took what might have been a containable fire and turned it into an out-of-control inferno.

Still on board the moving, burning *Bates*, which was now afire from every level of the decks, Beggs and his fellow firefighters had no choice but to abandon all efforts to save the ship and instead try to save themselves. Eugene Haas, a young store clerk caught up in the excitement of the moment, had joined the firefighters to help tame the blaze and was among those trapped. In the frenzy, Haas was knocked off his feet by a snapped rope and tumbled into the hold of the burning boat, where he lay unconscious. He later recalled: "The next thing I knew I felt water falling on my face and that aroused me. I got up and crawled out of there just in time, as the boat was then all afire and floating down a string of other boats."[18]

Now fully engulfed, the *Bates* was at the mercy of the Mighty Mississippi's swift current, which spun her out of control. She crashed violently into the *Belle Isle* and *Julia*, spilling burning cinders and hunks of wood onto their decks and setting them aflame. *Steamboat Directory* editor James T. Lloyd later wrote that "she appeared to be animated by some intelligent spirit which prompted her to involve the others in that destruction to which herself was doomed."[19]

Continuing on its perilous journey downriver, the *Bates* tumbled through an array of steamboats and towboats that lay in its path along the wharf. The *Montauk, Red Wing, Eliza Stewart, Timour, Alice, Kit Carson, Boreas Number Three, Mandan, Martha, Taglioni, Mameluke, Prairie State, Sarah, Saint Peters, Acadia, Alexander Hamilton, General Brooke, Frolic,* and *American Eagle* sat helplessly moored side by side as the fiery *Bates* moved toward them. Each caught fire before the *Bates* finally ran aground on the edge of Duncan's Island, a sandbar island that existed near the present site of the Poplar Street Bridge.

Frederick Colburn fought the Great Fire of 1849 along with nearly one thousand other men. He wore this ornate hat during firemen's parades and other ceremonial events. Painted fire hat worn by Frederick Colburn, ca. 1848. Missouri Historical Society Collections.

The scene must have appeared in person as though all hell had come to earth. When fireman Frederick Colburn arrived on the scene, he stood in awe as "the whole front of St. Louis seemed one vast sheet of flame." Likewise, a newspaper reporter for *The People's Organ* arrived on the scene to find the river "a sheet of flames." The blazing light from the burning boats was only occasionally masked by the immense clouds of black smoke that rolled off of them and into the growing crowd of firefighters nearby. Michael Fitzpatrick of the Liberty Company arrived to find that "you could not tell a man twenty feet away" due to the density of the smoke.[20]

But that wasn't nearly the end of it. The flames finally burned through the *White Cloud's* moorings, and soon she too had broken free into the river's current—but not before setting fire to her other closest neighbor, the *Eudora*. The *Eudora* was moored to the north of the *White Cloud*, but although the wind was blowing the flames away from her, the intensity of the fire was such that it made little difference. The growing northeast wind blowing across all three of the burning boats took the flaming cinders that had risen high into the night sky and sent them directly toward the shore.

Piled high on the levee were bales upon bales of dry hemp shipped in from the farms along the Missouri River. These bales made for perfect kindling, along with the piles of lumber surrounding them. The accumulating amount of lumber stacked upon the levee had concerned city officials for some time. A year earlier, then-mayor John Krum had tried to get the woodpiles cleared out, citing them as a fire hazard. Unfortunately, his pleas had fallen on deaf ears, and his fears had been validated: As the fire companies focused on saving the burning boats, the piles of freight and wood began to burn.

As if by some horrible design, neatly stacked among the dry lumber and hemp sat great quantities of barreled lard and bacon, which soon burst forth in the intense heat. A raging, grease-fueled dynamo of roaring fire now towered toward the sky. It formed a great wall of flames between the fire companies collecting near the levee warehouses and the burning boats. Colburn later recalled that "whilst our eyes were transfixed with this grand, but fearful sight, a heavy smoke bursting from one of the large levee stores gave notice of increasing danger to the City." The Naval Conflagration, as historian Edward

Edwards later termed it, had spread to the buildings along the levee. The fire was no longer just a threat to those whose livelihoods were dependent on the steamboats; it was now a threat to all.[21]

Flames Spread to the Streets

The continuous ringing of fire bells alerted St. Louis residents that this was no ordinary fire. At home with his mother on Tenth Street, John Leroy Carver, assistant engineer of the steamboat *American Eagle*, could hear the boats' bells sounding out the alarms. His immediate thought was that he needed to get to the levee to protect his employer's boat. He raced to the waterfront only to find the *American Eagle* already completely lost to the flames. "I saw that all that I had was burned," he lamented. Carver then joined his comrades in Mound Fire Company No. 9 to fight the blaze.

Members of rival fire companies dropped all notions of competition and quickly banded together against their common enemy. Franklin Company volunteer George Kyler heard the alarms from his room at a boarding house. He immediately dressed and ran to alert his fellow housemate, Hull Perry, who was a member of Liberty Company. Together they ran to the Franklin firehouse, situated a block over from their home. The two men grabbed the tongue of the fire engine and headed toward the scene. As they approached the levee, Perry saw Liberty men already fighting the flames and immediately joined them, leaving Kyler to continue on alone with the Franklin Company engine. Kyler struggled to pull the engine over the rough stones of Cherry Street toward the levee. He later commented, "I never could tell how I did it," but he did and was soon joined by the other members of his company.[22]

The Franklin, Union, Liberty, and Missouri fire companies were the first on the scene when the fire had been limited to the boats. But as the fire spread inland, other companies entered the fight. As Central Fire Company No. 1 approached the levee, flames broke through the roof of a two-story warehouse south of Green Street. The men of Central Company were able to extinguish these flames quickly, an action that proved critical in halting part of the fire's progress: At no other point in the night did the flames venture into the northern part of the city.[23]

The good fortune of the area north of the levee wasn't shared by the streets directly in the path of the increasingly high winds and flames. Although the firemen were attempting to halt any spread of the flames by dousing the roofs of the buildings along the levee, the fire's intensity was too much. To everyone's horror, flames soon leapt to shore once more, this time in a more central portion of the levee. Captain James S. Carlisle of the Franklin Company recalled, "It looked to us as if the city was doomed."[24]

At the corner of Locust and Front streets, smoke was soon seen rising from the roof of a foundry. Action to douse the flames was swift but to no avail because the fire had a new and abundant source of fuel—the multiple wood-framed buildings of the levee district. Although fireproof building technology was available, most of these structures had been put up decades earlier, which meant they were made out of clay bricks, native stone, and wood. The city's bricklayers had been hard at work building the emerging metropolis, but all of those brick buildings were held by wooden frameworks. Therefore, just as the dry wood construction of the steamboats often led to their doom, the wood-frame buildings of St. Louis were a perfect source of flammable energy.[25]

The Great Fire is most often described as one intense firestorm, but in truth it was actually two separate infernos. The north and south portions of the levee were halved by the South Market building, which served as the focal point of commerce for local farmers, traders, and auctioneers, in addition to hosting the city's town hall in its upper stories. Its loss would have been a devastating blow to the city's government and commercial interests. Understandably, firefighters gave the South Market building their full attention by painstakingly extinguishing small fires that continually erupted on its roof throughout the night. As a result, the building seems to have served as a sort of firebreak on the levee, which may account for the division in the Great Fire.

Although much of the attention was focused on the north end of the levee, where the original conflagration had spread from the burning *Eudora*, *Edward Bates*, and *White Cloud*, the boats on the south end of the levee burned with just as much intensity. Soon the buildings along Front and Main streets caught fire as flying cinders landed

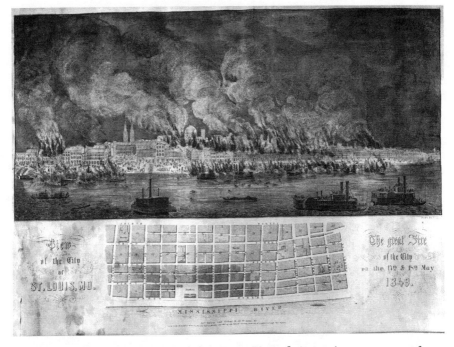

Because no photographs of the Great Fire of 1849 exist, we must rely on lithographer Julius Hutawa's illustration to understand the magnitude of the conflagration. Hand-colored lithograph by Julius Hutawa, 1849. Missouri Historical Society Collections.

on their roofs. The houses and buildings at the corner of Second and Main streets joined them as the flames continued their journey westward. One can only imagine the sense of panic residents felt as they saw their city burst into flame house by house and block by block.

As the hours passed and more and more buildings were consumed, it became clear that the city's ten volunteer fire companies couldn't fight the flames without additional help. Soon any and all able-bodied men were called upon for assistance. Captain Carlisle of the Franklin Company remembered coming across a group of about a dozen Irishmen watching the happenings from a spot on Battle Row, the rough Irish neighborhood situated near the levee's north end. He immediately sought to enlist them and shouted for help manning a hose. Carlisle was "told to go to Hell." He recalled their unexpected response when he offered them an equally curt retort: "They made a rush for me. I drew my [fire] trumpet and stood ready to do the best I could." Luckily for Carlisle, Captain Gorman of Union Company came up the street and shouted, "Hold on there boys. . . . If you hurt that young man, every one of you will be killed." Gorman, a greatly respected member of the Irish community, ordered the young men to man the hoses, and they promptly obeyed.[26]

Nearly one thousand men were actively battling the inferno at one point, but there still seemed to be little they could do to hold it back. Soon three blocks of warehouses on Front Street were burning along the levee. The flames then crossed Locust at Main Street and set fire to the businesses on the corner. In the midst of all the fire and smoke, the townspeople were in a panic. "Coals of fire larger than both of my hands fell over all the yard and house," observed stunned resident Frances Sublette, who was sure her home would be consumed by the flames that rained from the sky. The streets devolved into a chaotic scramble as individuals attempted to save what they could from the rapidly expanding fire. "Men and women acted like wild," recalled Carlisle. He watched as women and children ran through the streets terrified, calling for their husbands and fathers as the flames roared all around them. "Main Street was a roaring furnace, houses on both sides of the street were ablaze. . . . How it roared and bellowed—the crashing walls and houses."[27]

Business owners worked feverishly to move their stocks ahead of the encroaching flames. In order to do this, most needed the assistance of dray operators who could load their wagons and haul them to safety. Many accounts note that during this time the dray operators seized the opportunity to demand top dollar for their services. Dr. Simon Pollak recalled years later his attempts to assist two women who owned a clothing store on Main Street, near Vine. As the flames drew near, he secured the services of two furniture movers with carts at a cost of $30 each, which was roughly around $840 per wagon in today's dollars. (He may have found a bargain, because other sources mention that wagon owners were charging as much as $100 a load.)[28]

Pollak managed to get the clothing stock to his own offices and residence on Chestnut, nearly ten blocks from the fire. However, the flames were moving at such a pace that an hour later he found himself moving the items once again as the fire spread to his building. In the end, Pollak was able to save the ladies' merchandise, but his act of kindness came at the cost of his own property—he lost everything save one trunk and a box of books.[29]

Other property owners struggled to move things on their own. Those who didn't have the funds to hire temporary help sometimes devised their own methods for saving their merchandise. In a pinch, one German tailor threw his stock of material down a well—a decision that had him fishing out the clothing piece by piece for days afterward. Many merchants simply gave up and let the flames take what they had. Those who could afford it had insurance and knew that they would be covered in the end. Meanwhile, Captain Carlisle thought of his own business as he battled the flames. When he heard that the fire had already spread to that location, he took time out from fighting the fire to run to his own business. As he made his way through the streets, he witnessed a sort of surreal landscape, later recalling that "when I got up to Fourth Street, it was awful to see the goods and furniture piled all over the street from the Planter's House to Walnut Street."[30]

The panic and rush to save property allowed some to seek opportunity in the chaos. Looters began making their way through the streets, taking whatever might be left behind or momentarily set aside for retrieval. Trunks loaded with hastily grabbed valuables, silverware, and jewelry from burning stores—really anything that might be remotely worthwhile—were all fair game for the morally challenged segments of St. Louis's population. As the night wore on, the police arrested close to seventy individuals for looting.[31]

Successes and Failures

Back at the levee, the steamboats were still burning. Deckhands and others did what they could to quash the flames on several of the boats that weren't totally engulfed. Many of these still contained their cargo, including the *Martha*. As firemen on the levee fought to save the burning warehouses with their backs to the river, a powerful explosion suddenly lifted them off their feet and flung them like rag dolls. The flames had reached a cache of gunpowder stored below the

Martha's decks. A mushroom cloud rose above the levee as splinters and other burning debris rained down on the waterfront.[32]

Circumstances went from bad to worse as the night wore on when, overextended by the demands placed of the fire engines, the city's water system suddenly gave out. All across St. Louis, the hoses attached to the fireplugs ran dry. In some areas, small neighborhood reservoirs designed for just such an occasion were being employed by the engines, but they too were giving out. Only those near the river had a chance of battling the flames any longer. Fire captains from several companies ordered their men to assemble near the ferry landing at the foot of Market Street and pump water directly from the river. Here they would make their last stand and try to save what they could with the limited water available.

Meanwhile, every attempt was being made to save the South Market building near the ferry landing, but Mayor James Barry insisted on having the city records removed from the town hall anyway as a precaution. This job was placed in the hands of Sixth Ward alderman Isaac Sturgeon, who dutifully worked to carry out the mayor's orders. While Sturgeon concentrated on saving the city's archives, firemen continuously fought back flames from the surrounding buildings. Several times fires started on the South Market's rooftop, but each time the men were able to extinguish them before they got out of

Patrick Gorman served as president of Union Fire Company No. 2 for thirteen years. He escaped the Great Fire unscathed but was killed during the Civil War when a cannonball struck the steamboat he was piloting. Painted fire hat worn by Patrick Gorman, ca. 1840. Missouri Historical Society Collections.

control. Saving the South Market building was one of the firemen's greatest achievements in the face of the Great Fire, but yet another challenge was facing them just to the south.[33]

There, flames had begun to take hold at the rear of the Old Cathedral. Although the men of Captain Gorman's Union Company were valiantly trying to keep ahead of the blaze, they were fighting a losing battle. All around the Cathedral, neighboring buildings were completely engulfed. Seeing that they couldn't handle it alone, Gorman requested assistance from the Liberty Company, which was stationed close by. Michael Fitzpatrick served as the engineer aboard that company's engine. Hearing that the church was nearing the point of no return, he concluded that the Liberty Company should quit their current location and assist the Union boys.

Stopping in the alley adjacent to the church, they found the Union men exhausted and looking defeated. However, upon seeing the men of Liberty Company, their spirits were lifted and a shout of "three cheers for the Old Liberty; she has come in time" rose above the roar of the fire. Fitzpatrick and his men were close enough to the river that they could still use water to fight the flames, so the two companies worked together to throw jets of water upon the burning Cathedral and the roofs and façades of the buildings immediately surrounding it.[34]

Farther away from the river, residents were resorting to fighting the flames with wet blankets and whatever would hold water. Companies of men crawled on rooftops, extinguishing spot fires by throwing washbasins full of water and wet blankets on them. However fruitful this was is impossible to tell, but for most it was a last-ditch gamble worth taking. They only had to look around the crowded streets filled with those who had already lost their homes and possessions to find within them the drive to fight in any way they could.[35]

Over on Third Street, Captain Carlisle was relieved to see that his place of business was still standing. Instead of destruction, he found a group of wet, exhausted firemen from various companies attempting to restore their energy with a brief rest. As he and the others huddled together, they were suddenly jolted by the concussion from an enormous blast. At that point, Carlisle realized that those in charge had decided to attempt one last resort—blowing up buildings as a means of halting the fire.[36]

Captain Targee and the Firewall

With the water supply exhausted and the steady wind fanning the flames farther inland, city officials and firefighters alike decided it was time to take drastic measures to stop the fire's progress. At this point begins one of the most well-known chapters of the story of the Great Fire—and that of Captain Thomas Targee, an experienced volunteer firefighter and head of the Missouri Company.

In his day job, Targee served as the city weigher. He had arrived in St. Louis during the 1830s and had since gained a good reputation as an active member of the community. Based on his own understanding of the science of firefighting, Targee declared that the only way to stop the fire was to deny it the fuel it needed to continue by building a firebreak, a physical barrier that would slow the fire's progression. This was a dangerous proposition because it required pulling down buildings in the fire's path. The quickest way of doing this was by blowing up the surrounding structures with the only explosives at their disposal—standard barrels of packed gunpowder. Controlling the explosions' timing would be impossible; it was simply a matter of placing the gunpowder barrels and running. Nevertheless, everyone agreed it was the only chance they had of halting the fire.

To secure the necessary stock of gunpowder, Targee sent men and wagons to the St. Louis Arsenal, where the federal stores were located. Knowing full well that such an operation could be lethal, Targee spent the short time he had before the arrival of the powder kegs with his family. At his home on the south side of Fourteenth Street, he gathered his wife, Sarah, and their children around him. According to Joseph Boyce, founder of the Veteran Volunteer Firemen's Historical Society of St. Louis who later wrote of Targee's efforts, Targee explained the situation to his wife and asked her permission to proceed. For a father of six children whose ages ranged from seventeen to four, the decision couldn't have been an easy one, but if he indeed asked his wife for her blessing, she presumably gave it. With that, he kissed them all good-bye and headed back to the fire. At the corner of Main and Market, he met up with the team that had returned with the gunpowder.

Immediately Targee and his men went to work. Stacking the kegs for easy access and covering them with wet tarps to protect them

Captain Thomas Targee's heroic sacrifice in the fight against the Great Fire arguably made him the most iconic firefighter in St. Louis history. Painting by Mat Hastings, 1902. Missouri Historical Society Collections.

from the swirling sparks that filled the air, they began building a firebreak that would, they hoped, be large enough to contain the flames. Over the course of the next hour, Targee and other members of the Missouri Company lifted the heavy barrels of gunpowder onto their shoulders and ran into the buildings, placing them in such a manner as to weaken the buildings' structures as much as possible in an attempt to collapse them completely. Downtown, buildings shook as the thundering explosions did their work. Soon five structures lay smoldering in piles on the edge of the street, and the plan seemed destined for victory over the flames.

On the north side of Market Street, in a building known as Apollo Hall, stood a musical instrument store owned by James Phillips. Phillips had joined his fellow business owners in the mad scramble to save as much of his merchandise as possible before the fire could consume it. This turned out to be a wise move because in the early morning hours of May 18, Captain Targee had set his sights on bringing down Phillips's store.

Chapter Three

Taking no time to rest, Targee hoisted a barrel of gunpowder onto his shoulder and made his way toward the music store. Michael Fitzpatrick was manning his engine on Third Street when he noticed Targee run by him with a barrel that had a wet sack thrown over the top to protect it from the whirlwinds of burning cinders swirling through the streets like a blast furnace. Fitzpatrick watched him pass out of sight, then went back to his work, confident Targee had things under control.

Minutes earlier, Alderman Isaac Sturgeon had finished removing the city records from the town hall portion of the South Market building, but he had remained there in order to monitor the fire's progress. Climbing up on his horse, he surveyed the scene around him. Suddenly he caught site of Targee, "smoke-begrimmed and haggard through his grime," staggering past him on his way toward the block of storefronts. Sturgeon called after him, "Where are you going, Captain?" Without pausing, Targee yelled over his shoulder, "We are going to blow up Phillips's store!"

With axes in hand, a small group of men ran ahead of Targee toward the music store. They kicked in the door and battered it with axes to clear Targee's way before turning to run. Through the smoke, Sturgeon saw Targee enter the doorway, then almost instantaneously felt the impact of a deafening explosion. He caught the reins of his horse to try and turn away from the blast but saw "an object descending and with a sickening impact, it fell at my horse's feet." Upon regaining his composure after the shock of the blast, Sturgeon looked down to see that the object was Targee's leg, which had been severed at the thigh.

As feared, the barrel Targee held had exploded prematurely. Most likely he was the victim of the swirling sparks and cinders that filled the air. If even the smallest amount of gunpowder had been leaking from the barrels and connected with those sparks, it would have ignited instantly—Targee had no chance of escaping. Two local attorneys who shared an office near the music store were also hit by the impact of the explosion and badly burned. The men, Wells Colton and Russell Prentiss, lingered for some time before dying of their wounds.[37]

The Aftermath

As the light of dawn broke over the city, smoke poured from several blocks, but the largest portion of the fire was exhausted. The firewall had worked, as had the constant vigilance of the city's fire companies. Liberty Company engineer Michael Fitzpatrick recalled the fire captains finally telling the exhausted men that they could "limber up and go home." Fitzpatrick's company had valiantly helped save the Old Cathedral, and before the men left, "the priest came out of the rear of the church on a small porch, took off his hat, and raised his hands and said, 'God bless you men, you done good work and saved our church.'"[38]

Wet, cold, and tired, the men left the smoldering ruins along the city's waterfront to find rest. Mound Company fireman John Leroy Carver went home and cleaned up, only to return to the scene to examine the aftermath. He was most stricken not by the damage that the fire had brought upon the streets of his city but by the sight of the fire's many victims. Men, women, and children sat cold and exposed in the streets "without clothes to protect them" and with "nothing to eat." The image of these destitute individuals was forever etched into his memory. In 1909 he wrote, "It was a terrible sight—one I shall never forget—if I live to be one hundred years old."[39]

The Old Cathedral and South Market building, including the town hall, had been saved, but the remaining blocks of the riverfront north from Locust Street to Spruce and west from Front Street to Third were almost entirely unrecognizable. In all, 430 buildings were lost to the fire. The *St. Louis Daily Union* reported that the narrow streets of the city were "literally choked up with walls of fallen houses and destroyed property of various kinds." This scene of total devastation was recorded for posterity by St. Louis daguerreotypist Thomas Easterly. His glass-plate daguerreotype is the only known image of the aftermath; it shows a cityscape that closely resembles the images of Germany's bombed-out cities in the wake of World War II.[40]

Because these few riverfront blocks had long been considered prime real estate, many of St. Louis's most prominent businesses had been located there. Now a good portion of them had been consumed

Missouri Fire Company No. 5 firefighter William W. Branson's map of the city shows the extent of the fire (shaded blocks), the location of the firehouses, the site of Thomas Targee's death (#30), and the spot where the *White Cloud* was moored. Hand-drawn map by William W. Branson, 1891. Missouri Historical Society Collections.

by the blaze. Among the victims were three of the city's English-language newspapers, the *Daily Missouri Republican*, the *St. Louis Daily New Era*, and *The People's Organ*. George Knapp, owner of the *Republican*, managed to rescue files from his office but watched as the heat of the fire became so intense that the lead typeset melted and rolled to the floor, puddling in a solid mass. Also destroyed was one of the city's communications links to the outside world, the telegraph office.[41]

In the end around 280 businesses were destroyed, including two-thirds of the city's wholesale dry-goods merchants and half of the retailers, commissions, and grocery stores. Estimates for the total cost of the losses ranged from $3.5 million to $6 million, which equates to approximately $100 million to $170 million today. Business owners and investors were assured that all but two insurance companies were completely solvent and would pay 100 percent of their costs.

The remaining two, the St. Louis and Citizens insurance companies, would pay 70 percent of coverage.[42]

A fortunate circumstance was the fact that three bankers whose buildings were caught in the fire all reported that the fireproof safes containing their holdings had survived and that they would resume business immediately. Without an immediate flow of cash to local businessmen, recovery would have been a much slower process.[43]

At the river's edge, the burnt hulls of twenty-three boats lay in the current where they had been moored the previous morning, white and gleaming in the sun. The muddy-brown waters washed across the burnt decking and between the blackened wreckage, but closer to the smoldering warehouses onlookers were treated to a more surreal sight. Eugene Haas, the young store clerk who had tried to help extinguish the flames aboard the *Edward Bates*, recalled that "between the houses and the ruins of the boats was covered two feet deep with grease from the melted lard and bacon," which had been piled on the levee. "Such a sight you never saw in your life."[44]

Although the financial losses seemed relatively easy to calculate, the loss of life caused by the fire has never been completely clear. Some accounts note that three bodies were recovered from the wreckage of the *White Cloud* and another four were pulled from the ruins in the so-called Burnt District. The *Daily Union* reported at least one man killed on the levee by the debris scattered after the steamboat *Martha* exploded. It also told of a boy's corpse being carried into a police station. The *Reveille* ran a piece about a body pulled from the wreckage of a store whose pockets were stuffed with knives and other valuables; it was supposed that he had been pilfering the business when its walls collapsed.

Everyone in the city was aware of Captain Thomas Targee's tragic death. Many had witnessed the dramatic event Alderman Isaac Sturgeon described as the "finale to the fire." It was an act of heroism that has become the stuff of legend in St. Louis history. Many viewed his death as an act of martyrdom that ultimately saved the city. His sacrifice has never been forgotten: A dramatic oil painting of Targee valiantly standing with fire horn in hand graces the walls of the St. Louis Fire Department's headquarters.

According to Sturgeon, Targee's friends searched the rubble for his remains for days. His head was found nearly a block away from the site of the explosion. After all the pieces were located and placed together in a coffin, a ceremony was held at Christ Church. At long last, the hero was laid to rest. As a means of providing his widow and children with a constant source of income, as well as demonstrating the entire city's gratitude, Mayor Barry and the St. Louis City Council appointed Targee's widow as his replacement for the office of city weigher.[45]

News of the Great Fire spread as far as London. In the weeks afterward, newspapers across the country reprinted the accounts of the fire as they had appeared in the St. Louis papers. In cities such as Baltimore and Cincinnati, where investment in St. Louis's merchant and riverboat trades was heavy, the articles sought to soothe investors' fears by reassuring them that insurance companies were stepping up and covering damages.

In St. Louis itself, merchants almost immediately began plans to rebuild what they had lost. Local newspapers called on city leaders to widen the streets and improve the levee. Noted attorney Charles Drake wrote an open letter to the citizens of St. Louis from his home in Cincinnati, suggesting St. Louis take that city's lead and build large water cisterns in various corners to provide water supplies for fire companies. Meetings were called to gather resources for the relief of those who had lost everything to the flames, and donations arrived from the citizens of Quincy, Illinois, and Pittsburgh, Pennsylvania. St. Louis was on the path to recovery.

Arson or Accident?

Now that the fire was out and the rebuilding had begun, attention turned to determining a probable cause for the disaster. Unbeknownst to the public, police and city officials were conducting an investigation as early as May 23. Two men who worked on the levee were quietly arrested and brought before the St. Louis Recorder's Court for examination. These arrests were based on a charge of incendiarism (arson) committed upon the steamboat *White Cloud*.

Unfortunately, the record of these court proceedings, which would have documented the individuals' cross-examination, is lost to time. What remains are sketchy, incomplete accounts provided by the city's newspapers. From these published articles we can only try to piece together what might have happened that May night in 1849.

St. Louisans raised a variety of theories about the fire's origins in the days and weeks following the destruction, but according to the local newspapers, most people seemed to agree that the incident was likely the work of an arsonist. The motive? Collection of insurance money for the value of the steamboat *White Cloud*. However, Edward Edwards, who later researched the fire in order to write his history of St. Louis's volunteer fire companies, wasn't convinced by the arson theory. He points to Franklin Company fireman George Kyler's eye-witness description of another fire that had occurred along the levee on the morning of May 17. Kyler described seeing the following:

> I went down to the levee to buy some goods, and when there I was standing at the store door of Hamilton & McCarty, when the bell of the steamer *White Cloud*, rang out for fire, and I look up the levee and saw the boat laying about the foot of Cherry St., and on the upper deck were some matresses on fire, the men on the boat pitched some of them overboard, those that were supposed to be all right were carried to the cabin, it seems that the matresses had taken fire from sparks from passing stacks of boats.[46]

Based on Kyler's account, Edwards believes that the Great Fire was entirely accidental: The mattresses must have smoldered for hours inside the cabin before reigniting and eventually setting the boat on fire. Testimony later attributed to the watchman of the *White Cloud* noted that a fire had appeared in the ladies' stateroom during the ship's last trip. Given this situation, there may have been a mechanical explanation for the reoccurring fires in that space. The watchman implied that he naturally assumed the source of the fire was somehow connected to the events of that previous trip, although he later testified that he had heard it was a deliberate act. Even though an accident is still one possibility, the men who provided statements to the city's justice of the peace swore the fire was a case of insurance fraud.[47]

The *White Cloud* didn't appear to be a particularly lucrative boat. Her assessed worth after being declared a total loss was $3,000. This was much less than most of the other New Orleans and St. Louis traders, two of which—the *Sarah* and the *Taglioni*—suffered the same fate in the Great Fire and were valued at $35,000 and $20,000 respectively. It's likely that much of the *White Cloud*'s value was determined by her length of service. An earlier mention of a steamer named *White Cloud* appears in an 1844 article in the *Republican*. If this is the same boat, then she was around five years old in 1849, which was the average life expectancy for a steamboat. The older the boat, the more repairs she needed and the less reliable she became, factors that certainly would have affected her value. A large number of riverboats succumbed to accidents or natural decay prior to reaching this age. Perhaps her owner, Master Adams, felt that she had reached the end of her life and a convenient accident would allow him to recoup some losses.[48]

It appears from the steamboat arrival and departure reports printed in the *Republican* that the *White Cloud* had been sitting at the levee for several weeks when the Great Fire broke out on May 17. The ship's last reported trip, according to the *Republican*'s River News section, had taken place in mid-April. It wasn't her usual run to New Orleans but rather a short trip up the Illinois River to Peoria, Illinois. Ever since returning, she had been moored at the levee, and the later assessment of the boat noted that she had no cargo on board. However, this might be explained by one account that noted the *White Cloud* was undergoing repairs at the time of the fire. Whether the repairs could be attributed to the earlier fire mentioned by the watchman is unclear from the testimony.

In the days following the conflagration, the authorities believed they had sufficient evidence to begin a formal arson investigation. On June 2 they arrested the *White Cloud*'s watchman and engineer. Apparently fearing that the public might overreact to this news, the arrests were kept quiet. The two men were brought before what the *Republican* referred to as a "secret court" for questioning. According to the *Republican*, the watchman told the story of the "ragged Irishman" exiting the boat. But then he stated that after the fire had been detected and begun burning out of control, Charles Blount—whom he misidentified as the watchman of the *Eudora*—"came to him and told him that she was to be burned three days before." Blount also reportedly told the *White Cloud*'s watchman that he wished he had the money paid to the arsonist, thereby implying that he knew that the person who had set fire to the *White Cloud* had received a hefty sum for doing so. The *White Cloud* watchman also testified that the next day, Blount once again spoke to him about the arson and admitted that he knew who had done it, but the watchman didn't report this to anyone. In the meantime, Blount had shipped out on the steamboat *Marshal Ney*.[49]

Then on June 5, the *Eudora*'s actual watchman, Arthur Pentland, was brought before the city's justice of the peace, William W. Kitzmiller, to give his account of what had happened. Pentland's account follows:

> On the night of the fire, after I returned from supper, the carpenter of the steamboat *White Cloud* came on board the *Eudora* and took a seat on the boiler deck, and continued to look toward the *White Cloud*. I took a chair and sat alongside of him, when I observed that he appeared very much frightened, and trembled so violently that he shook the chair he sat in. He remarked to me—"Our watchman was discharged this morning; all the officers have gone to Alton, and took their things to shore, and, the captain left the boat in my charge." He remained aboard our boat about half an hour, looking aft towards that part of the *White Cloud* where the flames broke out; he then got up and going through our engine room, went on board his own boat. About an hour after this the fire broke out, but I did not see him (the carpenter) until after midnight, when I met him at a boarding-house on the levee, where he and I boarded. A chest was there: I asked him whose it was; he said, "Mine." I then remarked, "You have saved more than the boat." Next morning, at breakfast, I charged him with setting fire to the *White Cloud*, and he immediately got up from the table and left.[50]

Justice Kitzmiller asked Pentland several follow-up questions, including whether he knew the man. Pentland replied oddly: Despite the fact that he had testified that they had shared a boardinghouse and sat together talking that evening, Pentland said, "I do not know the man I have mentioned as the carpenter."[51]

The name of this carpenter singled out by Pentland is never mentioned in any published accounts; only Charles Blount is named in connection with the case. Accuracy doesn't seem to be the standard for newspaper reporting during this period, so it's unclear whether Blount and the carpenter are one and the same. However, the first person to testify, the watchman of the *White Cloud*, was the first person to finger Blount for the suspected crime.

Word soon traveled downriver and was received by Captain E. H. Gleim of the steamer *Marshal Ney*, the boat that had carried off Blount two days after the fire. Gleim notified the *New Era* that Blount had transferred to the steamer *Aramantha*, which would soon return him to St. Louis.[52]

Blount arrived on June 9 and immediately surrendered himself to the police. After questioning the young man, the police were convinced that he was neither guilty of setting the fire nor connected to it in any way. He was free to go. "Mr. Blount," reported the *New Era*, "we hear, is a man of family, and bears a character above suspicion." He could explain the meaning behind his exchange with the watchman who implicated him, and it was apparently misunderstood. Furthermore, he intended to publish his own account "which will no doubt throw some light upon the mystery that now clouds this affair." If Blount's account was ever published, it hasn't been found.[53]

In the end, no charges were brought against anyone, and no solid evidence was uncovered that could definitively point to the work of an arsonist. Thus, the origin of the Great Fire will forever be a mystery. But lacking this knowledge didn't seem to deter the people of St. Louis from moving forward—the city was fully back on its feet in a matter of months.

The Burnt District became a place of renewal, and the remnants of the fire were swept away. Like sprouting saplings after the ravages of a forest fire, new buildings rose within the charred city blocks, and life began again. This growth allowed St. Louis to accelerate its attempts to improve infrastructure and become a more modern urban center. It was a painful way of improvement, but in the long run it provided the means for a better city plan. St. Louis continued to grow rapidly in the years prior to the Civil War, and although new challenges and disasters lay ahead, none would ever again seize the city's soul quite like the Great Fire of 1849.

CHAPTER FOUR: WHERE WERE THE WATCHMEN?

n the January 6, 1849, edition of the *St. Louis Daily Union*, the crime beat reporter assigned to the St. Louis Recorder's Court lamented that since the beginning of the year "law breaking in our city seems to have been abandoned . . . we have looked over the docket for the last four days, for an interesting 'item' in vain." It was a slow start to the year, but reporters didn't have to wait long before trouble began to raise its ugly head.[1]

Cholera wasn't the only plague spreading through St. Louis in 1849. In the years following the Mexican War, the city's crime rate exploded along with its population. Newly arrived immigrants, westward-bound travelers and opportunity seekers, unemployed war veterans, and East Coast merchants were all converging on the Mound City (St. Louis's nickname before it became known as the Gateway City). Most of these new residents and temporary visitors were good, law-abiding individuals, but with the good often comes the bad, and local residents quickly learned there were plenty of bad apples in the barrel.

Almost daily the local newspapers contained stories of petty thefts, assaults, arson, public drunkenness, and murder. These acts of wrongdoing were frequently attributed to the supposed inherent bad qualities of wharf rats, tramps, and immigrants, but when viewed through a different lens, it's possible to discern modern urban issues such as alcoholism, drug addiction, poverty, and racism as contributing causes of crime. Further exacerbating matters was the fact that St. Louis's small-town infrastructure was ill equipped to deal with issues common to bustling industrial cities, as well as the unique challenges of life on the edge of the American frontier.

Robbery, larceny, and thefts were common crimes in 1849 St. Louis. Many of the thefts were as inane as the case of James Dolen, who was arrested and fined twenty dollars for loitering and stealing a sheep at the City Market. Local judges typically used heavy fines as a way of pulling petty criminals off the streets. If those convicted couldn't pay the fine, they were placed in the workhouse. This was likely an adequate solution in most cases—but only if the convicts actually made it there.

When John Clary, alias Moccasin John, was arrested and taken before the municipal court, this was seen as a major victory over petty crime in the city. Clary had a reputation as being "one of the most skillful and active of our hotel thieves and burglars," and when he appeared before the municipal court on a vagrancy charge, the judge saw his chance to store Clary away for a while. A jury convicted Clary of the vagrancy charge, and then the judge fined him $500, plus an additional security deposit of $1,000 to ensure Clary's good behavior for six months. Knowing full well that Clary couldn't afford either the fine or the deposit, the judge was sure he'd scored a win for the justice system. Moccasin John had the last laugh, however. Two days later, while he was briefly left unattended in a hallway in the calaboose (jail), he punched out a bar on a window. He was last seen heading south down the Mississippi aboard the steamboat *Sultana*.[2]

The Great Nisbet Robbery

The criminal elements in St. Louis quickly realized that the city and county law enforcement departments couldn't keep up with all the nefarious activity going on—an observation they used much to their advantage. There was a sense that with each major new crime St. Louis's criminals were becoming bolder. This was evident on the night of March 24, when five men pulled off a burglary that the *Weekly Reveille* called the most "extensive and daring" of robberies. As the city slept, and presumably while the St. Louis City Guard patrolled the streets, the vaults of a prominent banking house were almost completely emptied. Crowds gathered to see the damage in the morning, and the city's law enforcement officers were left blushing with embarrassment.

From roughly 10:00 p.m. on March 24 until nearly dawn the following morning, outlaws George Barnett, William B. Thompson, John Moran, Thaddeus Clark, and another accomplice had managed to bust into Wm. Nisbet & Co., smash holes through the walls, and pound their way into the brick-and-iron vault without anyone hearing a sound. Yet more confounding was the fact that although the

WILLIAM NISBET & CO.,
BANKERS AND DEALERS IN EXCHANGE
Bank Notes, Gold and Silver Coin, &c.,
North-east corner Main and Olive streets, St. Louis.

DRAFTS and notes on all prominent points in the Union, collected, and proceeds invested and remitted with the utmost promptness and despatch.

☞ Sight exchange on the eastern cities, for sale in sums to suit.

☞ Currency of all kinds bought and sold at best rate

EXCHANGE—SELLING RATES.

Boston	1 pm	Pittsburgh	1½ pm
New York	1 pm	Cincinnati	½ pm
Philadelphia	1 pm	Louisville	¼ pm
Baltimore	1 pm	New Orleans	½ pm

BUYING RATE.	CURRENCY.	SELLING RATE.
Kentucky ¾@1 dis	Kentucky	½ dis
Indiana 1 dis	Indiana	½ dis
Ohio 1 dis	Ohio	½ dis
Virginia 1 dis	Virginia	½ dis
Tennessee 2@2½ dis	Tennessee	1½ dis

Wm. Nisbet & Co. was one of the primary banking and lending institutions in 1849 St. Louis. Newspaper ad from the *Daily Missouri Republican*, January 8, 1849. Missouri Historical Society Collections.

structure was located in the heart of the city at the corner of Main and Olive streets and surrounded by occupied dwellings and office buildings, somehow no one noticed anything out of the ordinary. Considering the circumstances, it was clear to many that a robbery of this magnitude was an astonishing feat that only further revealed the weaknesses of St. Louis's approach to policing.[3]

The robbers' scheme had begun days earlier when a riverboat pilot by the name of Francis Couley was tempted by the promise of easy money. During the course of one of Couley's voyages on the Mississippi, four men approached him and offered up a share of a planned robbery if he agreed to assist them. These men, whom Couley later claimed he'd neither met before nor knew their names, told him that they needed someone to act as a lookout while they did their work. It's unclear whether they informed Couley of all the plans, but it can be assumed that he understood this wasn't going to be a simple smash-and-grab operation. Couley agreed, despite the risks of detection involved.

A few nights later, as the flickering gas lamps illuminated Main Street, Couley, Barnett, Clark, Thompson, Moran, and the unknown accomplice stood outside the Perpetual Insurance Company building, a structure that was also home to the city's chamber of commerce and, most important, the banking house of Wm. Nisbet & Co. As one of several private banking establishments in the city, it held significant deposits of paper notes, silver, and gold. These valuables were secured in the bank's safes, which were contained within a large walk-in vault in the building's cellar.

As a financial institution, Nisbet had a stable reputation, but perhaps no one but the criminals had considered that a recent development had made the building itself vulnerable. In the weeks leading up to that fateful night, a house adjacent to the Perpetual Insurance building had been torn down. This change in the landscape exposed the direct entrances into the banking house and allowed for easier access to the building—and likewise a more direct means of escape.

When the coast was clear, the gang of criminals made its move. The first obstacle was a heavy iron door, but this proved to be of little resistance as they wrenched it from its frame with a crowbar. All five men then entered the building and found only a glass door bearing the name of the Perpetual Insurance Company. Couley took up his lookout post in the hallway outside, ready to give his partners signals if someone approached or if they made too much noise.

Below the floor of the Perpetual Insurance office was the Nisbet vault. With picks and hammers, Couley's counterparts began to laboriously smash their way through the eighteen to twenty inches of brick that formed the vault's outer ceiling. Undeterred, the men managed to create a sizable hole only to discover that their planned passage was blocked by a heavy timber support beam. They then devised a new, more direct approach: They would break down the plain wooden door between the Perpetual and Nisbet offices in order to attack the vault's outer door.

Using crowbars, the group attempted to pry open the vault, but to no avail. Possibly motivated by frustration, the men briefly considered blowing apart the lock with gunpowder. They went so far as to pour powder into the lock before deciding that this was too risky. Resigning themselves to the fact that only determination and sweat would allow them into the vault, they once again pounded through eighteen inches of brick wall until they were able to create a hole just large enough for the men to enter one at a time. But, like the tomb raiders of ancient Egypt, they found themselves facing multiple chambers once they were inside. Now they had to break through the actual vault walls, which were three feet thick.

As the hours ticked by, the men pushed on, chipping away at brick after brick until another large hole appeared. One can only imagine the men's emotions when they finally reached the walk-in safe. Perhaps there was little joy considering they were now faced with breaking into a safe constructed of sheet iron three-eighths of an inch thick, but certainly they had come too far to let such a thing stop them. The men hammered away at the safe with chisels until they had a hole about three feet in diameter. One of the men crawled inside so he could pass the bank's treasures to his comrades' waiting hands. Inside were stacks of bank notes, bags of silver and gold coins, and an additional $1,500 in gold deposited by a returned California prospector. The total pot was nearly $30,000, which had a purchasing power close to $1 million in today's dollars.

The thieves, cash, coins, gold, and a strongbox belonging to the Citizens Insurance Company slipped away into the darkness of the predawn hours, leaving behind two coats; crowbars and other tools; and a mess of broken bricks, splintered wood, and metal fragments. Together they made their way to a rented room on Franklin Avenue, where they divided up the shares. For his work, Couley was given nearly $3,000 in bank notes, the modern equivalent of $80,000. The other men divided the remaining loot and went their separate ways.

The clerks of the Nisbet banking house arrived at work in the morning and found the doors to their establishment wide open. Word of the robbery traveled like lightning, and soon nearly a thousand curious residents had gathered in the street outside the Perpetual Insurance building. Soon the city marshal and police captain, J. E. D. Couzins, arrived to investigate the scene. It didn't take a detective to conclude that the perpetrators must have labored for hours to carry out the crime. The real question was, why hadn't the city's watchmen caught them in the act?[4]

City officials didn't answer publicly, but Couzins presumably sought to restore some manner of credibility to local law enforcement by moving as fast as he could to solve the crime. In the hours following the discovery, police picked up a number of individuals simply for being spotted out on the streets late the night before. Among them was a selection of St. Louis's usual suspects, who were questioned and then released. It appeared that the real culprits had gotten away. Nisbet issued a $1,500 reward for their capture, but little information emerged about the robbers or the whereabouts of the money.[5]

For city officials, the event was a public-relations nightmare. The *Daily Missouri Republican* published news of the robbery alongside an editorial about the state of the city's police force. With the headline "Where Was the Watch?" the editors noted how everyone was scratching their heads as to how "the robbery was committed in a populous, business part of the city . . . in full glare of the lamps and could not have been affected short of five or six hours' labor" yet it "escaped the notice, or was not detected, by the vigilant guarding of the night on that beat." This question wasn't new though. Controversy over the police department's competency and the number of officers required to patrol the growing city broke out regularly. The Nisbet robbery only added fuel to critics' fire.[6]

St. Louis's "Police" Force

In reality, St. Louis didn't have a true organized police force. Rather, it had a day and night patrol consisting of men appointed by the city council. The St. Louis City Guard was formed in 1846 to police the city 24 hours a day. It consisted of one captain, six lieutenants, and forty-two watchmen. By 1849 budget cuts had slashed the force to three lieutenants and thirty patrolmen who were responsible for maintaining order in a city whose population had grown to nearly seventy-eight thousand. In the daytime hours the city guard walked the beat with just one lieutenant and six patrolmen.[7]

Outnumbered and underpaid, the city's constables faced an uphill battle. Indeed, things had gotten so bad that the officers themselves were becoming victims, as Officer Saugrain Michau discovered when he walked out of the post office only to find that his horse had been stolen. The two horse thieves, Alexander Work and James O'Neill, were later caught, convicted, and sentenced to two years in the Missouri State Penitentiary.[8]

The city guard also lacked any real form of law enforcement training or skills. Then, as now, having the right set of skills could mean the difference between life and death for an officer of the law. Good intuition no doubt also played a role in managing dangerous situations, like the one Night Watchman Adams found himself in one evening outside the Tontine Coffee House on Main Street. Adams had encountered an angry, knife-wielding man by the name of Holdship and opted to diffuse the situation by trying to quiet him and convince him to put away the knife and go home. However, Holdship was too angry to stand down; he pulled out a pistol and threatened to shoot Adams. Reacting quickly not with a gun but with his nightstick, Adams "was at length successful" in putting Holdship in his place. Probably stunned from several good blows, Holdship was hauled off to the calaboose and fined fifteen dollars plus court costs the next day.

Some watchmen weren't as lucky as Adams. Officer Vogle was on routine patrol one Friday evening when an "insane man named James Nugent" suddenly attacked him for no reason. Nugent surprised Vogle, slamming him in the head with a heavy stick and then beating him severely. Others arrived on the scene and caught Nugent after a brief chase. Vogle suffered serious wounds to his head and hands and endured a slow recovery.[9]

Although citizens may have viewed the circumstances of the city's crime problem in clear-cut terms, it was a complex combination of inadequate training, municipal politics, and serious social issues in the emerging city that so often frustrated attempts by city leaders and constables to effectively deal with crime in St. Louis. Regardless, the public was demanding answers and solutions. A year earlier, Mayor John Krum had ordered an investigation of the police department to try to discover why it was so ineffective in curbing the growing crime rate. In his annual mayoral message to the city council, Krum lamented recent budget cuts and called upon the council to find more funding: "Our city is now so much extended that it is impossible, without great industry, for thirty men to properly guard the whole city. Burglaries, larcenies, and petty thefts of the most daring character have been committed of late in every part of the city."

Besides being of inadequate size to effectively control crime, examples of police brutality and corruption had convinced many residents that the city guard was part of the problem rather than the solution. Recognizing the public had little faith in the system, Krum added: "There are many defects in our present system which in my judgment demand immediate correction. If our City Guard cannot be made effective, it had better be abandoned altogether."

Yet despite the investigation and the mayor's call for reforms, little changed in the coming year. Near the time of the spring municipal elections in 1849, the *Republican* called upon the city to pass new policies that would result in the immediate discharge of officers found drunk on the job or otherwise derelict in their duties. One article stated that "it almost requires a search warrant to find a policeman in the night." That was certainly the case the night of the Nisbet robbery.

Bringing the Nisbet Thieves to Justice—Eventually

After two exceedingly long and quiet weeks with no clues or tips, Captain Couzins and his men finally received a break in the Nisbet case. This was good news, but now the pressure was on for Couzins to prove that he and his men were capable of solving serious crimes and dealing with troublesome criminals. It was a task that put Couzins's policing skills to the ultimate test—a test he nearly failed.

Two weeks after the Nisbet robbers had successfully vanished, the authorities in St. Louis received news via telegraph that some suspicious characters had arrived in the small town of Berlin, Illinois, located in Sangamon County near Springfield. Two men had come to the small town bearing saddlebags filled with money. They made an instant impression by carelessly purchasing an expensive wagon and waving around a lot of cash. The two crooks likely thought these rural folks were unaware of happenings in St. Louis, but however isolated little Berlin may have seemed, the world was changing. Telegraphs were closing the gap between towns and villages, and news traveled much faster than it had only a couple years prior. The citizens of Berlin were

J. E. D. Couzins was the lead investigator on the Nisbet case. Despite some blunders along the way, he managed to apprehend the perpetrators after a long chase across three states. Photograph by unknown photographer, ca. 1861–1865. Missouri Historical Society Collections.

well aware of a major news event like the Nisbet robbery, and these strangers seemed like natural suspects. When bank owner William Nisbet received the news that the perpetrators were close, he sent one of his clerks, David Foster, to accompany Couzins to central Illinois.

Couzins and Foster boarded a steamboat bound for Naples, a town on the Illinois River. On board they met a Mr. Spotswood, owner of the California gold deposit taken from Nisbet's safe. He had apparently learned of their mission and was determined to join them in hopes of reclaiming his lost property. After arriving in Naples, the three men made their way to Berlin and interviewed the townspeople. They were informed that the suspicious travelers had headed east toward the Wabash River. Immediately the St. Louisans rejoined the pursuit with the hope that they would overtake the outlaws. However, Foster, Couzins, and Spotswood, in their haste, took too little time to rest, and the journey wasn't an easy one. Difficulty finding available horses and an incident involving a broken wagon impeded their pursuit, and the constant push forward began to take its toll.

Overcome by exhaustion due to lack of sleep since leaving St. Louis, Foster collapsed while riding. Spotswood also became ill and decided to rest. Although the men knew that every minute allowed the criminals to gain more ground ahead of them, they had little choice but to stop. After sleeping a few hours at a local farm, the trio continued on their way toward the Indiana state line. Upon reaching Terre Haute, Couzins hired a buggy and driver and headed south, following a tip that the robbers had been seen in the vicinity. Some reported that the thieves had boarded a steamboat bound for Louisville—one that had left only a brief time earlier. Couzins and the buggy driver crossed back into Illinois and raced six miles on backcountry roads through the early morning light until they reached Hudsonville. There, standing on the landing, were two men dressed as farmers. Couzins immediately recognized them from the descriptions provided by the various witnesses.

Couzins made no attempt to hide from the two outlaws, who didn't recognize the man approaching them. With the help of the others, Couzins immediately seized the two men, handcuffing one and tying the other with a cord. One of the pair, in an attempt to abandon his loot, was able to reach into his clothes and throw a roll of banknotes amounting to $2,200 into a nearby fire burning on the levee. Couzins witnessed this move and was able to rescue the notes from the flames. Meanwhile, as Couzins was attempting to retrieve the burning cash, the other robber tried to bribe his way to freedom by tempting the buggy driver with a different roll of bills. The driver declined, and soon the men were headed up the gangplank of the steamboat to be searched and interrogated.

Using the ladies' cabins as an interrogation space, Couzins began to question the men, who turned out to be George Barnett and William B. Thompson. It wasn't hard to determine that they were the Nisbet culprits—their saddlebags contained the missing cash and coins. With the boat's captain acting as a witness, the money was counted for the record.

Evidently the two men had gone to some lengths to hide their identities from the boat's crew. They went so far as to arrange for a shipment of two hundred pounds of potatoes and dozens of chickens, procured from local farmers, so as to cloak their true intentions as travelers aboard the riverboat. If Couzins hadn't arrived, they probably would have gotten away with little problem.

It took nearly all day to sort things out, but Couzins managed to secure the men and, with the help of the buggy driver, bring them back to Terre Haute where Foster and Spotswood were waiting. Here Couzins faced a new set of challenges. According to the account in the *Republican*, Spotswood "demanded immediate possession of his money, and the warmth of his temper and his menaces, soon created excitement." Hoping to keep the evidence together, Couzins demanded that they wait to sort things out until after they had all returned to St. Louis. Spotswood had little choice but to go along with Couzins's plan, yet as soon as that problem was resolved, another arose. The buggy driver suddenly demanded a reward for his participation in the robbers' capture, threatening to take possession of the men himself if he wasn't paid. Couzins feared that the delay in getting the men back to St. Louis before they were charged might invoke a violation of the writ of habeas corpus, a law that the *Republican* reporter observed was "as useful a process for rogues in Terre Haute as it has been in St. Louis."

Seeing few options, Couzins paid the buggy driver a handsome reward of one hundred dollars. Then, in a scene straight out of an old western, the two crooks were handcuffed together, and passage was secured for Foster, Spotswood, Couzins, and the two prisoners aboard a St. Louis–bound stagecoach. At nightfall the coach stopped for a rest in Effingham, Illinois, where matters again took a turn for the worse. All three St. Louisans were still feeling the effects of their urgent pursuit. Exhausted, Foster and Spotswood got out of the coach and entered the nearby way station, hoping to get a few minutes of rest. Couzins remained in the coach with the two prisoners. Soon Barnett and Thompson were presented with a golden opportunity—in what the *St. Louis Daily New Era* trumpeted as the "gross negligence of the officer," an exhausted Couzins drifted off to sleep. Seeing their chance, Barnett and Thompson jumped from the coach and disappeared into the surrounding forest.[10]

Angry that Couzins still refused to hand over his gold, Spotswood returned to St. Louis and reported what had happened. Couzins and Foster remained in Effingham, where the local citizens formed a posse to search for the fugitives. A farmer reported that the men had stopped him for directions to Louisville. It was discovered shortly afterward that they had managed to get out of their handcuffs and were headed toward Vincennes.[11]

Meanwhile, Francis Couley had left St. Louis and reached Cincinnati, but so had suspicions that he was involved in the Nisbet robbery after a barrel was found in a home belonging to a riverboat pilot in Newport, Kentucky. According to the *Reveille*, "under circumstances that had excited suspicion," the barrel was examined and "found to contain $17,000 in gold." This wasn't Couley's cut of the money, but perhaps he had been hiding it for one of the others. Whatever the situation, Couley was arrested on suspicion of being involved in the robbery.[12]

Once again the telegraph office at the St. Louis Chamber of Commerce was buzzing with news of another suspected Nisbet robber. Immediately St. Louis police officer Saugrain Michau was put aboard a Cincinnati-bound steamboat with the intent of bringing home the latest suspect. Officer Michau found Couley in the Cincinnati jail, put him in shackles, and brought him aboard a returning boat. There he began to interrogate the suspect. It was at this point that a legal error occurred that would later have serious implications for the State of Missouri's criminal case against Couley. Michau, in his apparent eagerness to get to the bottom of the story, promised Couley that he would do whatever he could to convince prosecutors to go easy on him if he agreed to tell everything he knew. Couley took Michau's offer at his word and told him the whole story.

Back in Indiana, luck had run out for Barnett and Thompson. The local posse had found the two men, and once again they were headed for the calaboose in St. Louis. In the weeks that followed, the three captured men were indicted by a grand jury for burglary and grand larceny. Trials commenced in August, and all were found guilty. Barnett and Thompson were each sentenced to ten years in the Missouri State Penitentiary.

Couley's time in court, however, wasn't so cut and dried. Despite Michau's earlier promise of the possibility of a lighter sentence, Couley (who had no prior criminal record) was sentenced to fifteen years of hard time. Immediately his attorneys filed a motion for appeal based on the fact that Michau's promises had amounted to coercion. The case was pushed up the judicial line, and in the October term of the Missouri Supreme Court, the justices sided with Couley. His case was overturned, but he wasn't a free man. The following July, Couley was retried for the robbery and sentenced to eight years in the Missouri State Penitentiary, where he rejoined two of his companions in crime. Records show that they all worked together in the prison's hemp-processing factory until 1853. Barnett and Thompson escaped that year, but Couley didn't go along. He remained to toil away at his time, perhaps knowing that others were trying to lighten his sentence. Two years later, Governor Sterling Price pardoned Couley, freeing him from the last three years of his sentence—but there was a final twist to Couley's story.

It turns out that for all his trouble, Couley wouldn't have had anything to show for his effort even if he hadn't been captured. It seems that his partners in crime had swindled him too. Paper money in the first half of the nineteenth century was usually issued by state-sanctioned banks, not the federal government, so its value was determined by how solvent the particular issuing bank was. The $3,000 given to Couley for his role as lookout was made up of banknotes issued by a bank that had defaulted—the money was worthless. One wonders how much time Francis Couley spent thinking about this as he operated the hemp-spinning machines in the prison factory flanked by his "partners" who had talked him into the crime.[13]

Copycat Crimes and Substance Abuse

Even though Couley and two of his colleagues were caught, it doesn't appear that the other Nisbet robbers or the remaining cash were ever recovered. This situation did little to discourage people from attempting similar crimes in the city. In early May 1849 a number of businesses were hit by would-be safecrackers. On the levee, the property of Runyan, Hillman, & Company suffered damage when thieves tried, unsuccessfully, to break into the firm's safe by using gunpowder. Soon after this incident, robbers also tried to take the safe from Greely and Gale's Store.[14]

These bold crimes once again induced a reaction from the city's newspaper editors. The *Republican's* editors were particularly irritated: "The citizens of St. Louis pay annually a large sum to guard their property while they sleep, and here are four or five daring burglaries committed in rapid succession in the same neighborhood, and at a time when the whole night patrol of the city are on duty, and not the least clue or trace can be had to the perpetrators. There is certainly something rotten in Denmark."[15]

The St. Louis City Guard may not have done a good job of catching serious offenders, but its officers weren't completely idle. The *Republican* reported at the end of March that 147 individuals had been held in the city calaboose during the month and that 218 cases had been tried before the St. Louis Recorder's Court, which dealt with minor offenses.[16]

Most of the cases heard before the Recorder's Court involved the nuisance of public drunkenness. Typical was the case of Mrs. Rose Kelly, who was apparently a frequent visitor to the court. In April, Kelly appeared before the Recorder's Court judge for the second time in just two days, "charged with an excessive indulgence in spirits." When asked to present reasons for her frequent appearances, Kelly pleaded "as she had done on the previous day, poverty, trouble, weak head, and six small children." The judge was apparently unmoved by her story and fined her five dollars.[17]

The problem of alcoholism, or intemperance as it was called then, was a nationally recognized concern in antebellum America. Per-person consumption of alcohol during the early nineteenth century was so high among Americans that if similar numbers were duplicated today, alcoholism would be considered a national health crisis. When the phenomenon peaked around 1830, the average American was drinking nearly four gallons of spirits annually, mostly in the form of cheap whiskey. Nearly twenty years later, consumption had receded to an average of just over two gallons per person per year, but this didn't necessarily translate into diminished rates of alcohol-related offenses. Indeed, of the 147 arrests that found their way to the Recorder's Court in March 1849, 119 were for public drunkenness and disturbing the peace.[18]

Public reaction to the national alcoholism problem manifested itself in the growth of temperance societies, mostly notably in Missouri. One group of anti-alcohol crusaders, the Sons of Temperance, was founded in New York in 1842 and quickly spread throughout the country. The *Reveille* proudly reported that 6,800 Missourians had joined the Sons of Temperance, including 1,200 St. Louisans. Members were expected to abstain from drinking completely, and the membership's success, according to the *Reveille,* was measured by the fact that of those nearly 7,000 members only 36 had died in 1849 from alcohol-related causes.[19]

If temperance proponents needed instances of alcohol-related tragedies, they needn't look far. There were plenty of hard cases on the streets, and in the early summer of 1849, a sad tale played out on the levee. A middle-aged woman had been observed wandering about for two weeks with two small boys in tow. Being that there were few, if any, systems of support in place for women and families in similar states of destitution in pre–Civil War St. Louis, the outcome of her tale is hardly surprising: One July morning, as the wharf workers reported to the warehouses and riverboats for duty, they discovered the woman's lifeless body. The *Republican* reported that she was found ". . . in a secluded place at the upper part of the Levee, where she had probably taken lodging during the night." The story went on to note that "her two children were by her side, and seemingly unconscious of their mother's condition, no doubt from the fact of often seeing her in an insensible state of intoxication."[20]

A coroner's inquest was held, and it was determined that the woman was Mary Adeline Winngerter, who had only recently arrived in St. Louis from Pittsburgh. The inquest declared that she had most likely succumbed to cholera, but true causes of death were difficult to determine. Like so many other indigent cholera victims, she would have been buried in the potter's field in the former City Cemetery. What became of this woman's children is unknown. They most likely were sent to one of the city's orphanages, which were already swelling with the children of cholera victims.[21]

Other stories from the streets of 1849 St. Louis, like those of narcotics and homeless veterans, appear sadly familiar in the modern sense. On a cold January night, city officers came upon Mexican War veteran Christopher Youil, whom they soon recognized as being under the influence of opium. They arrested him, brought him to the calaboose, and then hauled him before the Recorder's Court. Youil was fined five dollars for possession, but the former soldier was in such a distressed condition and pleaded with officers so much that "his apparent suffering, from being deprived of the dreadful stimulus, induced one of the officers to return it."[22]

Life in the Calaboose

Alcoholics and the indigent often found themselves residents of the city calaboose. By most accounts, conditions in the stone-block building were less than ideal. One Sunday afternoon in February a man was arrested and locked in a holding cell. Jailers didn't check on him again until around 6:00 p.m. that evening, when they discovered that the man had died at some point in the day and that his corpse was being devoured by rats. In another instance, the roof of the jail was found to be in flames. A furnace pipe leading up through the roof had ignited the surrounding wood. Luckily firefighters extinguished the flames, but at no point did anyone attempt to remove the inmates from their cells.

During the cholera epidemic, however, the jail was portrayed as one of the safest places in town. As the city was experiencing the worst of the outbreak in July 1849, sixty-five individuals were confined to the jail. The *Republican* described this "fact worthy of notice": "Out of this large number of persons, confided together in a building about forty by eighty, and not by far the best ventilated in the city, not one death has occurred. . . . Their general health may be attributed to their regular habits and diet, and the total abstinence from intoxicating drinks."[23]

The inmates' good fortune probably had less to do with the lack of imbibing intoxicating beverages than with the fact that the jail's population was isolated from the rest of the city and that they were apparently provided with clean drinking water. Even so, it was best not to become a resident of this establishment if one could avoid it.

The Riot at Madame Clementine's

Grumbling letters to the newspapers and expressed anxieties by elected officials about the city's lack of ability to police itself may have signified there was a problem, but the actions of those who chose to take the law into their own hands—through mob violence in particular—seem to be the most emblematic symptom of the city's frustration with crime. Over the course of 1849, riots broke out on several occasions and for various reasons. Sometimes these riots had causes that went far beyond anything that could be controlled by city officials, such as the tensions that existed between Catholic and Protestant immigrants within the city's Irish community. Other times riots broke out simply because there were too many angry people and not enough police officers to control the crowd. When the masses became unruly, as they often did, the St. Louis City Guard could do little more than make arrests after the damage had been done.

Just how quickly an incident could escalate from the slightest of actions into a full-blown riot is illustrated by an event that occurred in late August at the intersection of Market and Thirteenth streets. On that corner sat an establishment operated by the city's most successful brothel keeper, a twenty-nine-year-old English immigrant named Anna Jarette Wright, who was better known as Madame Clementine. So profitable was her business that she had recently leased nearly the entire corner lot and expanded the brothel's footprint to cover almost an acre. A large privacy fence surrounded the property, no doubt to shield the premises and preserve her customers' reputations. However, the fence proved too much of a temptation for eleven-year-old John Kennedy, son of furrier Charles Kennedy, whose shop sat near the busy corner.

On that August day, the younger Kennedy couldn't help but to try to steal glances through the fence slats, but his curiosity didn't go unnoticed. One of Madame Clementine's bouncers, a German immigrant named Henry Meyercourt, attempted to chase the boy away. When Meyercourt confronted the lad, his threats were met only by the boy's laughter and returned taunts. The "German bully," as Meyercourt was later described, again ordered Kennedy to leave and threatened to shoot him if he didn't comply. The boy was unmoved by Meyercourt's seemingly harsh attempt to remove him from the fence row. Then Meyercourt, angered by the fact that his rebukes weren't being taken seriously, sought to make his intentions clear by taking a pistol from his pocket and firing it for effect. Kennedy may have finally gotten the hint, but others on the street were alarmed by Meyercourt's actions. Suddenly he was under attack, and before he could remove himself, someone brought the heavy end of a pitchfork down on his head. Meyercourt was waylaid briefly but managed to right himself and run into the brothel.[24]

Soon the street was filled with angry men shouting for Meyercourt to come out and face the consequences of his actions. In an attempt to defuse the situation, a policeman who arrived on the scene demanded that Meyercourt give himself up—a request the German man ignored. It wasn't long before many others were attracted to the scene and emotions began to run high. Unlike the police, many average residents weren't as willing to turn a blind eye to the city's various houses of prostitution. Events such as this one gave them a reason to vent their anger and take matters into their own hands.

Perhaps the gathered crowd recalled two recent events in Madame Clementine's house that had attracted attention earlier and seemed to highlight the city's growing crime problem. Just weeks before, Lizzy, one of Madame Clementine's working girls, was accused of stealing a gold watch and chain from one of her customers. When her accuser failed to show up to testify against her in court, Lizzy was released. A more serious matter involved a previous, though dismissed, charge against Meyercourt for shooting a man. Madame Clementine's establishment was no doubt seen by many St. Louisans as an immoral nuisance and a threat to the community's peace.[25]

As the crowd grew larger and angrier, it was obvious things were about to reach the boiling point. At this critical juncture, Madame Clementine decided it was time to address the masses. Appearing at the top of a flight of stairs on the outside of her house, she looked down upon the fuming crowd gathered on the other side of the fence. She revealed that Meyercourt was no longer on the premises and that he had exited the property through a back entrance. Almost instantly after the words were out of her mouth, a shot was fired from inside the fence. At that moment, the scene exploded like a powder keg on fire. A member of the crowd hurled a large rock at the stairs, which struck the unsuspecting brothel keeper so hard that it knocked her down the stairs. As soon as she could stand, Madame Clementine and the other residents of the house "took to their heels" as the furious crowd crashed its way into the house of ill repute.

The infuriated rioters let loose their anger on the contents of the house. Smashing whatever they could, they destroyed an expensive pianoforte; pushed over bookcases; and broke chairs, tables, and bedsteads. Pushing their way through to the rooms used by Clementine's charges, they gathered the girls' dresses and threw them into the open yard below. Still not satisfied, they set a torch to the piles of clothing. After all the contents of the house had been dealt with, they attacked the structure next. Men smashed the expensive woodwork before finally setting it alight.[26]

Details of the attack were printed the next day in the *Republican*. The editors sought to take the high ground by condemning the mob actions on one count, but they also added that Clementine's place "was an intolerable nuisance—not to be reached, it would seem, by the law—hence the summary mode of abating it." It would seem, in the opinion of the editors, that the end definitely justified the means.[27]

On the Sunday following the riot, Meyercourt was located, arrested, and taken to the calaboose to await his time before the Recorder's Court judge. A number of rioters were also arrested. Despite police officers' intentions to pursue those who were active in the attack, further violence was undeterred. The following Monday a crowd barged into a second brothel located near the corner of Ninth and Biddle streets. The "inmates," as the women were termed in the newspapers, were turned out of the building before the vigilantes "proceeded to demolish every article of furniture they could lay their hands on." Unlike the riot at Madame Clementine's, no arrests were made.[28]

Just a few days later, a grand jury was called upon to hear testimony from various witnesses in the case against Meyercourt, who was charged with attempting to shoot and kill Kennedy. The German bouncer was the first to stand trial. Despite the excitement incited by his actions, he was acquitted, perhaps because four witnesses testified that his actions were "ordered to be done by Madame Clementine." They also noted how he had merely fired the pistol into the air, with no clear intention of hurting the boy. In the end, Madame Clementine was charged with the crimes of operating a bawdy house and selling liquor without a license. She was ordered to appear before a judge, who set her bail at $200.[29]

Representing Madame Clementine at her trial later that week were attorneys A. P. Field and Pierce C. Grace. The two barristers certainly had their work cut out for them. Almost from the beginning, things weren't going well considering the court had a hard time finding unbiased jurors. Many prospective members of the panel declared they were convinced of her guilt because her unladylike reputation was widespread.

Madame Clementine's trial had all the trappings of good entertainment, and St. Louisans eagerly packed the courtroom to witness the proceedings. Normally answering to the charge of keeping a bawdy house wasn't such a major undertaking. Women were occasionally arrested on very similar charges only to be fined and let go, but the circumstances of this incident turned Madame Clementine into a sacrificial lamb. City officials and the police had allowed her to operate without interruption, but now her establishment was an embarrassment. To show the public that the city was doing its job to protect the community and discourage vice, St. Louis's justice system had to make an example of her at long last.

Despite surely understanding the situation, the defense attorneys were nevertheless appalled when the judge declared that Madame Clementine's past as a prostitute was admissible as evidence of her guilt. For three days the jury listened to Field and Grace present their case. Field even delivered a three-hour-long speech on his client's innocence, but to no avail. The jury handed the court a guilty verdict, and Madame Clementine was assessed a fine of $300 with no jail time. The defense immediately filed for a new trial on the grounds that her past shouldn't have been admissible, but the judge overruled the request. Field and Grace then appealed to the Missouri Supreme Court.

Before the court's October term began, Madame Clementine apparently had a change of heart about her path in life. No doubt tired of all the legal wrangling, unapproving glances, and rough customers—or perhaps simply longing for something better—she got married. On September 30, 1849, one of St. Louis's German-language dailies, *Deutsche Tribune*, announced that she had married a German immigrant and was now Mrs. August Loehner. The newspaper marked the occasion of her marriage by printing a message of well wishes that incorporated a famous German poem by Heinrich Heine.

Submitted.

On September 26 Anne Jeanette Wright, (born Clemen-
tina) married Mr. August Loehner, iron foundry owner.
May Heaven lavish its richest blessings on this new couple,

And may the words of one of our great poets prove to be
true:

"Time comes and goes,

Generations go to their grave,

But never weakens the love,

That those two have in their heart"[30]

August and Anne Loehner remained together for the rest of their
lives. He was a successful inventor of iron hardware and received at
least three patents in the years following the Civil War. She appears
to have become a respectable manufacturer's wife. In 1866 she was
awarded a prize for her entry in the St. Louis Horticultural Society's
garden show. The couple is buried next to each other in Bellefontaine
Cemetery.

When a Lost Cow Leads to Murder

As serious as the attack on Madame Clementine's establishment
was, everyday violence on a much more personal scale was a bigger
problem in 1849 St. Louis. At the end of the year, St. Louis County
reported that 14 persons had been locked in the county jail awaiting
murder charges while another 14 were held on the charge of assault
with intent to kill. This was a relatively high violent crime rate for a
city with a population of 78,000.

The local justice system seemed to struggle with a response to
all the violence as much as the local law enforcement agencies did.
Depending on the severity of a violent crime, the case would be heard
in either the Recorder's Court (such as an incident where Parks B.
Long was charged with "disturbing the peace and threatening to
shoot a German") or in the Circuit Court, where cases of a more seri-

ous nature were tried by the prosecuting attorney. The judges on the bench were determined by elections and political appointments, and often the pool of qualified jurists was quite limited. Additionally, the same cast of prosecutors and defense lawyers often switched places, depending on the prevailing political climate.[31]

But it wasn't just the legal structure that had its limits. The justice system itself lacked many of the tools it needed to objectively decide cases. Securing convictions was often a hit-or-miss situation because proving one's guilt or innocence was more reliant on the testimony of eyewitnesses than hard evidence. The lack of professional crime investigation in St. Louis in the mid-1800s made for weak cases and put pressure on prosecutors to prove a crime had been committed. Witnesses often didn't appear in court when summoned, leading to dropped cases.

Based on the outcomes of various murder trials presented in the St. Louis newspapers over the course of 1849, murder convictions weren't easy to come by. Even when someone was found guilty, that person received a varying degree of punishment, from a few months in the county jail to time in the state penitentiary to execution by hanging. Juries determined guilt or innocence, but judges decided what punishment fit the crime, hence the vast variation.

A case in point is the trial of George and Sarah Lambert, an unassuming immigrant couple who operated a dairy farm on rented property just northwest of St. Louis's city limits, in the area that would later become the Ville. Arriving in St. Louis from England earlier in the decade, the Lamberts established a seemingly quiet existence raising their small family and milking and tending to their dairy cows. It hardly seemed like the kind of environment where trouble would break out, but that's just what happened on the afternoon of August 17, 1849.

That day, Michael Donovan and his friend, who was identified only as Hefferman, were out searching for a stray cow that had wandered from Donovan's herd several days prior. Strolling down the dusty road that fronted the farm, the two men noticed a herd of cows in the Lamberts' yard. Donovan and Hefferman entered the farmyard and approached George Lambert to inquire whether he had seen Donovan's cow. While Hefferman conversed with George, Donovan walked over to the milk barn to speak with Sarah. The words exchanged between the two have been lost to history, but we do know that Sarah approached Donovan and struck him in the face before picking up a large stone. This immediately brought George and Hefferman into the quarrel. Circumstances escalated quickly, with Sarah yelling at the men to leave the premises before she and George entered the house and returned armed for battle. George was waving a gun at the two men, who were now backing out of the barnyard. Sarah, for her part, was making all her intentions clear by waving about a large meat cleaver.

Despite the obvious threat, Hefferman apparently wasn't one to back down. He lunged at George and seized the gun from his hands. At that point, Hefferman handed the loaded gun to Donovan, whom George attacked almost instantly. Hefferman came to his friend's aid, and soon all three men were struggling in the barnyard. While Hefferman attempted to pull George off of Donovan, the gun, which was in George's hands then, discharged. The contents blasted into the lower portion of Donovan's left leg, and he fell to the ground, seriously wounded. When the gun fired, Hefferman fell back and released George, who then tried to strike Hefferman in the head with the butt of the gun. Reacting quickly, Hefferman drew a pistol from his pocket, pointed it at George, and pulled the trigger. The gun misfired, and George grabbed it away. At that point, the gunplay was over, but the drama still hadn't ended.

Donovan lay in agony on the ground. Desperately wounded, he asked Sarah for a drink of water. Rather than provide him with aid, Sarah "sprang round, and raising the cleaver, which she held in her hand, said, 'I have a notion to cut your damned head off, you son-of-a-bitch!'" The Lamberts then turned and retreated to their house.

Hefferman managed to get Donovan home and summoned a physician. Donovan survived another six hours before finally succumbing to his injury. The next day, two officers of the law "were dispatched to arrest the murderer, and, by means of a stratagem, they succeeded without much difficulty." George Lambert was charged with murder; Sarah was charged as an accessory. The case went to trial two months later. The jury acquitted Sarah but found George guilty of murder in the fourth degree, the 1849 equivalent of involuntary manslaughter. Today in Missouri, involuntary manslaughter is considered a felony, and those convicted of it receive a sentence of ten years to life in prison. But in 1849, George Lambert was sentenced to three months in the county jail and ordered to pay a $100 fine—a light sentence for a deliberately aggressive set of circumstances. One could argue that the legal system wasn't doing itself or the public any favors by not pursuing more stringent punishments, but because the system wasn't equipped to truly investigate and try accused murders, perhaps it made no difference.[32]

Unfortunately for the people of St. Louis, crime was something they would have to adjust to rather than hope to eradicate. As the 1840s came to an end and the city's population numbers continued to surge, crime remained a serious issue. Those wanting a more effective police force would have to wait until 1860 for the establishment of the city's first professional law enforcement agency, the St. Louis Police Department. In the meantime, the St. Louis City Guard walked the beat and did what it could, as best it could, to keep the peace in a bustling community that bore little resemblance to the small trading post it once was.

CHAPTER FIVE:

NO RIGHTS AND FEW FREEDOMS

Recounting the experiences of St. Louis's African American inhabitants in 1849 is a difficult task given that so few of their voices were captured for posterity. Unlike the letters, diaries, and other written sources that have survived to document the lives of the city's white population, little such evidence remains for those persons of color who were enslaved or otherwise oppressed. We must rely mostly on printed sources from the period, such as newspapers and court records, or the occasional reference in the written record of a white author.

The very nature of the times accounts for the silence. Few African Americans in the 1840s could write well enough to record their experiences. Of those, most likely couldn't afford paper and writing utensils, things that were cost prohibitive for many individuals, regardless of race. Despite these obstacles, we can catch enough of a glimpse of what life was like for St. Louis's African American community to see that its everyday difficulties could be tempered by small successes—and that its limitations could be countered by those with a will to overcome.

What's most difficult for many people today to grasp is how pervasive slavery and racism were in the nineteenth century. Slavery touched nearly everyone's life back then and was deeply embedded in America's economic structure. After all, a system that exploited forced labor couldn't exist without strict laws to ensure that those who were enslaved couldn't resist. When the U.S. Supreme Court ruled in 1857 that anyone who was black, or who possessed any percentage of African blood, wasn't a citizen in the eyes of the law, it was a message intended to reinforce the understanding that America's black population had absolutely no rights. Without rights, attempting to use the law in order to gain freedom or to protect oneself from discrimination was futile.

Life in 1849 St. Louis was probably no different than most years for the city's African American population, aside from the tragedies that had befallen the city. Many simply tried to live their lives the best way they knew how, but others could sense that changes were on the horizon. Voices that had once been silent were starting to speak up. The power of the written word was at play, no matter how many attempts were made to suppress it.

Based on the belief that an uneducated population is an easily controlled one, Missouri's slaveholding politicians had always placed limits on black education. This created a situation in which only a small number of the state's African Americans could read and write. Groups such as the Roman Catholic Church and some black ministers had tried to provide educational instruction to the city's blacks in the 1830s and 1840s, but each time the authorities stepped in to shut down the efforts. As America's abolitionist movement grew and agitation against slavery increased, fearful proslavery interests in Missouri completely outlawed the education of all blacks in 1847 in hopes of diminishing their ability to communicate effectively. Yet some did manage to express themselves in writing, and they did so to good effect.[1]

In October 1849, Missouri newspapers passed along a small but curious piece of information for their readers: In Paris, M. de Tocqueville entertained Mr. Brown, a slave escaped from America. Despite the vague reference, St. Louisans required no further clarification about Mr. Brown's identity. They were well aware that the man in question was William Wells Brown, an individual known to many of the city's slaveholders because he had spent much of his early life as one of St. Louis's roughly 5,500 enslaved African American residents.[2]

No one in those years could have predicted that Sandford, as Brown was known during his enslavement, would become an international figure who humanized the face of American slavery. In 1847, Brown's autobiography, *The Narrative of William W. Brown, An American Slave, Written by Himself*, was printed in London. It told of his years in captivity, his escape around 1835, and his eventual rise to become a respected advocate for the abolition of the so-called peculiar institution. By 1849, Brown's narrative was in its fourth edition, and more than eight thousand copies had been sold since its first printing. Although this was a success for Brown and the abolitionist cause, it wasn't a pleasant reflection of life in St. Louis. Brown spared not the stories of brutal beatings, torment, sexual exploitation, and even murder of slaves at the hands of the city's slave owners. In desperation, Enoch Price, a St. Louis merchant who was Brown's last owner, wrote to Brown's literary agent declaring that most of the stories were pure fabrication, but Price's refutation did little to change the minds of Brown's audience.

Perhaps trying to take a bit of the sting off, the editors of the *St. Louis Daily New Era* used a little humor to lighten the mood: "'Was Mr. Brown a popular man when he lived in your town?' inquired a busybody of his friend. 'I should think he was,' replied the gentleman, 'as many persons endeavored to prevent his leaving—and several of them, including the sheriff, his deputy, and several constables, followed him some distance.'"[3]

Laying Down the Law on "Free" African Americans

The harsh realities of slavery affected not only the lives of enslaved African Americans but also those persons of color who were legally free. They too lived under the shadow of discrimination and institutional racism that pervaded all slave states.

From its time as a territorial entity, Missouri had permitted slavery while discouraging settlement by free blacks. When the Missouri Territory originally applied for statehood in 1819, one of Congress's main objections to its proposed state constitution was the exclusion of free blacks. Northern congressmen balked at the idea of laws barring free persons of color from settling on American soil. After considerable debate over the issue of exclusionary laws and the westward expansion of slavery in the United States, the general agreement known as the Missouri Compromise was reached. It allowed Missouri to enter the Union as a slave state so long as all prohibitions against free blacks were lifted—but it didn't provide clear provisions for protecting their rights. Consequently the Missouri General Assembly was free to enact whatever laws it felt were necessary to keep the existing African American population in line while also discouraging additional free persons of color from entering the state. Missouri's legislators—most of whom had settled there from the slaveholding Upper South—tried *very* hard to keep them out.

Slave owners viewed free persons of color as one of the most serious threats to the institution of slavery. A black man who didn't answer to anyone but himself was a bad example to those who wore the yoke of slavery. Such cases, they argued, encouraged dangerous ideas in the minds of their human property. They believed that keeping the number of free blacks at a minimum was necessary to reduce the negative impact that their presence might create. Over the next forty years, the Missouri legislature passed a series of laws aimed at minimizing that threat by keeping free blacks under very tight reins.

Creating this elaborate set of laws dictating what was and wasn't permissible for the state's African American inhabitants took a considerable amount of effort. Although many statutes were modeled after laws already on the books in other slave states or based on precedents that stretched back to the colonial laws that regulated slaves, legislators still had to be sure they were covering all the bases. First, they had to clearly define who was black.

In American slave society, where it was commonplace for white slave owners to father children with their slaves, it wasn't always apparent whether one was black. As Cyprian Clamorgan, a free member of St. Louis's African American community who observed the circumstances and culture of the free black population in the city, noted in his seminal history, *The Colored Aristocracy of St. Louis*, the situation in the Mound City was incredibly convoluted. He wrote, "Many of them [St. Louis's free African Americans] are separated from the white race by a line of division so faint that it can be traced only by the keen eye of prejudice—a line so dim indeed that, in many instances that might be named, the stream of African blood has been so diluted by mixture with Caucasian, that the most critical observer cannot detect it."[4]

Enslaved families often included children who were fathered by a white slaveholder, and many free families were descended from former slaves who shared similar lineages. The genetic maps of black families were therefore less than racially lineal. Their children often had very light skin tone and distinctly European facial features, which meant they could easily pass for Caucasian—a fact that was upsetting to those who subscribed to widely held beliefs that the African ethnicities were inherently inferior. This made it necessary to legally distinguish the Negro from the *mulatto* (a person who shared European and African parentage). The purpose of this distinction wasn't to provide any favorable rights or treatment for those with mixed blood. Rather, it was to prevent those with some African ancestry from attempting to declare they had rights because they possessed white ancestors.

According to Missouri state statute, mulattoes were defined as follows: "Every person, other than a negro, any one of whose grandfathers or grandmothers is, or shall have been, a negro, although all his or her progenitors, except those descending from the negro, may have been white persons, shall be deemed a mulatto; and every such person, who shall have one-fourth or more negro blood, shall, in like manner, be deemed a mulatto."[5]

With the distinctions clearly delineated, the law could then determine who was entitled to what freedoms. For those who were legally deemed to be Negroes or mulattoes, those freedoms were greatly restricted. Because race was weighed more heavily than one's legal status as free or enslaved, even free blacks were essentially, as historian Ira Berlin noted, "slaves without masters."[6]

Nearly every aspect of free blacks' lives was restricted in some form or another. For example, according to state law, free African American males between the ages of seven and twenty-one were required to be apprenticed and learn a trade, ensuring that all blacks were gainfully employed. (In the eyes of the state, an idle black person was either a threat or a burden.) Certainly learning a trade was advantageous, but like most things, it came with exclusions. Young white males were also entitled to apprenticeships, but unlike blacks they were required to be taught how to read, write, and perform arithmetic as part of the experience. In lieu of an education, black apprentices were to be given monetary compensation at the end of their apprenticeships. The law also stipulated that a black apprentice couldn't work alongside a white apprentice.[7]

Then in 1831 a small but horrifically bloody slave insurrection, the Nat Turner rebellion, put slaveholders everywhere on edge and made them eager to stamp out any future attempts at revolt. Meanwhile, growing pressure from the abolitionist movement in the North posed a further challenge, and efforts such as the Underground Railroad were slowly eroding the institution of slavery. Growing more concerned about the "threat" posed by free African Americans, the Missouri General Assembly sought to tighten controls on this troublesome population even further.

In 1835 Missouri legislators passed a new law declaring that all free blacks must be licensed to remain in the state. They now had to prove to a judge that they deserved to remain by stating that they had gainful employment and could be sponsored by a white inhabitant who could post a security on their behalf. Perhaps such demands weren't as degrading as living one's life as the property of others, but forcing native-born Americans to appear in court, convince a white man to sign a two-hundred-dollar security bond on their behalf, and declare before a judge that they were financially and morally responsible enough to live in their own state was certainly no less painful.[8]

In 1849 black men and women who had either come of legal age, been newly freed, or recently entered St. Louis County from another county within Missouri went before St. Louis County judges to plead their case for receiving the valuable "free Negro bond." It was up to each judge to decide whether a petitioner had "proved to the satisfaction of the Court that he/she is of the class of free Negroes who are authorized by law to be licensed to reside in this State, that he/she is of good moral character and capable of supporting his or herself by honest employment." If everything was in order, the petitioner was granted a license and allowed to remain in the state "during good behavior."[9]

Social Standards and Financial Opportunities

Interestingly, few laws segregated places of residence for free persons of color in the city. Unlike the post-Reconstruction period, when laws enforced segregation and demanded that whites and blacks live in separate parts of the city, in 1849 St. Louis blacks and whites lived in close proximity, although they didn't share dwellings. Often free black families lived in shacks built along alleys in the city or on the edge of town in communities such as Happy Hollow, a collection of homes that lay in a low section of land just west of Sixth Street.[10]

One rule that could be applied to residential situations was the ordinance prohibiting fraternization between blacks and whites. Indeed, Section 7 of the Negro and Mulatto and Slave Ordinances of the City of St. Louis declared that any white person over the age of ten who was found "associating with any negro or mulatto, bond or free" at any dance or other assemblage would be fined no less than five dollars and no more than fifty dollars. This prohibition was as much about preventing whites from sheltering runaway slaves as it was about separating the races, and the city made sure to enforce it. When one white man was caught for "having harbored free negroes in his house," he was fined $50, prompting the *Weekly Reveille* to comment, sarcastically, that this was "rather expensive hospitality."[11]

Certainly the city codes that existed at the time show that catching and punishing possible abolitionists was a top priority for St. Louis's leaders. According to the law, all blacks, enslaved and free, were required to obtain a written pass from the mayor if they needed to be on the streets between 10:00 p.m. and 4:00 a.m. Slave owners could also issue passes for free movement after hours. Anyone else found to be issuing written passes for blacks faced arrest and fines between $20 and $100—these fines were much more serious than most financial penalties for other offenses.

Another series of ordinances sought to lessen the possibility of blacks conspiring to escape or revolt. African Americans were not only prohibited from receiving an education but also from holding dances, meetings, and even religious services without the written permission of St. Louis's mayor. State law further barred an assembly of African Americans unless a white officer of the law or another authority was present; the manner of assembly didn't matter if more than a couple individuals came together. In August 1849 a group of gamblers tempted fate by organizing a card game in a private home. Someone, perhaps a sore loser or a belligerent neighbor, alerted the St. Louis City Guard. Afterward, the *Daily Missouri Republican* reported that "a party of negroes—some seven or eight—while engaged in cards yesterday at a house in the southern part of the city, were pounced upon by police and taken to the calaboose."[12]

In another case, an unauthorized "negro ball" was being held in the alley behind the State Tobacco Warehouse. When police caught wind of it, they raided the premises and arrested eight men and three women. The *New Era* noted that "numbers effected their escape by jumping through the windows and giving leg bail for their appearance." In the morning, the bailing out of the jailed slaves "presented a lively, amusing, and ludicrous scene" as slave owners came "calling for their negroes to get breakfast and to do other household work." Each of the slaves was fined one dollar for the offense.[13]

Selling liquor to slaves was also a crime, and those who ignored the prohibition were viewed as the dregs of society. The *New Era* reported on a suspected watering hole and hangout for black residents "both bond and free" on the levee. The bar, known as Harry of the West House, was a place where black men assembled daily to "play cards, roll ten-pins, and commit all kinds of debauchery." The editors sent a word of advice to the owner, identified only as an Italian, writing, "We would warn this negro with a white skin how he sells liquor to slaves, or he may be made to feel the penalty of the law."[14]

All the restrictive city ordinances aside, St. Louis was still a preferable destination for many blacks. Unlike small towns and rural counties, in St. Louis one could more easily blend into the community, joining the roughly 1,400 free African Americans present in 1849. Although this number wasn't large, it did represent the highest concentration of free blacks in Missouri, which provided a certain degree of freedom. Entertainment, places of worship, and a sense of community could all be found in St. Louis, but the lure of jobs and financial rewards was probably the most common draw.[15]

William Garrett, a thirty-six-year-old mulatto and Kentucky native, was one of those who sought opportunity in St. Louis despite the restrictions, perhaps because he was attracted to the port city's prosperity. As a drayman, the nineteenth-century version of a short-haul truck driver, Garrett was a crucial part of the city's economic structure. He and his fellow draymen were constantly hauling recently unloaded cargo from the bustling levee into the city or traveling in the opposite direction bringing produce, grain, or manufactured goods to the waiting steamboats.

The occupation of drayman was common among the city's free African American men, one held with considerable pride. For several years black draymen organized a parade through the streets of St. Louis as a way of showing unity and displaying their status in the community. Garrett was probably among those who participated in the draymen's parade in 1849. "The colored draymen of the city yesterday paraded our streets in their drays, the horses being decked in gaudy colors and the drivers in uniform," wrote the *Republican*.

"The line of drays, thirty-seven in number, each drawn by two horses sleeked up for the occasion, passed down Fourth Street about noon, preceded by a band of music, and under the direction of marshals mounted on horseback. The order in which they conducted their parade was marked by all who witnessed the procession."[16]

Punishments and "Protections"

Despite holding a place of economic importance to the community and establishing true legal residency, free persons of color still had no guarantee of freedom. Harsh penalties awaited those who couldn't immediately prove their legal status according to the law: Freedom papers had to be produced when demanded, or one could be arrested. Adding to the apprehension was the fact that bounties were paid for the capture of escaped slaves. This kept law enforcement officers—who were eligible to collect rewards—ever on the lookout for the opportunity to recapture slaves on the run. Even the city marshal had the authority to arrest without warrant any "free negro or mulattoe, or slave, who shall be found in the city violating any law of the State or ordinance of the city."[17]

The reality of life in the period before the passage of the Thirteenth Amendment, which granted citizenship to all persons regardless of race, meant that those who were considered of dubious status were at the mercy of those who enforced the laws. In 1846 the question of whether an African American was a citizen who enjoyed certain rights under the law was brought before a St. Louis court via a case challenging the constitutionality of the Negro license law. The judge in that case, John Krum, ruled that the law was indeed constitutional and that Charles Lyon, a free person of color who had filed suit against the state, was powerless to challenge it because he was black and enjoyed no legal rights.* Afterward the *Republican* noted that the county court

---

* John Krum was well known to those who opposed slavery. He was mayor of Alton, Illinois, when Elijah Lovejoy, an abolitionist and martyr for free speech, was killed by a proslavery mob in that city. Krum moved to St. Louis after the incident, where he was later appointed to the bench. Upon learning of Krum's ruling against free persons of color, the *Boston Daily Atlas* likened Krum to Philip III of Spain and his ruling to the Spanish king's expulsion of the Moors. In 1848, Krum was elected mayor of St. Louis and served until James Barry was elected to that office in April 1849.

should strictly enforce Judge Krum's decision, which would "free the city of a nuisance."[18]

The records show that the authorities frequently hauled suspected violators of the license law into court. In one instance Samuel Howell, "a free negro who has been fined and committed to the county jail for remaining in this State without a license," was brought before the judge. Howell was unable to prove to the court's satisfaction that he had the right to remain in Missouri. He was ordered to depart from the state, but not before receiving ten lashes on "his bare back" just to make sure he understood that returning wouldn't be a good idea—a typical punishment doled out for men in Howell's position. Later, James Lee and Lemuel Howard were each served twenty lashes for the same offense. Indeed, Section 28 of the acts relating to Negroes and mulattoes passed by the Missouri General Assembly stated that blacks who "appeared free" but lacked a license proving freedom in Missouri or citizenship in any other state were to be fined ten dollars and ordered to leave the state. The authority to inflict whippings for such offenses was left to the discretion of the judges, who almost always took advantage of this power.[19]

Nevertheless, there were cases when the ending turned out much happier than presumed. When Marshall S. Cockerill, a twenty-four-year-old steward, was arrested and placed in the county jail, he apparently couldn't provide immediate proof of his free status to those who had arrested him. When brought before the judge, however, he was able to substantiate his freedom and was discharged. City resident Charles Warfield found himself in a similar bind when he was unable to immediately prove his legal status. He was jailed and charged as a suspected runaway but later released upon a writ of habeas corpus when evidence was presented to the court that he was a free man.[20]

As precarious as the situation in St. Louis may have been, it's obvious from the actions of free men such as Charles Lyon that some people were willing to try to challenge the constitutionality of the Negroes and mulattoes laws in court. However, little to no progress was made given that using the legal system to one's advantage was quite difficult when one had no legal rights to begin with. Basic civil rights, such as those guaranteed by the Bill of Rights in the U.S. Constitution, simply didn't apply to African Americans.

A lack of basic rights made the black community vulnerable in many ways. For one, authorities could revoke a black person's freedom at will. Additionally, although laws meant to protect the public from violence applied to free blacks as well as whites, police didn't necessarily enforce them when white citizens were acting out against African Americans—and the consequences could be deadly. For example, when a young black man stepped out from a theater one evening in late June 1849, he "knocked" a white man standing on the sidewalk. In response, "the crowd immediately gathered round the negro; he was knocked down and stabbed—by whom it is impossible to say." He wasn't expected to recover, and there appeared to be no effort to find his killer.[21]

If or why the young black man bumped or shoved the other man will never be known, but the killing was the second white-on-black murder to occur that June, which makes one wonder whether the events were somehow connected. Only days before, a group of young white men had made national headlines for murdering a mulatto youth by the name of Collin Jones during an altercation. Details of the crime were printed in both the *Republican* and *The New York Herald*, but the two newspapers gave vastly different accounts.

The scene of the crime was described as a black brothel on Almond Street, the heart of the city's red-light district. It was a Friday night, and the place was likely as lively as any Friday evening in the summer. Seated at a table inside was Collin Jones, a young mulatto, who was playing cards with one of the young ladies of the establishment. As the two played, three well-known young men of the town entered the house while another stood watch outside the front door. The men approached Jones and seized him. He resisted and attempted to fight back. One or more of the young white men pulled knives and stabbed Jones in several places. He managed to break free and run screaming into the street. The men fled, and Jones was taken home for comfort. The authorities questioned him the next morning, and he gave them a statement that declared two of the men had stabbed him for no apparent reason. He died soon afterward. The *Herald* correspondent who telegraphed the story back to the New York office stated cynically that "no arrests have been made, nor will there probably be."[22]

A very different version of the story ran in the *Republican*. According to its report, three "citizens" entered a house on Almond Street where they knew they would find Jones, whom the paper improperly identified as Calvin Jones, for the purpose of finding some stolen property. Jones, "a notorious character," was found seated at a table "in the company of several mulattos, playing at cards." So as not to raise suspicions as to why these three men were in the house, one of the young men "jokingly picked up a pack of cards and insisted on having his fortune told." In response, Jones flew into a rage, grabbed the young man by the throat for having disturbed his card game, and seemed ready to inflict a beating on the now frightened "citizen." Fearing for his life, the young man drew a knife and cut Jones across the abdomen. Jones then "fell back" but "immediately rushed upon his opponent," who then plunged the knife deep into his lower abdomen once again. The story ends there by noting that Jones had died.[23]

The *New Era*'s account fell somewhere between the two previous stories. Apparently based on information provided by the local beat patrolman, the *New Era* reporter wrote that a gang of four or five men who had been "fleeced for considerable sums" organized a private patrol with the aim of finding the thieves. Around 11:00 p.m. that Friday, the men stopped Officer Fine of the night watch and informed him that they had found the location of a stash of their stolen property and that they were going to go get it. The citizen's patrol started down Almond Street, with Officer Fine following, and entered a small brick home. Fine reported that "soon after they entered, the inmates came rushing out, crying 'Murder,' followed by the white men, who in turned shouted, 'Stop thief!'" Then a black man came running past Fine, who gave chase. When he caught the man, the frightened individual told Fine that a man named Collin Jones had been stabbed along with the Negro woman who owned the home. Fine reportedly gathered everyone together but couldn't "ascertain who was the aggressor" and therefore didn't make any arrests. The woman was briefly jailed at the calaboose before being released. Jones, meanwhile, was taken into the house, and a physician was called. In the morning, Fine returned and learned from the physician that Jones was sure to die from his wounds. The officer took a statement "when it was determined to take his death bed confession."[24]

The truth was apparently somewhere in the middle of these three disparate accounts. Although Collin Jones's last statement wasn't revealed in the newspapers, Officer Fine must have felt that he had enough evidence of a crime with which to approach the city's prosecutor. Contrary to the *Herald* reporter's prognostication that no one would be arrested in connection with the incident, witnesses were interviewed, and the prosecutor's office brought the case before a grand jury. Four men were arrested and charged with murder in the first degree: Joseph Wilkinson; Joe Alvarez (or Alviris); Lyman Mower; and a familiar figure in 1849 St. Louis tales, Robert Mac O'Blenis.[25]

These men were well known around town because of their family connections and business reputations. Alvarez was a descendant of one of St. Louis's oldest families, which had settled in the area during the early colonial period and was part of the Creole community. His sister, Mary, married Robert Mac O'Blenis, a young man with a reputation as a gambler, street brawler, womanizer, and all-around troublemaker. Yet despite his checkered reputation, O'Blenis also ran a successful livery business and operated an omnibus service. This was most likely his tie to Wilkinson, who also operated an omnibus. (Wilkinson was already in trouble with the city at the time of the Jones incident because he was operating his business without a license.) Mower appears to have been a close friend of Wilkinson.[26]

This motley foursome seemed bent on either getting revenge or raising hell, but the fun came to an end during the legal proceedings. O'Blenis turned state's evidence against Wilkinson and presumably Mower. Also testifying against Wilkinson on behalf of the state was Madame Clementine, who was still in the midst of her own defense against the charges of keeping a bawdy house (as explained in the preceding chapter). Four of Wilkinson's friends, including Albert Jones (whose story appears in chapter 7), acted as his securities as the judge ordered a $10,000 bond. Three months later, Wilkinson sat in a St. Louis courtroom as a jury deliberated on his trial, but the jurors were unable to reach a decision. Apparently the circumstances of the event were as unclear to them as they are to us today.

The case did have lingering effects, however. Just after Christmas, O'Blenis encountered a drunken Wilkinson in the Empire Coffee House, one of their favorite watering holes. With bad blood between them, O'Blenis decided to shoot Wilkinson but missed and shot a bystander in the arm instead. O'Blenis paid for the man's medical bills and didn't have to go to court. Two years later, Wilkinson and Mower were again charged (but later acquitted) with assault with intent to murder after another violent incident. Six years after that, O'Blenis was sent to the Missouri State Penitentiary for the murder of Benjamin Brand at the Planter's House Hotel.[27]

The Emergence of the Black Middle Class

Even though the deck appeared to be stacked against St. Louis's free African American population, some individuals succeeded in owning businesses and land. Two of the most prominent were Jacques Clamorgan, a member of St. Louis's early Creole community and grandfather of community chronicler Cyprian Clamorgan, and a free woman of color known only as Esther. Jacques Clamorgan had died by 1849, but his children inherited his property and enjoyed the same rights as their father. Esther also benefited from earlier legal precedents. She was forty-nine years old in 1849 and remained the title holder of an early colonial Spanish land grant that contained several acres upon which Laclede's Landing stands today.[28]

A lucky few may have enjoyed special privileges and received income from lands and rents, but the majority of free persons of color performed manual labor as a way of making a living. The men often served as dray operators, and the women often ran laundry operations washing clothes for white clients. (In addition to owning land, Esther was a washwoman.) The Mississippi River was a deep source of employment for the black community, what with all the steamboat companies and shipping agents needing men to work in the warehouses along the levee or aboard the steamboats as porters, cooks, and waiters. Many of the steamboat lines hired free men of color but also contracted with slave owners to provide slave labor for many of the same jobs.

Of course, not all jobs required heavy lifting. Being a barber was one of the most profitable occupations for free blacks and mulattoes in 1840s St. Louis, often leading to prominent positions within the community. Thirty-two-year-old Albert White was one such man who ran a successful barbershop in the city. He and his wife, Charlotte, are

Bob Wilkinson was a barber at several of St. Louis's better hotels and was well known throughout the city. Daguerreotype by Thomas Easterly, 1860. Missouri Historical Society Collections.

listed in the census records as mulattoes who owned an impressive $1,500 in real estate. In 1850, White caught gold fever like many men and took his wife to the California gold fields. He ultimately chose to run a saloon instead of panning for gold or cutting hair, a decision that proved fruitful: He returned to St. Louis several years later with a sizable savings. In 1860, White's personal worth was estimated at $1,650, with an additional $20,000 worth of real estate to his name.[29]

A handful of other members of the free black community held a variety of jobs that required specialized knowledge or advanced skill. When A. N. Williams received his free license, it listed his occupation as tobacconist. Williams—who was most likely W. N. Williams rather than A. N. Williams, as listed in the records—was a Virginia-born tobacco merchant. George Hill and Andrew Hubbard both secured their freedom bonds in 1849 and worked as cooks. Patsey Meachum was a *mantua-maker*, an early term for dressmaker, as was Margaret Smothers. Anderson Lewis was a rectifier (someone who distills spirits), and Hardin Finley was a blacksmith. These skilled workers formed the foundation of a growing black middle class that continued to thrive well into the twentieth century.[30]

Abolitionism and Its Opponents

Free persons of color in Missouri—many of whom were former slaves, children of slaves, or the spouses of slaves—understood that they were fortunate; they also recognized that the majority of African Americans in the state were not. A large number of them felt a moral obligation to assist their enslaved brethren in escaping slavery. Historical records show that many free blacks were willing to risk their lives and personal freedom to assist enslaved blacks who couldn't gain freedom on their own by organizing escapes and building underground networks.

Slaveholders were obviously concerned about what they saw as the growing menace of abolitionism, a sentiment shared by the editors of the *New Era*. Their comment on yet another possible slave escape aided by the city's abolitionists was that "Negro property is every day becoming more insecure in our city." Abolitionist movements had gained momentum in the United States, particularly in New England and the Northeast, since the 1830s. One of the first abolitionist newspapers, *The Liberator*, was begun by Boston reformers William Lloyd Garrison and Isaac Knapp as early as 1831—a move that was seen as just another example of Northern meddling in the Southern way of life. In St. Louis slaveholders' anxieties were further raised when Elijah P. Lovejoy, editor of St Louis's religious newspaper, *The Observer*, shifted his editorial rhetoric away from the perceived evils of Catholicism and toward the promotion of abolitionism. Lovejoy's stance is ironic given that he had previously rented a teenage Sandford, later known as William Wells Brown, to assist him in his office when he was editor of *The St. Louis Times*. (Brown later praised Lovejoy as being compassionate and "decidedly the best master I had ever had.")[31]

By the mid-1840s, abolitionist sympathies were progressing enough that some St. Louisans saw a real need to lobby for legislation that might strengthen any protections of the institution of slavery in Missouri. The result was the St. Louis Anti-Abolitionist Society. On November 12, 1846, the group gathered in the rotunda of the Old Courthouse for an organizational meeting. Fifty-five representatives from townships in St. Louis County and wards throughout the city were elected to serve as vice presidents and members of the finance committee. This coalition of slaveholders consisted of some of the most prominent citizens of the region whose names are still recognizable today. Among them were Thomas Skinker, R. W. Hunt, John Sappington, James Bissell, W. McKelvey, and W. H. Dorsett. Enoch Price, Brown's former owner, represented the city's Third Ward, and Frederick Dent of Carondelet Township, who became the father-in-law of Ulysses S. Grant two years later, served on the finance committee.[32]

The group elected John O'Fallon as its president. He and his brother, Benjamin, were two of the area's biggest landowners and slaveholders. Brown mentions them both in his autobiography, claiming that Benjamin kept five or six bloodhounds for the purpose of hunting down runaway slaves and that John had sold one of his male slaves who was both a husband and a father of three, thereby forcibly separating the family.[33]

RUNNING DOWN SLAVES WITH DOGS. — Page 82.

The Narrative of William W. Brown featured Wells's recollections of slaves being pursued by bloodhounds owned by prominent St. Louisan Benjamin O'Fallon. Wells claimed O'Fallon kept hounds for just this purpose. Illustration from the 1847 edition of Wells's book. Missouri Historical Society Collections.

O'Fallon and the St. Louis Anti-Abolitionist Society had a clear objective: to call upon the Missouri General Assembly to enact a series of laws aimed at protecting the right to own slaves. The pre-amble to the group's constitution even said as much: "Whereas, the principles of all citizen governments rest mainly on the protection thereby afforded to life and property; and whereas, the utter failure to protect our citizens in the undisturbed possession of slave their prop-erty, has become notorious, and calls for prompt and decisive action from the people of this section of the State."[34]

Much of the St. Louis Anti-Abolitionist Society's concern was likely a result of enslaved people's increased efforts to use the legal system to sue for freedom. A number of freedom suits were filed over the course of the 1840s, including Edward Bates's victory on behalf of Lucy Delaney (described in chapter 6). Many of these cases dragged on and on. Charlotte, an enslaved woman owned by Pierre Chouteau, was winding her way through the appeals system trying to gain her freedom by claiming that because her mother was Canadian and therefore free, she should also be legally free. In the early months of 1849, Dred Scott was confined to a county jail cell like confiscated property while the courts decided when and how to proceed with his case. He was released in late March but continued to play the waiting game as the wheels of justice moved ever so slowly toward the deci-sion that would affect not only his life but also the life of every African American in the United States.[35]

Escapees, Their Helpers, and Their Hunters

Because the legal path to freedom could be arduous and lengthy with-out a guarantee of success, it was ultimately no different from attempt-ing escape. But escape, if successful, had the benefit of a quicker exit to freedom. Slaves who were willing to take the risk had friends—both black and white—stepping up to help them. Multiple stories in the *Republican* and the *New Era* show that an organized network of aboli-tionists was actively assisting enslaved individuals in the St. Louis area in 1849. Some of these escape attempts were successful; many were not.

Both papers took an unapologetic proslavery stance that's easily discerned in the wording and tone of the articles written about the escape cases. When it was reported that Benjamin Fowler had lost an enslaved woman and two boys the previous year, the *Republican* stated that the slaves "were enticed by abolitionists." When Fowler learned that his missing property had turned up in Will County, Illinois, he set off to reclaim it. Upon arriving there he secured a legal warrant to take possession of the three escaped slaves and managed to take hold of the two boys. However, reported the *Republican*, "abolitionists of that vicinity collected in strong force, and threatened violence if he should remove them." Fowler backed down and returned home on the steamboat *Ocean Wave* emptyhanded. The editors ended the story with an attempt to villainize the Illinois abolitionists by claiming the enslaved woman had expressed interest in returning home with her former owner, a wish "denied by her beloved abolitionist friends."[36]

St. Louis's location directly across the river from a free state increased the chances of a successful escape, but it didn't necessarily make escape easier. Vigilant eyes were always on the lookout for escapees, and just because one made it to a free state didn't always mean that the local authorities would be sympathetic, as was the case for a group of three enslaved men who successfully crossed the Mississippi at Gabaurie Island in early November 1849. With the assistance of two white abolitionist friends, E. J. Palmer and Isaac Shedeker, and a free black man and experienced absconder, Bob Williams, the three enslaved men raced through the countryside to try to get as much distance as they could between them and Missouri. However, "eight miles beyond Alton, they were arrested by a gentleman, who committed them to jail at Jerseyville." This man then proceeded to St. Louis to inform their owners of his discovery, no doubt expecting a handsome reward.

The abolitionist Palmer attempted to create greater distance between the escaped men and their owners by filing a writ of habeas corpus in Beardstown, Illinois, some seventy miles away from the Missouri state line. He also claimed that the men were actually free but had been illegally sold into slavery. With the filing of the writ, the men were allowed to continue to Beardstown for a hearing with a circuit court judge. They were accompanied by a local sheriff, who foiled the men's "several attempts to escape" along the way. The abolitionist Shedeker was allowed to drive the wagon carrying the men, and when they arrived in Beardstown, he attempted to make a break for it with the wagon. The sheriff, however, was able to seize the reins from Shedeker, thus stopping the desperate dash for freedom. The escaped enslaved men had no further recourse than to be taken before the judge.

Despite the considerable distance, their owners arrived in Beardstown to witness the hearing. The judge ruled that the abolitionists' activities and the attempted legal proceedings were illegal, and he returned the enslaved men to the St. Louisans. For his part in the attempted escape, Williams was also arrested and sent home to St. Louis. The *New Era* reporter covering the story surmised that he would "in all probability expatiate for his crimes in the Penitentiary in Jefferson."[37]

The Beardstown case was typical. If caught, authorities were eager to make examples of those who were escaping or aiding in the escape of others. These failed attempts usually ended with both the escapee and the abolitionist losing their freedom: Slaves were returned to their owners, and those attempting to "decoy a slave" were sent to the state penitentiary. Still, there were many who considered this an acceptable risk in return for the possible reward of freedom. In January 1849, John Johnson, whom the *Republican* identified as an abolitionist, was caught attempting to cross the river on the upper ferry with an enslaved person belonging to Edward J. Gay, a successful St. Louis merchant.

The story began in the days after Christmas 1848, when a man belonging to Gay and a woman belonging to Major Ryland attempted to escape together. Gay's man asked two white boys whether they would agree to take him and Ryland's servant woman to the residence of Captain Shreve. The two boys agreed, and the four of them set off for Shreve's home. As they were riding along, the man asked the boys whether they would change course and take them across the river to Illinois by way of the upper ferry. Though presumably he had provided some excuse for crossing the river, the two boys immediately suspected the man and woman were attempting to flee and ordered them off the wagon. Although the motive for the man's next action isn't clear, it can be assumed that he feared he would be arrested for playing a part in the attempted escape and so offered the woman to his owner and the authorities as a gesture of goodwill.

Gay summoned the police, who arrested the woman for attempting to escape.

The next day, Johnson was driving his hack on board the upper ferry when one of its back wheels ran off the ferry's apron. Some of the other men aboard the ferry offered to assist him in fixing it. In the process, one of the men looked into the hack and noticed a blanket and buffalo robe lying in the wagon. With "his curiosity excited" he examined them only to find a black man hiding underneath: It was Gay's man who had tried to escape the day before.

Both he and Johnson were taken into custody, where Gay's man confessed that two men in Illinois had paid Johnson to ship the slaves across the river. They had promised the man and the woman arrested the night before passage to Canada after they had entered Illinois. For his role in the attempted liberation, Johnson was sentenced to two years in prison; the enslaved man was presumably returned to Gay. Both men paid with their freedom, and Johnson ultimately paid with his life because he died halfway through his prison sentence.[38]

If some whites were helping slaves escape due to moral convictions, others were using the system to their advantage. A few realized that there was an opportunity to play both sides of the game and make a profit. One of these was former city marshal John Atkinson, who in October 1849 was accused of enticing slaves to escape to Illinois. He would arrange their passage and then hold them either in a secure location after they reached the free side of the Mississippi or in his own home in St. Louis. When a reward was offered for their return, he would take them back to their owner and accept the bounty. Likewise, he was encouraging free persons of color to enter Missouri with the promise of signing their freedom bonds as the security holder, but when they arrived in St. Louis, he sold them into slavery. The *Republican* commented that "an investigation has been ordered, and it will be, it is hoped, a thorough one."

Atkinson had been a law enforcement officer in several capacities in St. Louis County and the city over the years. He had even agreed to put forth his name on free Negro bonds for several members of St. Louis's free black community. Then out of nowhere he was identified as a possible lawbreaker. When the police came to his house to search for evidence, he became enraged and defended his home with a musket. The situation ended peacefully with Atkinson arrested and fined fifty dollars, but his story remains unresolved. Neither surviving court documents nor newspaper accounts reveal whether the accusations against him were proved accurate. He isn't listed as a prisoner in the state penitentiary records either. Perhaps an investigation found no wrongdoing, but why did the authorities look into him in the first place? Was he truly guilty, or were some angered by the fact that he was assisting free persons of color and therefore tried to frame him for false crimes?[39]

For their part, St. Louis's free African American community was pivotal in arranging for the escape of enslaved persons. These men and women had the most insight into the processes of planning escapes from a local perspective. They actively pursued opportunities to free slaves and communicated with white abolitionists to make escapes happen. One example was Mary Lot. A free black woman, she was arrested in September 1849 under suspicion of participating in the escape of numerous slaves. According to the *Republican*, "Thus far, in every instance, whether successful or not, she had managed her cards so well as to escape the closest vigilance." This time the authorities were hoping to collect enough evidence against her to make a conviction.[40]

Benjamin Savage and William Harris were two other active agents of the freedom struggle. Savage, a free Negro barber, had arranged for the escape of many slaves over the years before he and Harris were arrested in 1850. As the *Republican* noted that June, "There is a large gang of free negroes in this city and its vicinity in Illinois engaged in these operations . . . if the plans of our plan are carried out they will be soon be brought to justice."[41]

Having someone to make arrangements and connections was helpful, but it took time and planning to make it all happen, and time wasn't always something that enslaved people had plenty of. Some couldn't make contact with underground agents, nor did they want to miss an opportunity if one arose. Many simply decided when and how to break away on their own. Proof of these escapes can be found in the classified sections of the St. Louis newspapers, where reward notices were printed by slave owners hoping to reclaim their property. These ads remain the only record of many forgotten and unknown individuals who are otherwise lost to time.

In April 1849, James McFadin advertised a $200 reward for the capture and return of his slave, Jonas. According to McFadin's ad in the *Republican*, the owner was informed that twenty-year-old Jonas had either hopped aboard the steamboat *Swiss Boy* or *Time and Tide*, bound for the Illinois River. McFadin described the young man as five feet, eight inches tall and bearing a "grum [*sic*] countenance." He was dressed in striped cotton pants, a striped hickory brown shirt, a soldier's roundabout-style jacket, and a red plush cap. If he was aboard a steamboat heading up the Illinois, it's probably safe to presume that he was bound for Canada, although many escaped slaves found refuge in the small-but-growing town of Chicago.[42]

Four months later the St. Louis papers ran a reward notice offering up to fifty dollars for the capture and return of Maria. Her description provides a glimpse of the harsh realities of slave life. Maria was twenty-one years old, "a dark brown woman," and five feet, two inches in height. Her most distinguishing feature, however, was the fact that her hand was badly deformed: "Her left hand is so much burned that she cannot open the last three fingers of the same." The advertiser— Robirds, Brookes, and Company—stated that it would pay twenty-five dollars if Maria were captured within the state of Missouri or fifty dollars if she were taken outside of the state and lodged until she could be retrieved.

Some slave owners offered both substantial rewards for the return of their property and added bonuses if those responsible for aiding in the escape were also brought to justice. Four well-known St. Louisans joined together to offer a considerable sum for the return of five slaves who had presumably run away together. A total of $900 would be paid for their return—$100 for each individual, plus an extra $400 for delivering the persons who assisted them.

Through the descriptions provided for each runaway, we catch not only a glimpse of their physical presences but also a clue as to the value each held for the owner. Edward Bredell had lost a girl of twenty-two or twenty-three named Priscilla. She was "rather tall and square built; dark complexion" and "if confused, would have impediment of speech." Mrs. A. M. Perry was seeking the return of Amanda, a girl of about seventeen who was also described as having a "dark complexion; rather stout built;" a further characteristic was her "slow speech."

$300 REWARD.—Ranaway from the subscribers, on Monday night, the 7th instant, TWO NEGRO GIRLS, MARTHA and CAROLINE. Martha is a bright mulatto, short hair, medium size, about 24 years old, and the upper part of her upper front teeth decayed; she is quick spoken and intelligent; she has very small feet for a negro; dress not known.

CAROLINE is black; about 18 years old; small and slender; she has large eyes and very thick lips—the under lip hangs down; when she left she had on a muslin dress, of a light color, with a pink spot, a buff colored corded sun bonnet, and new shoes; she took with her also, a plain grey cotton dress, and a barege dress.

The girls ran away in company, and are supposed to have been enticed away by a free negro, the husband of Martha.

The above reward will be paid, if the negroes are apprehended without the State, and delivered to the subscribers at St. Louis; $150 if apprehended without the county, and $75 if within the county, and confined so that their owners can get them. A proportional reward will be given for the apprehension of either of them.

E. C. BLACKBURN,
JOHN LEE.

my11

Slave owners purchased ads in the *Daily Missouri Republican* and other newspapers posting rewards for the return of runaway slaves. These ads often contained the only known description of many enslaved African Americans. Newspaper ad, April 18, 1849. Missouri Historical Society Collections.

Nancy belonged to A. L. Allen. She was eighteen, "stout; thick set" with a "full face" and "flat nose." Apparently she was "quick spoken" and had been wearing a gingham dress with a "plain gold ring on her forefinger" when last seen. Bernard Platte sought to regain possession of his mulatto girl Theresa, whom he interestingly described as "17; well grown and very good looking." She could also be identified by the "small wen in the corner of her right eye." Finally, L. C. Dessaint had lost his man Martin. At thirty-eight, Martin was the oldest of the escapees. He was described as "spare built; about 5 foot 10 inches high; copper color; and his hair quite gray; quick spoken, and a pretty smart boy." The full stories of Priscilla, Amanda, Nancy, Theresa, and Martin remain unknown.[43]

We do, however, know that other enslaved St. Louisans tried to run away on their own but were unable to break free from the bonds of servitude. Ellen Turner was a slave in north St. Louis County. She and her enslaved husband were owned by the same person for the first few years of their marriage, but shortly after the birth of their third child, her husband was sold to another owner. Turner's owner then moved his family and hers to a new home some twenty miles from her husband's location in St Charles County.

Years later, Turner's daughter, Mattie J. Jackson, chronicled her parents' struggle to maintain contact in her own slave narrative. Apparently Jackson's father had been given permission to visit his wife each week, but this involved him walking twenty miles every Saturday night and making the return trip home each Sunday evening. He did this for two years until he decided that he could no longer live under the yoke of slavery. He promptly escaped, made his way to Chicago, and established himself as a preacher. According to Jackson, her father tried in vain to secure his family's freedom.

Turner was happy for her husband, but now her two surviving daughters had no father. Determined to seek her freedom and find her husband, Turner took her young girls one day and fled her owner's farm. She had to keep them moving to avoid being captured, which worked until the family reached the Mississippi. With Illinois only yards away, someone, perhaps a ferryman, began to question Turner. Apparently a reward poster had already been printed in the St. Louis papers, and bounty hunters were looking for her. She confessed to whoever was questioning her, was arrested, and was then jailed in St. Louis along with her children. Her owner, Charles Canory, handed her and her daughters over to Bernard M. Lynch, the notorious St. Louis slave dealer, who confined the family to his slave pen until William Lewis bought them. Lewis and his wife had a home in the city, and Jackson described them as harsh. The couple owned Turner and her daughters until the Civil War.[44]

Turner's situation was typical of many slaves who attempted but failed to escape to freedom. When they were caught they were often subjected to severe punishment or sold off. Turner and her family were fortunate enough—if it can be described that way—to remain together in St. Louis. Too often the consequences of escape involved being "sold down the river" to the large-production plantations in Mississippi Delta country. For enslaved men, women, and children, this was a sentence of hard labor that also likely meant a permanent separation from family.

Selling People for Profit

In the St. Louis newspapers, slave dealers regularly ran notices calling for large numbers of slaves. B. W. Powell, an agent in residence at the Planter's House Hotel, enticed slave owners with the promise that "the highest cash price will be paid for all descriptions of NEGROES." Others proclaimed a specific need. Dealer Joseph M. Heady, who ran his business from the City Hotel, regularly announced that he sought "300 Negroes—men, women, girls, and boys—from the ages of twelve to thirty, for which I will pay cash."[45]

The most prominent St. Louis slave dealer was Bernard M. Lynch. He had bought out a previous firm, White and Tooley, to establish a slave pen where men, women, and children were stabled like horses until they were purchased. From his business office at 104 Locust Street, Lynch, like his competitors, promised the "highest prices paid for good and likely negroes." He also offered the service of "boarding for others in comfortable quarters under secure fastenings." The wording of Lynch's advertisements, which refer to human beings in terms no different from those used for livestock and pets, reveal the inhumane reality of slavery.[46]

Enslaved people were no more than a means of profit to Lynch and others like him. What became of them or how they were treated was of no concern, an attitude that was the product of a system where the subjugation of an entire race of people was considered justifiable for the sake of monetary gain. In contemporary modes of thought, we find it hard to image that anyone could see fellow human beings as subhuman and undeserving of basic rights, compassion, and respect, but this was the very nature of slavery. Generations of Europeans were taught by means of science, religion, and popular belief that members of the Negro race were incapable of functioning as normal human

FOR SALE—An excellent MULATTO GIRL, about nineteen years old, a good cook, chamber-mai and washer and ironer. Enquire at No. 24 Water street. jan9 tf

NEGROES FOR SALE.—An excellent Negro Woman, a good cook, first rate washer and ironer. A very likely Negro Boy, aged about eleven years. For sale low. Apply soon to ['an5] WM. J. AUSTIN, 37 Locust st.

WANTED—300 NEGROES—Men, Women, Girls and Boys—from the ages of twelve to thirty, for which I will pay cash. Apply to the subscriber, at the City Hotel, St. Louis. [n14 3m3dp*] JOSEPH M HEADY.

Local papers ran daily notices from slave dealers and private sellers advertising the sale or want of slaves. The bottom ad shown here illustrates the common practice of buying lots of enslaved persons for shipment to large plantations in the southern United States. Newspaper ads from the *Daily Missouri Republican*, January 16, 1849. Missouri Historical Society Collections.

beings. They were brutal by nature, unintelligent, and without morality. It was only by force, servitude, and tight restrictions that blacks could be managed and rendered safe enough to live among the general population. By deeply instilling these beliefs and prejudices into the minds of all white Americans, both in the South and the North, it was much easier to rationalize leading men, women, and children onto an auction block to sell them.

The heartless treachery of it all is best illustrated by the story of a slave owner from the southern portion of Missouri who decided to take off for California with the hope of striking it rich in the gold fields. Before departing his home, he informed his male slave that he would take him along. The owner offered the desperate man a deal that he declared would benefit them both. In exchange for working for his owner for eight hours a day in the gold fields, the enslaved man would be given a remainder of each day to mine his own claim. With the money the enslaved man earned from his gold prospecting, he could purchase his freedom for $800. With an additional $600 he could buy his wife's freedom; for another $400 for each of his children, the whole family could be freed. Ecstatic at the prospect of gaining freedom for himself and his family, the enslaved man eagerly agreed, and he and his owner began the journey upriver. When they arrived in St. Louis, the enslaved man discovered the true nature of his owner's proposal. His owner had no intention of taking his property with him. Needing money for the journey west, he'd made arrangements for a slave dealer to take possession of the enslaved man, who was promptly sold for $750.

A reporter for the abolitionist newspaper *The North Star* spoke to the angry and deceived husband and father after the transaction was completed. The enslaved man said, "My heart was high as I thought of the prospect of becoming free, and having my wife and children, but think how I felt when massa sell me to get money to carry him to the gold mines." The reporter concluded the article with his own commentary that "the story was heart rendering, but it is a scene of every day life among slave traders."[47]

In St. Louis, the ultimate fate of enslaved individuals was determined on the eastern steps of the Old Courthouse, where the slave auctions were held. Slave dealers gathered at one corner of the steps, along with horse traders and real-estate auctioneers who competed for the attention of the assembled crowds on sale days. On one of these afternoons, a correspondent from *The National Era*, an abolitionist newspaper based in Washington, DC, witnessed one of these sales. In dramatic terms he captured the scene as three enslaved women of differing ages were sold on the block. The reporter sought to show his readers the irony, the cruelty, and the barbarism that occurred among people who considered themselves good Christians and upholders of democracy.

Three auctioneers were assembled, each selling a different article of merchandise "old furniture; another, horses; and the third, living images of the Almighty Father—a bureau, a horse, a WOMAN!" The narrative continues:

> "How much for Maria, gentlemen, a very valuable woman, and sold for no fault?"
>
> And Maria was much more white than black—more Amer-

ican than African blood in her veins. Some white man's daughter, doubtless, was here sold. Maria stood in the centre of a crowd, her eyes cast down, her bosom heaving; in silence she stood under the eastern porch of the desecrated Hall of Justice, while men, trafficking in their kind, bid upon her flesh, and bought, with dollars and cents, a sister of "Mary, the mother of Jesus." Then came into the circle, at the word of command from *the man who sold other men*, another woman, whose flesh, not so fair as Maria's, was not prized so highly, and brought less per pound, though something more, I observed, than did the animal with four feet, sold at the same instant under another hammer.

At last, the circle of buyers and sorrowing lookers-on opened again, admitting a girl of seventeen; and now the greedy and hateful eyes of some brightened up as with a reflected glare from Satan's keener glance. The bids run rapidly up; this young woman will work for years; never mind her tears. . . .

As the girl of seventeen left the circle to follow the purchaser of her body, I observed that she took from her fingers three rings, and, with a look of unavailing sorrow, handed them to a boy who stood near, with a word of anxious whispering, which I could not hear—probably she sent them as token of a last farewell to friends held dear. She followed out of the crowd and down the street the man who had bought her. She had no halter on her head; it was on her soul.[48]

Powerful scenes such as this one provided abolitionist newspaper editors the ammunition they needed to evoke readers' emotions and further the spread of antislavery sentiment. In a world devoid of visual media, the abolitionist press relied on its correspondents throughout the slave states to provide masterfully written descriptions of the horrors of the slave existence. This tactic proved an effective tool in the fight against the peculiar institution.

As the slave economy flourished in the South, it wasn't difficult to find examples that could illustrate the greed, moral bankruptcy, and sexual exploitation that existed among those who bought and sold human beings. Missouri was no exception. Historians have argued that Missouri's system of slavery existed on a much smaller scale than the rest of the slaveholding South, but as shown by *The National Era's* account, it was no less tragic or inhumane.

Thomas Hart Benton and the Free-Soilers

Although slaveholders were trying their best to hang on to the old system, there were signs that the end of slavery was inevitable. As the country evolved and expanded, many questioned slavery's relevance. European countries were slowly abolishing the practice at home and in their colonial possessions, yet this dying institution was deeply ingrained in the American economy. Abolition would have harsh financial repercussions for many parts of the United States, and the beneficiaries of the slave system weren't willing to simply roll over.

A group of slaveholding planters and merchants in central Missouri controlled much of the state's politics. This faction of the Democratic Party, known as the Fayette Clique, occupied many of the statewide offices and dominated rural politics. In 1849, fearing that Northern antislavery forces were gaining too much ground in the fight to halt proslavery attempts to expand the peculiar instituion westward into the territories acquired during the Mexican War, the Missouri General Assembly passed the Jackson Resolutions. Drafted by allies of Claiborne Fox Jackson, a leader of the Fayette Clique and a staunch supporter of slavery, the resolutions were created to instruct Missouri's delegation of U.S. senators and congressman in Washington on how to vote when challenges to slavery were brought up in Congress. Many of the Missouri delegation fell in line, but despite the obvious political consequences, Missouri's senior senator refused to do so.

Thomas Hart Benton, one of the most prominent men in American politics at the time, had come to believe that slavery was a drag on the country's potential for growth. A true believer in manifest destiny—the idea that God had ordained the United States of America to occupy the North American continent from sea to shining sea physically, politically, and economically—Benton was unwilling to sacrifice national expansion for the sake of keeping the institution of slavery intact. Growing pressure from Northern interests on the slavery issue

Senator Thomas Hart Benton's stand on prohibiting the westward spread of slavery wasn't supported by many of Missouri's slaveholding elite. Painting by George Caleb Bingham, ca. 1850. Missouri Historical Society Collections.

threatened to block Benton's aims of constructing a transcontinental railroad and establishing American dominance in the Pacific.

Back in Missouri, other individuals also sought the end of slavery not for humanitarian reasons but for simple economics. These antislavery proponents wanted to end the institution because they believed in the concept of free labor, a political philosophy based on the idea that hard work and ambition are the keys to personal success. Proponents of free labor despised slavery because they felt it was part of a rigged system that favored wealthy landowners at the expense of the common man. They concluded that slavery took jobs away from hardworking white men and allowed rich planters to prosper without sharing the wealth. A separate coalition of antislavery forces was also coming together under the banner of Free-Soilism, a political faction that opposed the expansion of slavery westward and supported gradual emancipation nationwide.

Free-Soilers and abolitionists were often considered one by their opponents, and being associated with them was political suicide in

Missouri. Benton spent 1849 touring the state to defend his refusal to support the Jackson Resolutions. His enemies attacked him at every turn, publishing sharp rebuttals to his speeches and declarations and holding their own counter-rallies. In the end, Benton lost his January 1851 re-election bid and was replaced by prominent St. Louis attorney and proslavery advocate Henry Geyer, the Fayette Clique's preferred choice. However, although the clique won the battle, it literally lost the war. Jackson was Missouri's governor by the time the Civil War began in 1861, but he and many of the clique's remaining members were forced to flee the state when federal forces took control of Missouri that year.

The Connection between Colonization and the White House

Although many in St. Louis supported gradual emancipation, they didn't necessarily want liberated slaves living among them. Fearing that freed slaves and free persons of color would cause racial unrest in America, certain factions of the antislavery crowd supported the idea of creating a colony of former American slaves and American free persons of color on the African continent. Even in 1849 this was a controversial stance among some abolitionists, both black and white. Abolitionist newspapers often condemned the effort as proslavery and un-Christian. J. B. Vashon, the noted abolitionist and activist, wrote to Frederick Douglass after learning of a colonization meeting organized by free persons of color in St. Louis. Stating that he had always considered that "Slavery and Colonization are *twin-sisters*," he was dismayed that some blacks were openly embracing the idea. Vashon believed that the "main desire of the friends of Colonization is, to drain free colored people from these United States, so that the chain of slavery may be riveted more tightly upon its victims."[49]

Vashon's suspicions had a basis in truth. Early leaders of the colonization movement had promoted the effort as a way of ridding the country of free blacks. However, instead of totally resisting efforts to send them abroad, some blacks chose to take advantage of an opportunity to establish a country free from slavery and open to self-determination. Congress had initially rejected efforts to establish a colony for freed American slaves, but a similar effort by the British government to colonize its own freed slaves had persuaded some Americans that this might be a good option after all. In the 1820s the American Colonization Society was formed for the purpose of establishing a permanent African colony for freed slaves based on the model of American democracy. The result was Liberia, a country whose name was taken from the Latin word for "land of the free." In 1824 a party of mostly free persons of color sailed to Africa with the hope of making the experiment a success.[50]

In St. Louis, those who supported gradual emancipation embraced colonization enthusiastically. A meeting of the Missouri Colonization Society was held in March 1849 at the Second Presbyterian Church. The featured speaker was Hugh Garland, a former Virginia state legislator, attorney, professor of Greek, and author of *The Life of John Randolph*. The purpose of Garland's speech was to promote the Liberian cause. The *Republican*'s editors encouraged the public to attend and realize the importance of this endeavor. Success in Liberia, they said, "will revolutionize three continents."[51]

Presiding over the jam-packed meeting was attorney Edward Bates. Reverend Finley, the society's secretary, spoke on the increasing support for the colonization cause, including a growing interest taken by members of the city's free black community. Indeed, a group of St. Louis's black citizens was there to listen and observe what these seemingly friendly white men had in mind for them. Finley concluded his remarks and introduced Garland, who took the stage and launched into "a speech of some length." His subject, he told the attentive crowd, was "freedom and liberty—human liberty." Upon hearing of his aim "every patriot's heart beat high, every freeman's soul expanded."

Garland then proceeded to rail against slavery as a blot on the American landscape and explain how it was created by tyranny and the wicked and how it went against God's design for man. Yet, when it came to enslaving the people of Africa, Garland reassured the crowd of slaveholders that God "designed from this evil to accomplish good to the whole human family, and most especially to the African race itself." He went on to proclaim that "not many generations are yet to come before Africa will lift up her hands and rejoice at the day her sons were led into captivity." Ironically, Garland's argument was the same one used by defenders of slavery to justify its existence, one that said African peoples were savage and ignorant and should count themselves lucky that they were taken from the darkness and into the compassionate, loving bosoms of their white masters.

Garland then continued on the idea that "work shall set you free." Because the South had mastered the production of cotton, source of the world's textile industry, clothing manufacturing would be the savior of the world. Teach the savage to wear clothes and provide him with the resources to produce his own textiles, and prosperity and modernization would follow. Such an endeavor, Garland told the attentive listeners, would make the job of missionary work much easier in Africa, given that "to Christianize a people without first providing them suitable raiment to hide their nakedness, is an impossibility." This was the path to freedom—hard work and clothing.

Finally, Garland praised the successes of the Liberian colony, stating, "The experiment has proved successful and we find that the Liberia colony has grown and flourished beyond that of any other colony ever established on Africa's shores." To illustrate the enormity of the endeavor, he declared that "the success of our pilgrim fathers is nothing to be compared to the success seen in this colony." He observed that these victories were due only to the guiding hand and intellectual influences of the colonists' white benefactors, despite the harshness of their earlier experiences: "Before the spoiler went among them, burned their villages and dragged them into captivity, they were more like animals than human beings, having no conception of moral existence or moral being, with intellects little beyond that of the elephant or the lion that roamed their plains. It would have been impossible to make an impression upon such intellects." Now they were spreading civilization across the so-called Dark Continent and influencing the native tribes surrounding the colony. "So the glorious work spreads, consequent upon the existence of slavery in this country." The message was clear: Slavery may indeed be evil and now should be gradually abolished, but nevertheless it has all been a practice in tough love.[52]

Garland's performance was a splendid defense of the end justifying the means, but his speech may have been less about convincing the audience of the benefits of the peculiar institution than about rationalizing his own relationship with slavery. In 1840, Garland left his native Virginia, his political career, and his failed attempts at becoming a gentleman farmer in order to try his luck in the West. Leaving his family behind, he arrived in St. Louis eager to start new enterprises. But life in St. Louis proved to be no more successful than his days in the Old Dominion. Despite being unable to establish a steady flow of income, he sent for his wife, Anna; his children; and the family's slaves to join him in St. Louis. One of those slaves was a woman named Lizzie, who had been a possession of Garland's in-laws since her birth. She was later passed to Garland's wife and had resided with his family for several years. Better known to history as Elizabeth Keckley, Lizzie would become Garland's saving grace.

Keckley published an autobiography in 1868 titled *Behind the Scenes; or, Thirty Years a Slave, and Four Years in the White House*, in which she described her tribulations as an enslaved woman in Virginia and St. Louis. Within her descriptions of life with the Garlands, Keckley sheds light on the attorney's dire circumstances. She recalled her arrival in St. Louis, where she found Garland "so poor that he was unable to pay the dues on a letter advertised in the post-office for him."[53]

Seemingly deep in debt and just scraping by, Garland looked for ways to improve his lot. Finally he concluded that the only way in which he could generate a steady income would be to hire out his ten slaves, including Keckley's elderly mother. Keckley was appalled by the thought of her aged mother toiling away for hours, so she approached Garland and asked him to allow her to bear the full burden for the family instead. Aware of her talents as a dressmaker and seamstress, he wisely consented, and soon she was creating dresses for the wives of some of St. Louis's leading citizens. "With my needle I kept bread in the mouths of seventeen people for two years and five months," Keckley later wrote. She was an intelligent and resourceful woman who was devoted to the welfare of her family, both black and white, and driven by the goal of one day gaining her freedom.

Keckley had endured many humiliations and hardships as an enslaved woman, not least of which was rape at the hands of a white man in Virginia whom she refused to identify in her autobiography. A previous owner had beaten her severely, and although the Garlands hadn't treated her harshly, she was still expected to know her place. Despite the hardships and setbacks, Keckley's hope for freedom became a reality—but not until after Garland's death.

The man who derided the evils of slavery before the crowd at the Second Presbyterian Church and called for its extinction refused to allow Keckley to purchase her freedom. When he died in 1854, his wife took the advice of her cousin, the executor of Garland's estate, and consented to granting Keckley and her son, George, their freedom in exchange for $1,200. In 1855, Keckley presented the money to Anna Garland and walked away a free woman, an achievement of which she was very proud. Later, as dressmaker and maid to First Lady Mary Todd Lincoln during the Lincolns' years in the White House, Elizabeth Keckley became one of the most well-known and successful free black women in America.[54]

Yet Keckley's labor wasn't the only way in which Garland reaped the rewards of the slave system. In 1845 he conceded his failure in other pursuits and returned to practicing law. In 1849 his cousin, attorney B. S. Garland, recommended Hugh replace him as counsel for a client whose case had been dragging on in court for several years. Irene Sanford Emerson, widow of Dr. John Emerson, was continuing to fight a freedom suit filed by Dr. Emerson's longtime slave, Dred Scott. As the courts were tied up with many important cases, Scott's trial was repeatedly set back until it finally appeared on the docket in December 1849. The following month, Garland and his junior partner, Lyman Norris, lost Emerson's case, and what seemed to be an apparent victory for Scott turned out to be just another stop on his long journey toward Chief Justice Roger Taney's historic U.S. Supreme Court ruling.[55]

Remembering St. Louis's Enslaved Men, Women, and Children

For the great majority of enslaved persons, neither manumission nor escape was an option. Most lived and died in slavery. With but a few exceptions, we'll never know their names. Their deaths were seldom recorded, and most were buried in unmarked graves. This was typically true even for those slaves who were held with some genuine regard by their owners. One exception can be found in a corner of Mount Olive Cemetery, where a stone marks the final resting place of a man identified only as Dick. He was the property of John Withnell, an English immigrant who came to St. Louis in 1831. Withnell was a stonecutter by training. After he arrived in St. Louis, he was soon employed to help with the stonework of the Old Cathedral, which was then under construction. In 1838 he received the contract to supply stone for the new state capitol building in Jefferson City.[56]

Landing such an important government contract was a profitable venture, and Withnell's overhead must have been minimal because most, if not all, of the actual stonecutting appears to have been performed by his fifteen slaves. With no wages to pay, most of the money would have gone straight into Withnell's pockets. Capitalizing on his achievements, he lived comfortably at his home on Carondelet Avenue and was elected alderman of the First Ward in 1842, serving two terms. He also diversified by opening the Fulton Brewery at 21 Almond Street with fellow Englishman Samuel Wainwright, later a leader of the St. Louis brewing industry.[57]

Success seemed to follow Withnell, and no small part of it can be attributed to his use of slave labor. Perhaps he realized this, which is why when his trusted slave Dick fell victim to cholera, Withnell chose to honor him by laying him to rest among some of the county's earliest white settlers. A handsome tombstone, though broken, still marks his grave. It reads:

Here
Lies the body of
Dick
Coloured Servant
of John Withnell
He Died of Cholera

Dick obviously didn't live to see his people go free, but a great many other enslaved persons did. Given the everyday burdens of slavery and prejudice that existed in St. Louis in 1849, it could hardly have been conceivable to those who suffered the realities of its existence that the country would free its slave population and establish constitutional recognition of African Americans as citizens less than twenty years later.

Many more heartaches and pain would occur before slavery's eventual demise, but when the Civil War came to Missouri, large numbers of African Americans fought for their freedom. Colored infantry units swelled with former Missouri slaves, and they proved to be some of the Union's best soldiers—perhaps because they were fighting to reverse the injustices that burdened Dred Scott, Elizabeth Keckley, Mattie Jackson, and all the enslaved who in 1849 could only dream of such a day.

CHAPTER SIX: THE STRANGE CASE OF NATHANIEL CHILDS JR.

By the end of the 1840s, St. Louis was a dangerous place. Becoming a victim of armed robbery or burglary was a very real daily possibility, but crimes weren't always perpetrated by rough characters on the muddy streets of Battle Row or in the seedy saloons along the levee. Theft of a much more subtle sort could likewise occur in the respectable corners of the city—namely the financial sector.

Community Cornerstones: Banking and the Law

As the nation's market economy turned westward, St. Louis became more prosperous, attracting all manner of entrepreneurs, investors, and opportunists. Money flowed into the city with each arriving steamboat, but all that money would do little unless it was invested, cultivated, and secured. New financial institutions naturally followed the influx of commerce, supplying credit and nourishing the capital needed to make it all happen, but creating those financial institutions wasn't always an easy venture. Banking was a controversial topic in the early nineteenth century, particularly in the strongly independent American frontier, and money lending was seen by many as the means for a selected few to control the country's wealth at the expense of common farmers and laborers.

Settlers in the West tended to hold very strong Jeffersonian beliefs that banking institutions were the epitome of the elitist, aristocratic system the Founding Fathers had fought to topple in America. Merchants and budding manufacturers in St. Louis, however, were in favor of establishing local banking institutions. A good number of these businessmen had only recently arrived in St. Louis from Boston and other eastern cities where banking had long been an accepted means of operation. Now that they had relocated, they didn't want to have to rely on the banking centers back East.[1]

Throughout the first decades of the nineteenth century, political factions fought over the necessity of establishing and maintaining a public banking system in America. Democratic president Andrew Jackson spent much of his administration deriding banks and finally managed to kill the Second Bank of the United States. In Missouri, Old Hickory's philosophy was well received, and his followers held much of the state's power. However, some factions in Jackson's party didn't fully embrace his antibank philosophy. A group known popularly as the Locofocos was willing to accept a state-chartered bank.

A coalition of St. Louis business interests fought to establish such a bank, hoping to fill the void left by the defeated Second Bank. The farmers, attorneys, and merchants who made up the elected body of the Missouri General Assembly went back and forth over the issue for several years. Many of them remembered two earlier attempts at starting local banks, both of which failed due to poor management and questionable lending. Nearly twenty years had passed since those days, and now bank supporters had won the opportunity to establish a bank—but only by agreeing to a series of measures designed to keep the bank as transparent as possible and within the confines of state control.

The resulting Bank of the State of Missouri was a compromise between public and private interests. With half the stock owned by the State of Missouri and the other half publically sold, the bank was an experiment in business and government cooperation. A board of twelve directors led by a president was charged with the institution's management. The General Assembly was given the power to elect the board's president and six of its members, each of whom would serve two-year terms. Private stockholders had the power to select the remaining six board members at an annual stockholders meeting in St. Louis. The bank could issue notes; do business by means of bills of exchange, checks, and drafts; and manage private deposits. Payment on demand in either gold or silver was permitted on all banknotes. Those who pushed for the bank and those who were skeptical seemed to be equally satisfied with these arrangements. On February 2, 1837, Missouri governor Lilburn Boggs signed the bill into law, and St. Louis's merchants and businessmen finally had the institution they had been pining for.[2]

The opening of the Bank of the State of Missouri was one step toward progress in the natural development of St. Louis, given that banking institutions were necessary cornerstones of successful communities. So too was the presence of a stable system of laws and justice. St. Louis had firm foundations as a regional justice center, reaching back to its time as the capital of the French colonial territory of Upper Louisiana. When the United States took over the west side of the Mississippi after the Louisiana Purchase, St. Louis became home to the Superior Court of the Territory of Missouri, which later transitioned into the Missouri Supreme Court. Naturally, due to the city's size and importance, the federal courts were also located in St. Louis.[3]

Circuit courts, county courts, and the city court provided a near-endless source of business for area lawyers. Many of these men argued before judges who presided over courtrooms within the Old Courthouse on Fourth Street before rising to the top of the legal profession. Among the attorneys plying their trade in St. Louis was Edward Bates.[4]

Attorney Edward Bates and the Court of Public Opinion

Born on a Virginia plantation in 1793, Edward Bates sought to achieve success on the American frontier by moving to the remote fur-trade center of St. Louis in 1814. Frederick Bates, his older brother, had ventured west before him and was already serving as secretary of the Missouri Territory. A few weeks after his arrival, the younger Bates took up the study of law under the direction of frontier attorney and land speculator Rufus Easton.

Six years later, Bates had grown in prominence enough as a lawyer that he was elected to Missouri's constitutional convention, which was responsible for drawing up the state's first proposed constitution. While juggling law and politics he gained both wealth and stature, becoming a figure respected not only on the local level but also on the national political scene. In the tumultuous environment of pre–Civil War politics, he stood as an unapologetic moderate. His middle-of-the-road stance and deep belief in the sanctity of the law were very attractive to many Americans.[5]

On the most divisive issue of the day—slavery—Bates favored gradual emancipation. He had emancipated his own slaves, as had

Attorney Edward Bates was busy in 1849. He served as the defense lawyer for accused embezzler Nathaniel Childs Jr. and suspected murderers Gonsalve and Raymond de Montesquiou. These high-profile cases helped propel him onto the national political stage. Steel engraving by F. Garsch, ca. 1855. Missouri Historical Society Collections.

his mother and his sister, but he was careful not to associate himself with abolitionists. Still, when it appeared that a young African American woman named Lucy Ann Berry had solid legal grounds on which to sue for her freedom in 1842, Bates argued her case in court and convinced a jury to release Berry from bondage. In her memoir (*From the Darkness Cometh the Light; or, Struggles for Freedom,* which she wrote many years later under her married name, Lucy Ann Delaney) she not only praised Bates as a man willing to stand up for the cause of freedom but also for being a polite and respectful individual.[6]

Despite his willingness to fight for the freedom of African Americans when the law allowed, Bates, like many notable Americans at the time, was a member of the American Colonization Society. This group believed that if and when slavery was abolished, all free men and women of color in the United States should be returned to West Africa so as not to create racial disharmony.[7]

Many of Bates's contemporaries believed him to be one of the nation's great legal minds. Citizens listened when he expressed opinions, and he often stepped forward to lend his support to important—yet mostly safe—subjects, such as promoting St. Louis as the terminus of the proposed Pacific Railroad or upholding sacred observances of the Sabbath in the city.

Although Bates may have done what he could to promote himself as a leader of men, on a personal level he was rather fragile. He worked diligently for his clients at the cost of his health. Tough cases drained him physically, and he often had to take time to recover from fatigue and what appeared to be bouts of depression. His personal diary includes many entries in which he speaks of his cases taxing him greatly. Whenever he needed time to relax, he usually either left for his farm on Dardenne Prairie in St. Charles County or gardened at his Grape Hill estate, which sat on what is now the Barnes-Jewish Hospital complex in St. Louis's Central West End.[8]

By late 1849, Bates's ability to work through stress and fatigue was put to the test when he became the lead defense attorney in two sensational cases. In both instances his clients were accused of committing crimes that greatly stirred St. Louisans' emotions. Bates found it necessary to invest his full strength and legal prowess into both cases with little or no rest in between because they were practically back to back. The fact that the accused in the two high-profile cases sought to secure him for their defense was a testament not only to his capabilities as a defense attorney but also his prominence in the court of public opinion.

The first of these crimes was discovered just days after the cholera epidemic ended in early August; the second crime, covered in the next chapter, followed two and a half months later. Both stories spread nationwide. Americans who didn't know who Edward Bates was in the fall of 1849 certainly did by the spring of 1850.

The Case of the Missing Coins

On August 10, 1849, two of the city's money-brokerage firms sent separate requests to the Bank of the State of Missouri branch on North First Street for routine cash withdrawals. These seemingly insignificant actions ultimately revealed that a major crime had been committed right under the noses of the bank's management. This time it wasn't a robbery carried out by some motley gang but rather embezzlement committed by a stealthy insider. This time, unlike the Nisbet robbery described in chapter 4, the pursuit of justice wasn't a matter of chasing down fleeing outlaws but rather examining clues, motives, and bank practices to catch a two-faced criminal.

When the bank opened that August morning, a clerk working for broker E. W. Clark requested a withdrawal of $50,000, to be paid out in coins. Because the amout was so high, the bank's cashier, Henry Shurlds, instructed one of the tellers, L. C. Hurschburg, to pay out the request in gold sovereigns, a British coin of higher value that was used as a stable currency even in the United States. Later that afternoon, a clerk from another firm, Page and Bacon, came to the bank asking for $40,000 in coins. Shurlds again instructed Hurschburg to pay out the request in sovereigns, but the teller knew that the morning's earlier withdrawal had substantially depleted the amount of gold coins in the cashboxes held in the bank's main business office. He now had to go into the vault to retrieve a reserve box of coins.

Hurschburg returned from the vault, opened the box, and began to remove the bags of coins but paused when it appeared that the box's contents had been miscalculated. A quick count of the bags revealed that the cashbox didn't contain the amount listed on its manifest tag. Believing that the missing bag of coins could be a simple clerical error, Hurschburg opened a second box—it too revealed an identical loss. The teller quickly grew concerned because, as far as anyone knew, the boxes hadn't been removed from the vault since they had been placed inside during the full audit of the bank's deposits earlier that spring.

The institution's four-step process for securing the boxes also seemed to have been followed. The first step was to count the coins in each bag before placing them inside the box. Then the amount of coins and number of bags were written on a paper tag attached to the outside of the box's lid. Next, the box was nailed shut. Finally, a wax seal was placed over the seam. An unbroken wax seal meant that the box hadn't been opened since it was secured, and both boxes Hurschburg had removed from the vault bore intact seals.

Shurlds, whose role as cashier essentially made him the bank's manager, wasn't present when the discovery was made. He returned that evening after closing only to be met at the door by a nervous

Hurschburg. Shurlds ordered another box opened for inspection. He later testified in court that "we went into the bank, and found that there was but four bags of sovereigns in the box instead of five."[9]

Later that evening one of the bank's directors, Edward Walsh, arrived to personally investigate the situation. When he was satisfied that this was more than an accounting error, he requested everyone on the bank's board of directors be summoned to assist in the inspection of the remaining boxes. The entire board had participated in the audit earlier that spring and was therefore familiar with the deposits and contents of the boxes. Walsh also summoned a former employee of the bank, the recently resigned teller Nathaniel Childs Jr.

Creating a Sterling Reputation

Nathaniel Childs Jr. came to St. Louis from Baltimore in 1835. Like Edward Bates, Childs had brothers who had made the journey to the city before him, allowing him to settle into the community much more easily than others. Childs first landed a job in a printing office; shortly thereafter he became a clerk in an insurance company. To his credit, he seemed to have many qualities that his new neighbors found endearing. For one, they respected that he was a member of an old Maryland family. His father, Nathaniel Childs Sr., had fought in the War of 1812 and witnessed the shelling of Fort McHenry while serving in a militia unit that was defending the city against the invading British.

By all appearances, Childs was an ambitious young man ready to establish himself in the commerce center of the West. Like many eager achievers of his day seeking to prove themselves as worthy, civic-minded, and upstanding, he joined a debating society, the Franklin Society of St. Louis, and quickly began serving as the group's secretary. In one meeting announcement published in local papers in 1836, Childs notified members that the topic of discussion would be "Has the press greater influence in society than public men?" (This was a topic of great irony given that one day the public would form opinions of him based on what was reported in newspapers across the country.) Childs continued to stand out, and by 1837 he had the honor of presenting the opening prayer at the city's Fourth of July celebration.[10]

Religion, particularly the Methodist faith, was a passion of his. He was an ordained minister in the church and became a leading member of Fourth Street Methodist Church, one of the largest Methodist congregations in St. Louis. In 1841 he was elected secretary of the newly established Centenary Methodist Church, which was formed by a group of former Fourth Street congregation members. Childs

Centenary Methodist Church, where Nathaniel Childs Jr. was treasurer and a junior pastor. Photograph by unknown photographer, date unknown. Missouri Historical Society Collections.

also served on the new church's building committee and was there when the structure's cornerstone was laid in May 1842. He became very active in the church's Sunday school academy and sometimes preached to the full congregation at the invitation of the minister in residence.[11]

Because being a family man was a sign of stability and respectable living—and because Childs had vast ambitions—he married soon after arriving in St. Louis. His bride, Eliza Tibbs, was an English immigrant who had traveled to America with her parents. At the time of their wedding, Childs was working as an insurance clerk, but he presumably sought a more stable source of income to support his new family. His sterling reputation in the community likely helped him secure the job of second teller at the Bank of the State of Missouri's St. Louis branch when it opened for business in 1838. The specific job of the second teller was to complete all the transactions that required coin payouts. Childs also served as the paying teller who handled check cashing for customers. He likely didn't expect he would have to defend himself publicly twice in his first two years on the job.[12]

Two Suspicious Incidents

Twice a year the Bank of the State of Missouri submitted a detailed expense account to the governor for inspection and published a list of public accounts in the newspapers. A governor-appointed committee also audited the bank's books and supplied a detailed report to the Missouri General Assembly prior to each session. Last but not least, the bank submitted quarterly reports to the state auditor. In this climate of close scrutiny, any irregularities in the bank's daily business had the potential of making big news, and two such incidents had Childs standing up for himself in the public arena of the press.[13]

The first situation led to questions about the competency of the bank's tellers. In 1838 a young man claimed that his employer, a local brokerage firm, had sent him to the bank to cash a check for $43.50. As he was leaving, he noticed that the stack of bills handed to him seemed rather thick. He proceeded to count the money and soon realized that he had actually been paid $4,300. The young man, along with the brokerage firm's owners, returned to the bank to report the error. When confronted, Childs denied that any mistake had occurred. He also published his side of the story in the St. Louis papers in an attempt to protect his reputation. The bank stood by him, but some in the community stated that it smelled like a cover-up. The excitement soon passed, and in the end all was forgotten.[14]

Then in 1840 a much more serious incident occurred that required the bank to disclose full details to the state. In a sworn affidavit presented to the Missouri senate, Childs described the events of January 16, 1840. He and his co-worker, George W. Dent, had been asked by cashier Shurlds to bag and crate $100,000 worth of foreign gold coins, which were scheduled to be shipped to a bank in New York City. As Childs counted, bagged, and tagged each cache of coins, he asked Dent to recount a bag of American gold coins. Both men swore that each bag was properly counted and a slip of paper noting the amount of each bag was included in the sacks. Each bag was then placed in a shipping keg that the bank used regularly. Dent and the bank's porter loaded the keg onto a wagon. The keg's destination was the steamboat *George Collier*, but it never arrived there. It had vanished, and its whereabouts were never discovered.[15]

Despite these two embarrassing episodes, Childs's reputation remained solid in the larger community—but not so among the bank's directors and senior staff, who had started to become suspicious of the reverend's personal affairs. They knew that his salary was $1,200 a year, which was a moderately good salary for the time but certainly not one that allowed for excesses. Yet by the late 1840s, Childs and his wife had four children, two household servants, and three slaves. He had also amassed some property around the city and purchased roughly fourteen acres of land near the southeast corner of Grand and Laclede for use as a graveyard by the Centenary Methodist Church. The bank's directors confronted Childs about his assets sometime in late 1848, but he assured them that he was living within his means and could account for all of his purchases.[16]

The board ultimately renewed Childs's position as teller, but its skepticism didn't disappear entirely. Some of the directors felt that further investigation was needed. Under the guise of needing to count the available coinage in preparation for a scheduled shipment to the East Coast, they initiated a count of all the bank's deposits. In order to remove Childs from the actual accounting process, they carried out the audit themselves beginning in February 1849, but their plan didn't quite work.[17]

The directors had set themselves up in the cashier's office to conduct the audit, which meant they needed someone to bring the bags of coins to them from the vault. Even though he was removed from the accounting portion of the count, Childs still had to participate in the process of sealing the boxes. Because it was Childs's responsibility to ensure that the bags were placed in the vault—and because he held keys to the vault—each box of coins was handed over to him and another teller after it had been counted. The two tellers attached a tag noting the amount held in the box before hammering the container shut, placing a wax seal on it for security purposes, and placing it in the vault. Nothing out of the ordinary was detected, and by all accounts Childs didn't seem to exhibit concern or anxiety at any point. Near the end of the count, however, he announced to his co-worker, L. C. Hurschburg, that he intended to resign later that spring. Hurschburg later testified that Childs had asked him to keep this information secret, promising that he would recommend Hurschburg as his replacement after he had officially resigned to the directors.[18]

The count was finished in March with no deficiencies detected. Childs announced his resignation to the directors soon afterward, and they accepted it. Just as he had promised, Childs put in a good word for Hurschburg, but getting the directors to follow this recommendation apparently required some convincing. A few of them didn't feel Hurschburg was qualified because the German immigrant still spoke broken English. They wanted to hire someone else, but Childs told them that the personality of their first choice, a Mr. Duncan, was unsuitable for public-facing work and that Hurschburg's command of English would soon improve. His argument must have been persuasive enough because the young German was hired to replace Childs as second teller.

As cholera raged through St. Louis in the late spring and early weeks of summer, at least two of the bank's tellers fell ill, so the directors asked Childs to return while these men were incapacitated. He agreed, even though he was technically no longer bonded as required by the bank's policies. After the men had recovered from their illnesses,

Childs left St. Louis to travel east, most likely to visit family in Maryland. By late July he had returned to the city and was working with his brother in the building-materials business. Presumably he was at his place of business on the afternoon of August 11 when someone from the Bank of the State of Missouri summoned him to return to his former place of employment for a conversation with the directors.

Guilty Until Proven Innocent

Director Walsh, board president James Hughes, and the remaining directors arrived at the scene of the crime to begin the task of determining what was going on. Childs also arrived as requested and entered the building. The door was locked behind him. Shurlds and the directors were ready to start the emergency audit. Forty-seven boxes were hauled out of the vault and into the bank's boardroom, where they were opened one by one. As Childs waited in the main banking room, the investigators found that "from 14 boxes abstractions had been made." Most of the missing bags had contained either silver German thalers or gold sovereigns, both of which were the most valuable coin types on deposit at the bank. All in all, a total of $120,900 was missing from the carefully sealed boxes—the equivalent of roughly $3.7 million today.[19]

After the loss of funds was confirmed, Dr. Isaac Forbes, one of the bank's directors, was understandably upset and decided to question Childs himself. Forbes wanted to believe that some mistake had been made in the accounting process. While the other dismayed and confused directors remained in the boardroom, Forbes sought out Childs. The director found him leaning against a desk in the main banking room, seemingly waiting for the outcome of the audit. Forbes gave him a summoning nod, so Childs followed him to the back of the banking room, where they both took a seat.

Based on the details of Forbes's questioning, there's little doubt where he placed the blame for the abstraction. This was a "horrible affair," remarked Forbes to Childs. He then asked Childs whether he thought this was some gross mistake. "No," replied Childs. This prompted Forbes to ask, "Then the money is gone?" Childs replied, "Yes, 'tis gone." "You know why I [am] questioning you," said Forbes.

According to Forbes, Childs stated that he "knew my feelings toward him." The director asked Childs whether he could tell how such a large sum of money could have been taken in such a short time. Childs answered that he could not, which prompted Forbes to ask who would have had the ability to carry out such an abstraction. Childs replied, "The cashier, Mr. Hurschburg, or myself alone." But he followed this reply with: "I am innocent."[20]

Someone came out of the boardroom and called Forbes aside. Soon afterward Hughes, the board's president, informed Childs that he was to be arrested and that he would have the chance to defend himself in court. Childs repeated that he was innocent and asked when he might be arrested. At that point, a policeman entered the bank and took Childs into custody. Hughes and Shurlds had visited a justice of the peace earlier to make the arrangements to place Childs under arrest, meaning the directors had already decided that Childs was guilty.[21]

As Childs sat in jail, a grand jury was called, and all the directors testified as witnesses. On August 18, 1849, the grand jury charged Childs "with feloniously and fraudulently embezzling from the Bank of the State of Missouri, the sum of $121,000." When the preliminary hearing was held soon afterward, Childs answered the indictment with a not-guilty plea. Bail was set at $25,000, which was an enormous sum of money for the time, but this was no ordinary crime. Five friends of the accused collected the necessary bail, though not without some difficulty. Two of them later claimed that some of the bank directors approached them immediately following the indictment and asked that they not supply bail to Childs and instead simply accept that he was guilty and headed to prison. Unsurprisingly, the directors denied this accusation in court.[22]

The fact that so many men stepped forward to help post Childs's bond was also no surprise. In the larger community, the idea of anyone insinuating that Childs was capable of such an outrageous crime was a crime in itself. Members of his Methodist congregation, as well as a large number of bank customers and friends, viewed Childs as an upright Christian and good-hearted person. Few could believe that this man—an ordained minister, an active participant in civic circles, and a husband and father born of a good family—was capable of perpetrating such a devious crime. As Columbia's *Weekly Missouri*

Statesman printed at the announcement of his arrest, "No man in the community stood higher than Mr. Childs as a citizen, nor none in whom all denominations of Christians had greater confidence as a man of piety and a preacher of the gospel." Surely this whole incident was a misunderstanding.[23]

When news of Childs's arrest broke, newspapers across the state picked up the story and reacted to the charges. The *Statesman's* editors pointed to the bank's Locofoco connections as reason for the misappropriated funds. The Locofoco faction of the Democratic Party was the main proponent of the bank's charter, and the bank's directors and officers were largely members of this faction. "Here's a beautiful spot of work!" wrote the *Statesman*. "It really does seem that Locofocoism can prudently manage nothing. The Bank of Missouri, purely a Locofoco concern, at last falls a victim to Locofoco speculation to the tune of $120,000! Will not the people long outraged and insulted by official delinquencies and crimes look to these things?"[24]

The case threatened to erode public trust further than what was safe for the bank. Politically it was a nightmare because antibank resolutions had been debated in the Missouri General Assembly as recently as March. Those resolutions had been defeated, but the editors of the *St. Louis Daily New Era* noted that "preaching against banks for the purposes of demagoguing is first rate capital in some parts of Missouri." The last thing the directors needed was more political pressure and bad press. Given what details they knew of the misappropriation affair, they feared that when the evidence presented itself, they would all suffer, both personally and professionally. As is so often the case in the history of public-relations crises, the bank's administrators immediately launched an effort to cover themselves and make sure the focus remained on someone else, namely Childs.[25]

The bank's directors were all prominent members of the community and had been for many years prior to the bank's inception. Some had held statewide or municipal offices; others were successful businessmen or responsible civic leaders. Nearly all were connected to the state's political machine, and each of them knew that by serving on the Bank of the State of Missouri's board of directors they risked exposing themselves to ridicule from those who still rejected state support for banking. With all of this in mind, the directors personally took it upon themselves to conduct a criminal investigation in an attempt to gather as much evidence as possible against Childs while also controlling the damage from the scandal. They carried out their investigation in a rather amateur—and somewhat legally questionable—manner.[26]

When the men learned that physician Joseph Nash McDowell was going east for a trip, they asked him to stop in several cities along the way to inquire whether Childs had deposited large sums of money in their banks. They recalled the former teller's earlier vacation trip and wondered whether it had been a convenient excuse to remove the funds from St. Louis and spread them around for safekeeping. Ultimately they found no evidence to suggest anything of the kind.[27]

In a more immediate action, fearing that Childs might try to flee or secret away his loot somewhere, the bank's attorney hired members of the St. Louis City Guard to serve as the financial institution's private security force. Guard officers were stationed outside Childs's home after he made bail and outside the home of one of his friends. It was this move that ultimately came back to haunt the directors, because many members of the public viewed it as a misuse of power. It was exactly the kind of tactic that voters of the time feared: Give too much power to a corporation or institution, and it will use that power against the people.[28]

Bates versus Geyer

Childs clearly needed legal counsel, and he sought out the best. He didn't have to look far because he had a friend in the esteemed Edward Bates. The two men had known each other for some time. In his volunteer role as director of Centenary Methodist's Sunday school, Childs had once rented a steamboat for a day to take the children on a river excursion to Alton, Illinois, and back. Along for the trip was special guest Edward Bates, who entertained the children with stories. So, when Bates learned of Childs's predicament, he agreed to take the case.[29]

In early September the trial date was set for the first week in November. This provided Bates with plenty of time to review the evidence and prepare his case and his team, which consisted of Trusten Polk, Uriah Wright, Roswell Martin Field, and R. S. Blennerhasset. All four men had stellar reputations as skilled attorneys. They were also well-respected members of the community, three of whom— Polk, Wright, and Blennerhasset —had served as members of the Committee of Public Health during the cholera epidemic earlier that summer. It was a skilled, and costly, defense team for a former teller to employ. For his part, Bates noted in his diary that "there are quite too many counsel in defense." Nevertheless, he seemed gratified that "as yet we get along very well," which may have been because the other members of the defense team were willing "to adopt all my propositions."[30]

The number of attorneys was no less for the prosecution. The state assigned Henry Geyer as chief prosecutor along with Willis Williams, the bank's attorney, and five other assistant prosecutors. Geyer was one of Missouri's rising political stars in his own right. The very next year the explosive political situation that existed in Missouri over the slavery question allowed him to defeat the state's iconic lion of the U.S. Senate, Thomas Hart Benton. Geyer is best remembered, however, for another matter relating to slavery: He volunteered to represent Missouri before the U.S. Supreme Court in one of American history's greatest legal cases, *Dred Scott v. Sandford.*[31]

Attorney Henry Geyer was also a top-notch legal mind and rising political star. He defeated Thomas Hart Benton to become Missouri's next U.S. senator in 1851. Six years later he successfully argued against Dred Scott's case for freedom before the U.S. Supreme Court. Photograph by George Stark, date unknown. Missouri Historical Society Collections.

Given the attorneys involved, *State of Missouri v. Nathaniel Childs, Jr.*, which began on November 4, 1849, was destined to be a true battle of the best legal minds. The case was also destined to be played out in the pages of the city's newspapers, because everyone was interested in the trial of a preacher accused of robbing a bank. The *Daily Missouri Republican* printed a daily transcript of the trial's proceedings and ran a full copy of the previous week's testimony on Sundays. It was a popular move, as evidenced by this statement from the *Republican*'s editors: "The run upon our bank of daily papers, for some days past, has been larger than we anticipated and more than we are prepared to meet . . . that anxiety seems to be to read the testimony in the case of *State vs. Childs*."[32]

Geyer's Arguments: Suspicious Wealth and the "Other Woman"

The prosecutors placed a number of considerations before a jury made up mostly of men with humble backgrounds, including a carpenter, a jeweler, a bookkeeper, and more than one farmer. It was a group that appeared to have few pretensions, and each side of the case was likely hoping to seize on this side of the jurors' nature. The prosecution began by presenting Childs as the most logical employee to pull off such a heist. He had access to the bank's vault, he maintained the bank's accounting of coins on a daily basis, and he began his time as second teller with few assets and little money but was now much better off. Geyer and the others would present a mountain of evidence, they said, to prove Childs was the guilty party.

One logical means of obtaining the funds was by secretly taking them from the boxes. Because some evidence suggested that the sealing wax on the boxes appeared to be altered, the prosecutors argued that perhaps Childs had unsealed the boxes, extracted a bag from each, and resealed them. He had access to the bank's wax and seal, and on more than one occasion he was allowed to enter the bank to work alone after hours.

The prosecution called Mr. Fisher, the owner of a local bookstore, to the stand to testify about Childs's purchase of sealing wax. Fisher noted that in January, around the time of the count, Childs had come to the store to buy wax. He told the storekeeper that it was necessary for securing the money boxes. He bought a large quantity, but the next month he was back for more. Fisher commented to him that he surely hadn't used up all the wax that he had purchased previously for the bank. Childs, Fisher declared, didn't comment. He simply bought the wax and left. When the missing bags were discovered, some claimed that the wax on the boxes appeared to be a slightly different color. Fisher testified that Childs had purchased two different varieties of wax: Hibernian wax the first time and government wax on the second occasion. This could, the prosecutors contended, account for the differences in the wax.[33]

These accusations seemed plausible, but where was the money? Why did he do it? With no direct evidence of Childs's execution of a crime, the prosecutors had to make do with what they had—and what they had raised some serious questions about the good reverend's personal affairs.

Although Childs seemed to be a happily married man, there were rumors that he had more than just a friendship with a young widow from Centenary Methodist's congregation. Stories circulated that he had purchased a piano, an expensive gold pencil, a silk dress, a portrait, and even a servant girl for Mrs. Margaret Whitlock. Furthermore, after the report of the possible embezzlement was discovered, someone reported that Childs had passed money to Whitlock for safekeeping. Her residence was the second house guarded by the watchmen.

When the bank's attorney, Willis Williams, and one of its directors, James Yeatman, learned of these rumors, they approached a judge so they could get a warrant to search Whitlock's home for the missing gold. The warrant was granted under one condition: It was for the seizure of any gold in question and nothing else. Yeatman and Williams agreed and left to confront the young widow along with fellow directors Dr. Isaac Forbes and John Ryland, plus a couple police officers.

Margaret Whitlock lived with Marie Haydon, her adoptive mother. The circumstances of Whitlock's married life aren't easily discernable, although it's safe to reason that her husband had died fairly recently because her only child was about one year old. Given the conventions of nineteenth-century life, approaching Whitlock regarding her

James Yeatman served on the board of the Bank of the State of Missouri during Nathaniel Childs Jr.'s tenure and was an active participant in the bank's internal investigation of Childs. Photograph by unknown photographer, late nineteenth century. Missouri Historical Society Collections.

business, public or private, with Childs wasn't an enviable task. Both individuals were respectable middle-class citizens; to imply anything improper without solid evidence was risky. All four gentlemen realized they had to proceed with caution.

With what they viewed as a carefully orchestrated plan, Yeatman, Forbes, Ryland, and Williams rode in a carriage to Whitlock's street. Because Williams was already acquainted with Whitlock, it was decided that he would go to her door while the other three men waited in the carriage for the signal to proceed. The policemen remained out of sight. Williams would knock, and if the others saw him enter the home, then they would know that Whitlock was present and they could approach as well. They later stated that by proceeding in this manner they had hoped to avoid arousing any suspicion, but given that the Childs affair was already widely known—and being that St. Louis was still small enough that most people knew each other's business—it's likely everyone who lived on that street was watching the scene unfold.

The three men saw Williams walk up the street to Whitlock's door. He knocked, the door opened, and Williams stepped inside. Ryland, Yeatmen, and Forbes piled out of the carriage and made their way to the front door. The conversation with Whitlock began with pleasantries, but then Williams turned to business. Forbes later stated on the stand that "Williams remarked he had come on a very unpleasant duty—that as an attorney for the bank he had come to inquire whether, according to rumor on the street, Mrs. Whitlock had in her possession any papers, documents, or money belonging to Mr. Childs."

Whitlock surely knew this visit was coming. She tried her best, it seems, to remain calm during the questioning. No, she replied, she didn't have anything belonging to Childs. Reframing his question, Williams then asked whether she had ever received any gifts from Childs. No, she again replied, she hadn't received gifts from "Brother Childs." Did she not receive some books from him? No books, but she did recall that he gave her a pencil—a gold pencil. What about a piano? Whitlock replied that there was a piano, but it was an exchange. Childs had bought her a new one to replace an older one, and she had paid the difference in the cost. Rumor has it, stated Williams, that she received from Brother Childs a "handsome silk dress" from Rutherford's store. "Was it, was it so?" she asked herself. She then said to Forbes, "You know it, Brother Childs did give me that striped silk dress."

What about "the negro girl?" asked Williams. Getting slightly indignant, Whitlock asked, "Has it come to this, that Brother Childs is to be charged with making me all these presents?" She then continued to deny the validity of the claim while stating that anything between them was purely business. Childs had bought the servant for her, but he was to be repaid through the collection of rents on a building Whitlock owned. He had transacted several business arrangements on her behalf. Not dissuaded, Williams pressed on. From his line of questioning, it's obvious he felt she was hiding something. He even turned up the heat, reiterating that this was all unpleasant business and then stating that "he had come as a friend" and that he didn't "desire that anything unpleasant should be done." However, he continued, there are officers waiting at your door with a search warrant and "if needs be, [they will] search your very person." Whitlock held fast for the moment, once again denying she had received anything from Childs.

At that moment, the bank cashier Henry Shurlds arrived at Whitlock's home and asked to speak to Ryland. He and Williams exited the house, leaving Yeatman and Forbes with Whitlock. She informed them that she needed a drink of water and left the room. When she returned, Williams had reentered. This time it was Yeatman who asked whether she was holding anything for Childs. Miraculously, Whitlock seemed to have a sudden recollection. As a matter of fact, she proclaimed, she did have some papers that Brother Childs had given her just that morning. It seems she had spent the previous night in his home and before she left, he had asked her to take some documents for safekeeping. They were upstairs, she claimed, moving to go retrieve them. Williams stated that he would have an officer join her, but she said, "Oh no, no, you go with me, Mr. Williams." When the two came back downstairs, Williams had the documents in hand. They consisted of property deeds, promissory notes, a certificate of deposit for $2,000, and an account book on which was written "E. W. Clark & Bros. in Account with Margaret A. Whitlock, Cr, May 15, 1849, to currency $2,000."

Williams and the others had what they wanted, but had they received it legally? The search warrant was for the seizure of gold, not papers. When Forbes was cross-examined by Bates on the stand, he was asked whether there really was a search warrant or police officers at the ready. Forbes stated that he knew officers were summoned, but he never saw the search warrant himself.[34]

The evidence presented by prosecutor Geyer, despite being entirely circumstantial, was pretty compelling: Childs appeared to be hiding something, and his private life was a little shady. Geyer and his fellow prosecutors attempted to stress the questions about Childs's personal affairs to prove that he needed the money to support his extravagant lifestyle. The questioning returned to the earliest suspicions of Childs's acquisition of personal property and the directors' actions to find the truth.[35]

Shortly before Childs resigned, he was asked to furnish a statement of his personal assets. He did so and passed the statement along to Shurlds, who inspected it and declared it acceptable. Shurlds testified that after he'd reviewed the document, Childs had asked for it back so he could make a copy for his own files. When Shurlds inquired about the document later, Childs refused to return it. He declared that it was his right to retain it now that the review was over. Prosecutors demanded that it be produced for the court, but the defense retorted that it wasn't a true legal document because the bank had no legal authority under its bylaws to demand such a document from Childs in the first place. Childs had provided it as a courtesy and had burned it after the review—it was conveniently gone.[36]

Bates's Arguments: Incompetence and Overreach

In the first round of the trial, the prosecution had produced some credible witnesses and some compelling testimony, but now the defense team had its time for rebuttals, and the accused's attorneys declared that they could easily provide counterevidence to discredit anything put forth by the prosecution. This crime wasn't the work of a faithful, longtime bank employee like Childs. Someone else in the Bank of the State of Missouri was surely the real crook, and Bates declared that before the trial was finished, charges would be filed against the truly guilty party.

Childs, they argued, could account for all acquisitions of real estate and increased deposits of his personal wealth. The truth was that he wasn't really a poor man when he came to St. Louis, contrary to the prosecution's portrayal. Childs had saved money from the time he was a very young man in Baltimore. In fact, he had saved so much money, his brother Joshua testified, that Childs was able to provide Joshua a loan soon after his arrival in St. Louis. Childs had diligently saved money from each paycheck. Supporters testified that he was a wise and shrewd investor in real estate and had acted as a business agent for several people who paid him percentages of their returns. Whitlock was just another of these clients. Nathaniel Childs Jr. was a genuine recipient of the fruits of the free-labor system, a model of the Jacksonian ideal of the self-made man.[37]

As any good defense attorney would have done, Bates turned the focus away from his client and toward the bank's practices. What followed was some eye-opening testimony about the everyday happenings at the institution entrusted with Missouri's personal savings and business accounts. First and foremost, security didn't appear to be one of the bank's top priorities, either in its accounting practices or in its securing of deposits. Bates asked whether Childs was the only person allowed after-hours access to the facility; it turns out he wasn't. Clerks, watchmen, bank porters, and several others also had easy access—though not all of these were authorized—including Shurlds, whose home was connected to the bank by a door that opened right into the building.

A watchman testified that on at least one occasion, Shurlds's wife had taken the keys and entered the bank while her husband was out of town so she could retrieve something she had left inside. When asked whether she had used the key any other time, the watchman confirmed that she had been called on by the directors on several occasions to deliver keys to them when her husband was out of town. But Mrs. Shurlds wasn't in the habit of delivering the keys herself; one time she had them delivered by a servant girl!

Clearly the keys were being passed around among several individuals, none of whom had the authority to have them, even the directors. It was the duty of the cashier, the second teller, and paying tellers to keep the keys secured. Yes, the defense contended, Childs had a set of keys to the vault, but he kept it at the office (although he claimed to have lost one key that was never recovered, and the corresponding locks weren't changed). But like the other clerks, he had to be let into the building itself by the night watchman—a position that faced steady turnover. Over the course of a year, even in the short time since Childs had left the bank, several different individuals had served as night watchman, a job that required sleeping inside the bank. Any of these men could have accessed the vault during the night if they had obtained copies of the keys kept in the office.

Security was also loose when it came to the bank's official seal, which was used to mark the wax for securing the cashboxes. The clerks testified that for several weeks the seal was left out on a table in the bank's counting room. Given this fact, Childs's attorneys didn't even have to make the assertion that anyone could have taken it and returned it without suspicion.

The defense also wished to answer the questions concerning Childs's behavior during the completion of the February count. Why had he asked Hurschburg to keep his planned resignation a secret? Bates explained that Childs simply worried that Hurschburg's chances of getting the job would be diminished if word got out that the second teller position was opening soon. There would be many applicants for such a job, and Childs already knew that the directors had a certain prejudice against Hurschburg. Bates and his team contended that through his actions, Childs was simply protecting his friend.

What, asked the defense, about the bank's accounting practices? When accounting errors were detected, how were they reconciled? The answer wasn't very satisfying. The tellers bore full responsibility for shoring up the daily transactions, and Childs was in charge of tracking the coins. The directors relied on the statements produced by the second teller to confirm the daily deposits and other business. The only way to detect a discrepancy was to perform a count on all the deposits. This was done just once a year, and sometimes the count was conducted not by an actual count of the coins but simply by weighing the bags.

Although these revelations could still easily point to Childs as the culprit, they also left the door open for any number of perpetrators. The directors' lax and incompetent leadership was further proven after one witness, when pressed, admitted that when he had cleaned the cashier's office during the course of the February count, he had had to pick up several empty sparkling-wine bottles. The cause of the clutter? Loring Pickering had been appointed as a new director during the course of the count, and several rounds of drinks had been ordered to celebrate. Just how accurate was a count carried out by inebriated directors? It was an embarrassing claim, and it didn't help that not long before the Childs affair was revealed, Pickering had skipped town after facing charges of murder and embezzlement from his own business.

Public sentiment about the role of the banks was the next weapon in Bates's arsenal. He proclaimed that Childs—not the bank—was the victim. It was a clear abuse of state power on the part of the bank to try to cover its mistakes and mismanagement with accusations against a lowly clerk. The bank was using its clout to carry out a campaign of lies against his client and had even broken the law to achieve its aims. Citing the investigative tactics used by the directors, Bates went in for the kill.

Some of the directors' actions, whether intentional or not, could be seen as nothing less than pure intimidation. John Hogan, an acquaintance of Childs, testified that after the charges had become public knowledge and rumors began swirling about Childs and Whitlock, he and his friends were astonished to find themselves in hot water for simply being nosy. After church one evening, Hogan and two friends were gossiping about the stolen money's whereabouts. One of the men claimed he had heard the gold was being held by Whitlock. Hogan and his other friend, Edward Gay, knew Whitlock's mother and decided that because they were close to her home, they would drop in and ask some questions. When they arrived on Whitlock's street, they realized that they weren't sure which house she lived in. They began to inquire of the neighbors, who directed them to more than one residence.

Finally they passed through the gate in one of the yards, and a door to one of the houses opened. A man's voice called out to them, "Is that you, Mr. Gay?" Edward responded yes and went to the door. The man asked whether Gay wished to see Mrs. Haydon, Whitlock's mother. Gay said yes, and the man turned to Hogan and asked the same. He also said yes. The man then said, "You shall see Mrs. Haydon—come on, Lawler [referring to a fellow policeman], we will take these gentlemen to the calaboose." A surprised Hogan then defensively declared, "Well, I reckon you won't!" It was now clear to Hogan and Gay that they were dealing with the assigned watchmen. The officer responded to Hogan's defiance by saying, "Well, I reckon we will."

On the stand, Hogan stated that, "I then said, if I am going to the calaboose, I want to know why and want to see your authority for arresting us. 'You want to know my authority?' said he, holding up his club. 'This is my authority.' I said, it had not come to that yet, that people, should be arrested by virtue of club authority, and demanded to see some other authority. The man replied he had authority to arrest anyone inquiring for this house." Despite their protests, Hogan and Gay were taken to the jail and held for half an hour before being allowed to leave.[38]

For the defense, the inappropriate measures taken by the bank's directors to protect themselves were inexcusable. They were using the police to bully Childs and his friends; they obtained evidence not authorized by a search warrant; and, most disturbing, they had no scruples in implying that Childs and Whitlock were engaged in an inappropriate relationship. This was the work of supposedly upright people abusing their powers and privileges. The directors were destroying the innocent to protect their own reputations. The *Republican's* editors proclaimed what many felt, that the trial was "useful in demonstrating the impropriety of mingling political purposes with the conduct of the only commercial and financial bank in the state—a lesson not yet sufficiently understood in this state."[39]

Final Arguments and the Fate of Nathaniel Childs Jr.

Final arguments began on November 30, 1849. Depending on who was speaking, Childs was either a wolf in sheep's clothing or a true victim of unbridled state power. The state's case, at least in Bates's opinion, was extremely thin. The prosecution "seem to have no unity of counsel, nor settled plan of operation," he wrote in his diary during the trial's last days. He was particularly perplexed by the fact that although Henry Geyer was the State's prosecuting attorney, the legal arguments and cross-examinations were largely carried out by Willis Williams, the bank's counsel. It seemed like a civil case rather than a criminal trial—and a poorly executed one at that. As Bates noted, "There is no show of a case made against the accused."[40]

With fingerprinting and other forensic investigative methods yet unknown, proving Childs's guilt was difficult. The prosecution did have strong, though circumstantial, evidence, but its case was weakened by the embarrassing revelations exposed during the course of the witness cross-examinations. Despite this, the prosecution fought on, trying to find any weak spot where it might crack Childs's upstanding reputation.

Although Williams hadn't explicitly declared that Childs was straying from the path of righteousness in his relationship with Whitlock, he clearly hoped to raise doubts about the reverend's behavior. Williams, whose own ethics had been questioned by the defense, made no attempt to hold back his contempt for Childs during the trial's final arguments. "Childs," Williams told the jury, "was not the first minister of the gospel [who] had been accused of high crime; nor was it entirely new that those wearing the livery of Heaven could fall." Sounding like a minister himself, Williams reminded the jury that "Lucifer was an angel in Heaven, enjoying the very presence of God, and he fell, and to that fact, we owed the existence of a hell, for the punishment of sin." The comparison left nothing to the imagination: Childs had taken advantage of his employer and the community by claiming to be a man of God, and now he must pay the price of his deception.[41]

Defense counsel Uriah Wright rose and countered with an attack on the bank's actions against Childs's character for the sake of the directors' own "instincts of self-preservation." They could prove nothing, he argued, so it was easier to deflect attention from their incompetence. Everything presented by the prosecution was therefore circumstantial.

The jury listened to the final arguments presented by six of the attorneys over the course of a week and a half. The last two attorneys to approach the jury were Bates and Geyer. Bates stood before the weary jury and, over the course of two days, reiterated that the "indictment was wholly defective." The prosecution of Childs was a tactic to cover the truth of the bank's own mismanagement. "Because," he told the jury, "if they can fix suspicion upon Childs, they acquit themselves. They may lose their money indeed, but they save their reputation."

On Friday afternoon, December 7, Geyer got up to take his turn and make the final address to the jury. He began by telling the twelve assembled men his intention was to "argue the case upon the facts—a course of argument not yet attempted by the gentlemen on the other side." He spent the first half of the address answering Bates's accusations against the bank and charging the defense with turning the jury's attention away from the facts—that he was spending nearly the entire day defending the bank's actions didn't bode well for the case's outcome.

It wasn't until the following afternoon that Geyer finally told the jury he was putting Childs's fate in their hands. A complete transcript of the trial published the following year notes that Geyer "committed the case to the jury, with the hope that they might be enabled to exercise such judgment in its decision, as would be satisfactory to the country, and in after years, be satisfactory to those who may have a review and examination of the facts." The transcript ends simply with this description of the trial's conclusion:

> The case was then (at half past 5 o'clock) given to the jury, without instruction from counsel, and the court took recess for half an hour. At a quarter past six the court was again opened, when the jury returned the following verdict:

> "We the jury, find the defendant NOT GUILTY, as charged in the indictment."

> Great applause succeeded the reading of the verdict by the clerk, and a number of Childs' friends crowded around him to offer their congratulations. The court then adjourned.[42]

In the end, the facts of the case were truly lost. The prosecution had displayed nothing but disorganization and incompetence, despite all the legal minds involved. Bates had truly bested Geyer and Williams, and he'd had a feeling the jury would vote to acquit all along, writing, "I think they would have given their verdict, spontaneously, from the box." Yet still he gave the case his all, recording in his diary on the night of the verdict that "the case of Mr. Childs has occupied my thought intensely day, night, and even in my dreams."

Was Childs guilty? If the evidence is considered in total, it's likely. He understood the practices of the bank, probably better than anyone. He knew where the weakest links existed in the accountability chain and was aware of the lax security measures. It's also hard to believe he was able to live so well on such a meager salary.

After the criminal trial, the Bank of the State of Missouri attempted to recover the funds by means of a civil case, but this too was unsuccessful. Childs responded to the whole affair by countersuing. He managed to win partial damages against the bank for defamation of character. For her part, during the course of Childs's trial, Whitlock filed a defamation case against Willis Williams, contending that his actions taken during his visit to her home were no less than a damning slur. In the end she was successful too.

All in all, it took nearly two years for the dust to settle, but just like the Nisbet robbery, the story had a final twist. In September 1851, weakened by the stress of the trial and public questions of her husband's fidelity, Eliza Childs died. Oddly enough, only two months after the death of his wife of nearly twenty years, Reverend Nathaniel Childs Jr. married Margaret Whitlock, the young widow from the congregation who held those important banknotes for him and swore that her relationship with him was nothing more than business.

Over the next few years, Childs's financial situation deteriorated. Despite his legal victory, his reputation had taken a severe hit from which it never recovered. Facing hard times, much of his property was eventually sold at public auctions due to delinquent taxes and unpaid debts. The successes of Childs's past had disappeared. Perhaps driven by desperation or old habits, the next series of events might have provided his former accusers with some sense of satisfaction.[43]

Exactly ten years after the 1849 embezzlement case, Childs walked into a bank in St. Louis and cashed a check for $270 drawn on the account of P. Crow & Sons. After Childs departed, the bank clerk looked more closely at the check he had just cashed. Something didn't seem right, so he chased down Childs and questioned him. Further inspection of the note revealed that it was a forgery. Childs soon found himself sitting in a jail cell once again.[44]

This time the evidence was clear: Nathaniel Childs Jr. was found guilty of forgery and sentenced to four years in the Missouri State Penitentiary in Jefferson City. The St. Louis correspondent for the *Daily Alta Californian* noted in his column of October 27, 1859, that "sixteen years ago no man in the community was held in higher esteem, no man engaged a greater share of public confidence, no man's prospects appeared brighter."[45]

Only one of Childs's old friends came to his defense. Over the course of several years, even during his term as U.S. attorney general, Edward Bates petitioned for a pardon for Childs. Finally, just before the reverend's sentence was up, Missouri's governor granted the pardon, and Childs quietly returned home where he and Whitlock remained until leaving St. Louis for Washington, DC. From there, Childs secured a clerkship for a time with the Postmaster General's Office and finally with the U.S. Patent Office. He remained a clerk until his death in 1880.[46]

CHAPTER SEVEN: THE MONTESQUIOU BROTHERS MURDERS

A s 1849 entered its final months, the rapid course of harrowing events seemed to show no sign of slowing down. By the time the Nathaniel Childs Jr. case (described in the preceding chapter) finished in December, attorney Edward Bates was exhausted, but he had little time to rest because even before the Childs trial opened, an incident occurred that would eventually call Bates to the defense once more.

In the city's center, at the corner of Third and Vine, sat St. Louis's largest and most respectable lodging establishment. Opened first as the Mansion House in the late 1820s, it changed ownership twice before Theron Barnum became its proprietor in 1840. Barnum's first action as owner was to rename the establishment the City Hotel. This was a calculated act of branding because Theron was the nephew of famed hotel proprietor David Barnum, owner of Baltimore's City Hotel. The Baltimore City Hotel was considered—by those who could afford it—to be the best hotel in America, so naturally Theron and his wife, Mary, sought to model their St. Louis hotel after Uncle David's great success.*

Through hard work and investment, the St. Louis Barnums prospered, and the City Hotel became visiting dignitaries' lodging of choice. Over time, many notable guests checked into Theron Barnum's establishment and were impressed by its comfortable rooms and good food, including a signature stew that was one of its biggest draws.[1]

The City Hotel's first-class reputation attracted the attention of two visiting Frenchmen, brothers of noble birth who, like so many others of the European leisure class, sought adventure in the rugged wilderness of North America. The Montesquiou brothers had arrived in New

---

* David Barnum's Baltimore City Hotel attracted many important visitors, including Charles Dickens during his 1842 tour of America. Dickens eventually arrived in St. Louis during that tour but stayed at the Planter's House Hotel instead. Barnum and his establishment later came to hold a more dubious place in American history: The Baltimore City Hotel was where John Wilkes Booth gathered his co-conspirators in early 1865 to plot the assassination of President Abraham Lincoln.

York City sometime in late spring before traveling up and across the vast wooded expanses of Quebec and Ontario. Like so many tourists before and since, they couldn't pass through the region without stopping to see the majesty of Niagara Falls. Next, they proceeded down through the Great Lakes to the prairies of northern Illinois, where they hunted ducks, quail, and prairie chickens. Their route took them southward to Springfield, then farther down to Alton, where they hunted in the surrounding prairies and reportedly bagged 250 prairie chickens in one afternoon.[2]

On October 27 the two men crossed the Mississippi River and arrived at the door of Barnum's City Hotel. They had a considerable amount of baggage consisting of their luggage, hunting equipment, and guns, as well as their hunting dogs—all of which was hauled not by packhorse or buckwagon but by buggy. Although they were a conspicuous pair, the Montesquious seemed to purposely avoid attention and social interaction. Twenty-nine-year-old Gonsalve de Montesquiou and his twenty-six-year-old brother, Raymond, were later described by those who did interact with them as handsome but neither friendly nor particularly interesting in character. No one at the time knew that they were members of one of the most ancient and respected families

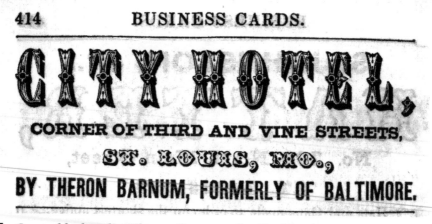

414 BUSINESS CARDS.

CITY HOTEL,

CORNER OF THIRD AND VINE STREETS,

ST. LOUIS, MO.,

BY THERON BARNUM, FORMERLY OF BALTIMORE.

Created by hotelier Theron Barnum, the City Hotel gained a reputation for being St. Louis's most accommodating and upscale hotel. Newspaper ad from the *St. Louis Business Director for 1850*. Missouri Historical Society Collections.

in France: The brothers were directly descended from D'Artagnan de Montesquiou, who was appointed marshal of France under Louis XIV, and also great-grandsons of the Duke of Rochefoucauld, author of the book *Maximes morales*. To top it off, each was a count in his own right.[3]

Over the course of the next two days, neither man exhibited any unusual behavior, although there were two small run-ins with the hotel's management. The first involved the kenneling of their dogs. The Montesquious apparently wished to keep the animals in their room, but Kirby Barnum, the hotel manager and nephew of the proprietor, took it upon himself to remove them while the Frenchmen were away. When the brothers returned and discovered the situation, they complained bitterly. The second incident speaks perhaps to a sense of entitlement. After the brothers entered the hotel's dining room and seated themselves, Barnum informed them that they had taken a reserved table and asked them to move. Gonsalve took this as a personal affront and became incensed. Both of these were minor incidents in the everyday operation of a public house, but what happened next at the City Hotel was anything but typical.[4]

The Night Gunfire Rang Out

Late on the night of October 29, Kirby Barnum and the hotel's steward, John Macomber, retired to their room after their workday ended. The two young men shared quarters situated among the regular guest rooms near the rear of the hotel, where a long veranda stretched the building's length.

Around 11:00 p.m., the corridor was seemingly quiet, but only minutes after Macomber had crawled into bed he heard a tapping at the window, which opened onto the piazza. He looked up to see a figure standing on the dark veranda. After seeing a gun in the person's hand, Macomber "called on Barnum to give the alarm." Barnum reacted immediately by turning to run. As he did so, the quiet hallway was shaken by the blast of a shotgun. A heavy lead ball passed through Barnum's lower back while the rest of his torso was peppered with buckshot. The large ball exited his body only to hit Macomber in the arm (Macomber later testified that he heard two simultaneous blasts, as if two men were firing at the same time). Barnum was crawling out of the room into the hallway at the moment Macomber realized he had been shot. In the excitement, one of the victims, probably Macomber, began shouting, "Murder!" Fearing for his life, Macomber had briefly run into the hallway but then returned to the room and locked himself in—leaving Barnum wounded and in agony in the corridor.

The shooter or shooters began to run, but the explosion of gunfire and the cries for help aroused the attention of the three men occupying the adjoining room. Most likely in a panic, the gunman fired again just as Albert Jones threw open the door to see what was going on. A spray of shot once again fanned out, and Jones took a direct hit to the heart, falling dead instantly while the room's other two occupants— Captain William Hubbell and H. M. Henderson, who were standing just inside the door—suffered wounds to their heads and hands. In a flash, the incident was over, and the gunman had fled.[5]

Alerted by the gunfire, the alarmed guests of the City Hotel began to stream into the halls and onto the piazza, where they could hear the sounds of the frightened and wounded men. While someone ran to find a watchman, hotel owner Theron Barnum arrived to find his nephew lying on his side, insensible from shock. Macomber indicated to Barnum and a group of men who had gathered that they should go to the adjoining room. Barnum and the others entered the room to find Jones doubled up against the wall, lying as he had fallen.[6]

Four constables eventually arrived at the hotel, where suspicion had fallen almost immediately on the two Frenchmen. They found Raymond de Montesquiou fully dressed and standing in the hall only a short distance from his room. He was arrested and at first denied his involvement in the shooting before confessing that his brother had fired the shots—and was presently locked inside their room.

With the assistance of Officer Flanagan, Barnum and the others forced open the door to find Gonsalve in bed. He quickly made a jump for his shotgun but was seized by Flanagan before he could do any damage. Gonsalve put up stiff resistance at first; he and Flanagan wrestled so much that Gonsalve "was stripped almost entirely of his clothes." Finally, Flanagan secured the Frenchman by force and put him in irons. As he removed Gonsalve from the room and walked him down the hall, the man reportedly cried out on several occasions,

"God save the Queen!" causing some to believe that the Montesquious were actually French Canadians and not French nationals.[7]

Followed by nearly two hundred angry citizens, the police took the brothers to the city's calaboose (jail). The *St. Louis Daily New Era* reported, "It was with great difficulty that the officers could prevent the now infuriated crowd from taking summary measures with the prisoners."[8]

Noble Brothers Under Guard

The following morning, attending physician John B. Johnston provided the conclusions of his autopsy on Albert Jones to a coroner's inquest that had been called at the hotel. Coroner Esrom Owens listened to Johnston's testimony, along with accounts provided by Macomber and Hubbell. Johnston's description of the condition of Jones's body added to the horror of what had happened.

> Upon the surface of the chest, auteriorly, and towards the left chest, were observed sixty-three holes, apparently from large-size shot. . . . Also one large wound, apparently made by a large musket ball, over the cartilage of the third rib, about one inch to the right of the meridian line of the sternum. On dissection, found to extend through the mediastinum into the upper portion of the heart, entering at the posterior part of the left ventricle, and passing obliquely backwards, severing the aorta at its origin; passed through the left side posteriorly, fracturing the ninth rib near its angle, and made its egress at that point through the common integument. . . . A large quantity of coagulated blood was found in the cavity of the thorax (probably amounting to 30 ounces).[9]

News of the incident spread quickly through the community and was wired to newspapers across the country. Once again, another tragedy was turning heads toward St. Louis. The violent, senseless nature of the crime was shocking, but just as baffling to the public was the fact that the suspects had interacted very little with anyone since their arrival. It had all the elements of an intriguing mystery— one compounded by the fact that Gonsalve wouldn't talk. This left

Raymond to try to explain everything despite speaking little to no English.

He informed police that the brothers were members of the celebrated French noble family of Montesquiou—this seemed an unlikely story to some who believed that the brothers were everyday con men. The following afternoon a unit of men consisting of the mayor, several police officers, Theron Barnum, and several citizens and members of the press entered the brothers' City Hotel room, which was filled with a great quantity of expensive clothing, jewelry, equipment, and toiletries. A reporter for the New Era confirmed the two were anything but frauds by describing the room's contents: "Their baggage consisted of four large leathern trunks, four carpet bags, and a great variety of trumpery, such as hunting apparatus, fishing tackle, gun cases, ammunition, & etc. . . . They were well supplied with every convenience, comfort and luxury appertaining to young men, and some of their effects were really costly." Adding to the proof that the Montesquious truly were important people were letters of introduction and correspondence from prominent individuals, including Bishop Hughes of New York. Also discovered were two large buckskin bags containing $1,454 in gold coins. Clearly these men weren't traveling lightly, nor did they want for money.[10]

Members of St. Louis's old French Creole community had no problem believing the story of the young men's noble birth because the Montesquiou family was well known to anyone familiar with French history. One local newspaper, the Daily Missouri Republican, tried to convince the public of the pair's ancestry, reporting that "they descend from a family in France not only of great historic fame, but distinguished for private virtue." Further confirmation of the brothers' noble claims came in the form of a letter to the Republican written by someone identified only as G. S. A. The writer translated an article taken from the Courrier des États-Unis, a French-language newspaper published in New York City: "The two men, whose names are mutilated by the dispatches, can they be Gonsalve and Raymond de Montesquiou? We would think so, for these gentlemen were in New York a few weeks since, started for the West on a hunting excursion, and the description just given would most unfortunately apply to them."[11]

The *Republican* sought to further legitimize the men's claims by printing a genealogy of the family that outlined its long contribution to French history, but the paper didn't go so far as to fully sympathize with the brothers. "The fate of the two young men in confinement affords a melancholy contrast to the glorious lives of their forefathers," declared the *Republican*'s editors. The Montesquious may have been young men of privilege in Europe, but now that one of them had committed a crime in the United States, they were to be "cast into prison to answer, for their lives."[12]

Any sort of sympathy shown by the city's French descendants was hardly shared by the general population. Albert Jones, the victim who had died instantly, was a popular figure. An ambitious young man, he was a coach maker who had been elected to the St. Louis City Council as alderman for the Sixth Ward. Jones was seen as a rising star cut down in the flower of his youth. His story was made more tragic by the fact that he was to be married the next day.[13]

Instead of a wedding on October 30, Albert Jones was laid to rest following a funeral procession that began at the front of the City Hotel. According to the *New Era*'s report the next day, the mourners were plentiful: "Long before the funeral train moved, Third Street, in from the Hotel, was crowded for a distance of two squares. . . . We have seldom seen a body of men that displayed so much feeling." At three o'clock, a group of pallbearers carried the coffin through the doors of the hotel to a waiting hearse. The *New Era* wrote, "There was no noise—the most profound silence reigned, and the vast concourse gazed upon the coffin . . . then quietly dispersed to their respective homes."[14]

As the funeral proceeded, there was a palpable feeling of tension in the air. Jones's death had stirred up a lot of anger among the young men who knew him as a friend and community leader. As his friend Isaac Sturgeon rode along in a carriage with several other men to the graveyard, he overheard a conversation led by one of the other passengers. Robert Mac O'Blenis, who was known throughout St. Louis as a notorious troublemaker, mentioned to the other men that after the funeral, a mob of citizens was planning to storm the jail, take the Montesquious from their cell, and hang them. Feigning sudden illness, Sturgeon excused himself and raced to inform City Marshal

Theodore LaBeaume of the plot. LaBeaume immediately set about foiling the mob, motivated not only by the need to maintain order and justice but also by his native sympathies as a member of the city's old Creole elite. It was clear to him and other members of the Creole community that the Montesquious would need their full protection.[15]

Acting quickly, LaBeaume pulled Judge James B. Colt away from his supper to approve a removal order to release the brothers from the confines of the calaboose. By the time Colt signed the order, a jailer had arrived with news that the calaboose was already completely surrounded. The entire police force was present to try and protect the jail from a crowd that had grown to some 1,500 persons. It was now impossible to remove the Frenchmen from the jail through the front

Thomas Easterly's daguerreotype of the city's calaboose. It was a temporary home to many of St. Louis's vagrants, drunks, and criminals. It also held the Montesquiou brothers while they awaited trial. Daguerreotype by Thomas Easterly, 1850. Missouri Historical Society Collections.

doors because the crowd could easily surge forward and seize the prisoners before anyone could stop them. As the city marshal and the others reviewed their options, LaBeaume realized that the jail's back door opened into the backyard of the residence of St. Louis's Episcopal bishop, Cicero S. Hawks.

The so-called Right Reverend agreed to allow the use of his property for the escape. Because people were constantly coming and going from his residence, he advised that the Montesquious be ushered into his parlor and then each brought out separately with two other men by their sides. LaBeaume and the jailers removed the nervous Raymond and Gonsalve from their cell as the crowd grew outside. As inconspicuously as possible, each man was walked through the yard, into the house, out the bishop's front door, and into a waiting taxi on Walnut Street. The ploy worked. Immediately the brothers were whisked off to the protection of the St. Louis Arsenal. However, LaBeaume's ordeal wasn't over yet. At the Arsenal, the commanding officer told the city marshal that he didn't have the men to protect the prisoners. If word of their new whereabouts were to leak out, the brothers would be just as vulnerable at the Arsenal as they had been at the jail. He advised that they proceed to Jefferson Barracks, where they could receive the full protection of federal troops.

Meanwhile, back at the calaboose, the crowd continued to swell, and an intoxicated individual, whom the *New Era* described as "a man somewhat notorious for the active parts he generally takes in such proceedings," arrived at the scene. This was no doubt Robert Mac O'Blenis, the man who had originally stirred up the crowd.[16]

Mental Illness or the Word of a Dying Man?

The Montesquious arrived at Jefferson Barracks after new carriages were procured to make the longer journey. With them was Officer McCullough, of the city guard, and a posse of six men sent to guard the brothers and act as an escort upon their return to the city. Neither the sympathetic LaBeaume nor prosecutors wanted to take any chances of endangering the men.

When the door to Gonsalve's carriage was opened, he made a weak attempt at escape but was easily caught. With the Frenchmen safely locked inside the military compound, everyone waited for the crowds at the calaboose to disperse and the tensions to subside.

After the situation stabilized and cooler heads prevailed, a formal investigation was launched. City Marshal LaBeaume, who spoke fluent French, led the questioning of the two men in hopes of learning what had motived them to commit such a violent and unprovoked attack. What he discovered was both enlightening and disturbing. During the course of the questioning, Gonsalve told LaBeaume that he took full responsibility for firing upon the innocent victims. When asked what motivated him to carry out such an act, he replied: "I was merely fulfilling a mission. One year ago two of my relatives were killed by a mob in Paris; the idea had often occurred to me that their death should be avenged; I know it was my duty to avenge them. Now it is done, and I am satisfied. I have fulfilled my destiny, and I have nothing to reproach myself." Furthermore, he admitted that Raymond had been present when he fired the fatal shots, but only because he was trying to dissuade him from following his impulse.[17]

When Raymond was questioned, he told the same story. It was a tale that reflected the turmoil of a changing Europe and the pain of a family illness. France, like much of the continent, was in the throes of political upheaval. Revolutions and violent demonstrations had broken out in the German principalities, Italy, and Hungary as the citizens of these nations demanded more democratic forms of government. The brothers' native France had seen angry mob actions against what many viewed as attempts to return power to promonarchist groups. In fact, during the June Days uprising in 1848, many Parisians had been killed. The Montesquiou brothers were therefore traveling in North America as a way of passing time until things back home calmed down, but that was only one reason.

On a more personal level, they were traveling so that Gonsalve could regain a more stable mental state. Raymond insisted during questioning that his brother had displayed unusual behavior for some time before the incident. He recognized Gonsalve's behavior as a manifestation of an all-too familiar trait that ran in the Montesquiou family. In 1847 their father had committed suicide; an older brother also suffered from mental illness and was confined to an institution. Mental illness was certainly a plausible explanation given Gonsalve's claims, but the authorities weren't so quick to absolve Raymond of any kind of guilt. Too many question marks remained about the details of the murder.[18]

Investigators decided to question another key individual—the first shooting victim, Kirby Barnum, who was still capable of speaking. His recollection didn't match Gonsalve's version of the story. Barnum insisted that when he looked through the window that night, it was Raymond who had stood before him holding the gun. This insistent testimony by the dying man wound up hampering Raymond's defense for the duration of the brothers' legal battle.[19]

As the story unfolded, Arthur de Montesquiou, the men's youngest brother, serendipitously arrived in New Orleans. He had sailed from France for his own visit to the United States with a prior planned arrangement to meet his brothers in the Crescent City. Instead, he was greeted with news of the murder and its aftermath. Immediately he left for St. Louis. Meanwhile, news of the tragedy had also reached family in France. Upon hearing of her sons' predicament, their mother, Madame de Montesquiou, widow of Count Alfred de Montesquiou, quickly set diplomatic instruments into motion by contacting the closest thing to nobility in St. Louis—the Chouteau family.[20]

After the Chouteaus learned of the Montesquiou brothers' plight, they stepped forward to act as a local base of support. This initiated a sequence of correspondence, eventually establishing a close relationship between the two families that lasted for many years. Madame de Montesquiou contacted Charles Chouteau to express her gratitude and relief that someone was looking after the welfare of her children. She also announced that two individuals would soon arrive in St. Louis to assist her sons: Charles Oliffe, a family friend, and Viscount Gerard de Cessac, brother-in-law to the Montesquious.[21]

Enter Edward Bates

It wasn't long before attorney Edward Bates also received a parcel of letters from Madame de Montesquiou, forwarded by William Cabell Rives, the American minister to Paris. In them she begged Bates to help defend her sons. He soon agreed to meet with Arthur de Montesquiou, who had just arrived in St. Louis. The young man immediately echoed his mother's plea. "I declined talking on that subject [for] now," he informed the brother, wanting to assess the situation himself before taking on such a difficult case.[22]

Soon after this meeting, Bates was joined by LaBeaume and Arthur for his first visit with the accused. The defense attorney, upon entering Gonsalve's cell, found the young Frenchman "sick in bed—on rather a mean pallet on the floor." Gonsalve didn't speak to Bates or anyone else. Bates found that Raymond was able to speak some English but described him as a "dull, leary man." Altogether he seemed little impressed by the two noblemen and noted that "none of them I learn, show any of that smartness & vivacity so common to Frenchmen."[23]

As Bates contemplated the men's case, he received letters of support from important relatives, including the brothers' uncle, the Duke de la Rochefoucauld, and French general Nicolas Charles Oudinot, who took time to write on the brothers' behalf even as he was successfully laying siege to Rome in an effort to crush that city's republican revolution. Despite the impressive family connections, Bates didn't welcome the letters; he felt they would actually work against the men. Writing in his diary, Bates observed, "They are evidently under a mistake in trying to enlist the influence of great names." He worried that the rabble of St. Louis would look upon this as a flagrant attempt at using privilege to thwart justice. In St. Louis, Bates concluded, "it is probable that the known good wishes of great men may" actually adversely injure the brothers' case by "exciting a counter feeling."[24]

The family obviously didn't feel the same way. In December, at the urging of Madame de Montesquiou, two more men arrived in support of the brothers: Louis Borg, the French vice-consul in New York, and Justin Paillard, another family friend. According to Bates, Borg informed him that he was commissioned to investigate the murder on behalf of the family and at the urging of Napoleon II. Bates was told to keep Borg fully informed of all developments. As Bates had worried, the presence of these two men gave the appearance of unwelcome outside meddling. The odds of the brothers receiving a fair and impartial trial were quickly evaporating.[25]

Bates didn't need more variables that could further endanger an already difficult case that would, perhaps, be the most challenging one of his career as a defense attorney—should he take it on. There could be no argument about what happened that night: A murder had been committed, and the man or men responsible had been caught. Typically on the frontier, this was obvious grounds for a guilty verdict, followed by a sentence of death by hanging, but this case didn't rest simply on the men's actions. It also took into account their motive, and Gonsalve's mental state turned the whole matter on its head. Bates knew that the only recourse was to prove that Gonsalve was mentally ill at the time of the murder, writing, "The facts are manifest, & not denied; and unless insanity can be made out, there does not yet appear any ground of defense or even mitigation."[26] A successful insanity plea was a long shot, but Bates decided to accept the case anyway and set about building a defense aimed at proving Gonsalve de Montesquiou was indeed insane and incapable of knowing right from wrong.[27]

The use of the insanity plea was uncommon in the early nineteenth century. In 1849 most American jurists would have been aware of its use in two high-profile cases: the trial of Richard Lawrence in Washington, DC, and the trial of Daniel M'Naghten in London. These two cases not only educated the public as to the existence of the insanity plea but also established precedence for determining insanity as a defense, as well as the treatment of the accused. Lawrence was tried for the attempted assassination of President Andrew Jackson in 1835, declared innocent by reason of insanity, and hospitalized. M'Naghten's case went further in establishing insanity as a legitimate defense. The Scotsman was put on trial for the attempted assassination of British prime minister Robert Peel. When the verdict was reached and M'Naghten was declared innocent by reason of insanity, the precedents for determining the parameters of one's mental state as a defense were set into English law in what became known as the M'Naghten Rules of 1843. Certainly Bates would have been aware of these, but it's unlikely he used such a defense often during his career.[28]

According to the M'Naghten Rules, Bates would have to prove his client was "laboring under such defect of reason, from disease of the mind, as not to know the nature and quality of the act he was doing, or if he did know it, that he did not know that what he was doing was wrong." Simple enough, what with evidence of mental illness in the Montesquiou line that could easily be proven by presenting the fact that their elder brother was committed to a Paris insane asylum and their father had committed suicide. Bates himself had witnessed Gonsalve's behavior and observed on one of his visits to the jail that "Gonsalve is in a bad fix again, yesterday & to day—decidedly mad— Poor fellow!" He could also employ the testimony of an expert witness, Dr. William Carr Lane, who had examined Gonsalve and declared "that his mental disease is permanent, and that no hope need be entertained for his future restoration."[29]

As Bates began to piece together the case, he gathered depositions from a number of credible and respected witnesses who had come into contact with the brothers, including Jesuit Father Pierre Jean DeSmet, who had acted as the brothers' confessor. Father DeSmet stated that he came to know the brothers well because he visited them about every two weeks while they were in jail. When he initially encountered Gonsalve, he observed that the Frenchman was in "very low spirits." The first time he took Gonsalve's confession "he appeared to be altogether out of his mind; his hand was trembling in my own." The priest discovered on subsequent visits that Gonsalve's mental state would fluctuate between visibly disturbed to seemingly normal: "In several of my other visits I remarked occasionally that he was in a great taciturnity or melancholy state of mind. At other times he would appear reasonable and make answers to my conversations."[30]

An Indecent Proposal

As the year 1849 came to a close, Bates was gearing up for the trial that the new year would bring. In January 1850 a grand jury was called, and charges against both men were recommended: one for the murder of Albert Jones, another for the murder of Kirby Barnum, who had finally passed on during the course of the investigation. The trial was set for the April 1850 court term.

In the days following the grand jury's recommendation, Bates was suddenly approached by an attorney representing the Barnum family. Mere days after the shooting, the Barnum family had expressed interest in a civil suit seeking compensation for the loss of income resulting from Kirby Barnum's death. Now that Kirby was dead and a charge of murder had been levied against Bates's client, the Barnums

Theron Barnum, owner of the City Hotel, sought to profit from the loss of his nephew by asking for a cash payment in exchange for not testifying against the Montesquiou brothers. Daguerreotype by Thomas Easterly, date unknown. Missouri Historical Society Collections.

approached the esteemed attorney with an audacious offer. Theron Barnum wished Bates to know that—for a sum—the family would refuse to testify against his client. Bates was aghast and disgusted that they would suggest such a deal, writing "the relatives of the deceased . . . eagerly seek to turn the whole affair of blood suffering into a mere speculation." When Bates asked the Barnums' attorney what that price might be, he replied that the family wasn't yet sure but that he thought it would be in the range of $20,000—just over half a million dollars in today's currency! In his diary entry describing the proposal, Bates simply wrote, "Poh!"

The Barnums' incredulous efforts to profit from the tragedy enraged Bates not only because "they have let down the truth and majesty of justice & the dignity of grief to the vulgar level of a money bargain" but also because it risked undermining the credibility of his case. He worried that if even rumors of a possible bargain leaked out, the validity of witness testimony would be called into question.[31]

The Montesquiou Trial, Round One

When the trial for the murder of Kirby Barnum finally began, its promise of high drama made it the hottest ticket in town. Once again the public was to be entertained by a cast of the city's best orators and legal minds. James Lackland was arguing the case for the State. Bates was the lead attorney for the Montesquious, joined in counsel by Charles Gibson; Wilson Primm; and, ironically, Henry Geyer, whom he had just faced off against in the Childs trial (described in the preceding chapter).[32]

Many months had passed since the murders and those vengeance-charged days following the crime, yet the whole affair still had St. Louisans' full attention. Bates described the public excitement in his diary: "Large crowds attended during the greater part of the speaking which was long. Through snow, rain, and mud hundreds of ladies attended, especially while Geyer & myself were speaking."[33]

Proceeding over the trial was Judge James B. Colt, brother of the famed gunsmith whose firearms bore the family name. Colt was a respected man of the bench, known for his fairness and sound legal opinions. A later biography of Colt noted that during the Montesquiou murder trial, he was "straight and just, neither bowing to the wild prejudice engendered against the accused nor cringing in the least to the high and influential power brought to bear in their favor."[34]

As the April trial progressed, neither the solid evidence of Gonsalve's unstable mental state nor the even hand of Judge Colt's presence in the courtroom seemed to help Bates in his efforts to sway the jury. He presented his witnesses and read his depositions declaring that Gonsalve had a prior history of mental instability. Gonsalve's own admission of guilt and his acknowledgement that Raymond was attempting to stop him, along with his outrageous claims of acting on behalf of God's will, Bates argued, proved that Gonsalve was the only responsible party for the murder. But Kirby Barnum's deathbed claim that Raymond was the true gunman dogged the younger brother's defense. To the public, Raymond's guilt was apparent despite his sibling's obvious insanity. This shocked Bates, who wrote, "Never have I witnessed a more vindictive public prosecution than this."

Issues of class distinctions and prejudice hung heavy over the trial. All the resistance to Bates's arguments invoked in him both a sense of determination to fight on and a looming sense of defeat. In his mind, the evidence was overwhelmingly clear that Gonsalve couldn't be held accountable for his actions and that Raymond was completely innocent. The possibility of Raymond's conviction particularly bothered him, causing him to remark in his diary that "never in my practice of 34 years, have I felt an interest and excitement so deep & intense." He found that he couldn't even look upon Raymond's face without feeling despondent. "I am overcome with sorrowful emotion, too strong for my control," he lamented.

As Bates saw it, the case against his client was based on "low minded prejudice," which he blamed on the feelings of the "rougher sort" who still sought vengeance rather than true justice. Over the course of the trial, it became apparent to him that in the court of public opinion the lines were clearly drawn between those who were better educated and those who weren't. The "educated and intelligent" were 10-to-1 in favor of acquittal, whereas the others clearly had no interest in anything that might allow the brothers to escape the hangman. Bates hoped, however, that even the rougher sort would eventually cool down and come around to sense.[35]

When the case was given to the jury for deliberation, it came back without a verdict. Nine jurors had voted to acquit Raymond, but three were unconvinced of his innocence. As far as Gonsalve's fate, seven voted to acquit on the grounds of insanity, but five held out. One juror, a known member of the local Know-Nothing Party, was suspected of allowing his anti-immigrant feelings to cloud his opinion. With a hung jury, a new trial was set for June 1850.[36]

The Montesquiou Trial, Round Two

While the city waited for the second trial to begin, Bates suffered from total exhaustion. He had spent weeks defending Nathaniel Childs Jr. only to launch straight into the investigation of the Montesquious, followed by their April trial. He complained of "feeble health" and expressed that he had "no energy to do anything." Yet he had to press on. There was very little recovery time before he once again entered the old brick courthouse and stood before a new jury.[37]

Because there was no clear physical evidence linking either brother with the crime, eyewitness testimony was the key to the case. As news of the murder had spread, other witnesses came forward who had dealings with the Montesquious over the course of their travels. One individual who provided a deposition was the renowned New York restaurateur Lorenzo Delmonico, of Delmonico steak fame. When the brothers first arrived in America, they stayed at Delmonico's hotel on Broadway in New York City. Delmonico and two of his waiters painted a very different picture of the Montesquious. All of them declared that the brothers were perfect gentlemen who showed no sign of troubling behavior. Delmonico testified that they had stayed at his establishment for five days at the end of the previous July, only three months prior to the murders, and that during their stay he saw them every day and "they always appeared like gentlemen and very quiet." The waiters testified to the same: The Frenchmen proved to be nothing more than sober and gracious.[38]

A second set of testimonies showed the brothers in an entirely different light. As the Montesquious passed through Illinois in mid-October on their way to St. Louis, they had stopped for lodging in Springfield. At the Carrigan Hotel, the men found that they had to share a room with another traveler, J. E. Jackson. Taking the second bed in the room, the brothers went to sleep, but in the early morning Jackson observed some truly chilling behavior from Gonsalve, noting that ". . . soon after daylight, one of the accused raised himself in his bed directing to me a vacant look." Jackson reported that Gonsalve had lain down again only to do the same thing a few moments later, this time "muttering in an undertone some French expression." It was then that Raymond awoke, the two brothers conversed in French, and Gonsalve arose and began to dress. Jackson noted, though, that Gonsalve "kept his eyes on me, and my bed. Frequently approaching the foot of my bed, as if to satisfy himself of some point." When Gonsalve was dressed, Raymond got up and also dressed. Gonsalve waited for Raymond to finish, and then the brothers removed two guns from the bed and left.

Jackson afterward went to breakfast and spoke to the hotel's owner, Henry Carrigan. His deposition describes their conversation:

"I inquired who these men were, he had brought into my room? When he informed me, he did not know them—that they had stopped at his house about 12 o'clock the night before and he having no other vacant bed in the house was obliged to put them in my room. I remarked to him, 'You may depend upon it, one of them is not right in his mind.'"[39]

Carrigan also supplied a deposition and gave an equally unsettling account of his first encounter with Gonsalve. When the two men appeared at his door around midnight, asking if they could lodge for the night, Carrigan agreed to let them in: "They called for supper, after which I took a light, and at their request two guns, and went upstairs and showed them a bed. The bed was in the room occupied by Mr. J. E. Jackson. When we first entered the room the tallest of the two startled as if suddenly frightened, and looked wildly around the room, as if searching for some place to escape, or for some hidden enemy. I remained in the room longer than I should have done if I had not witnessed the strange actions I have just related."[40]

The eyewitness account of Gonsalve's irrational behavior seemed to soften the new jury and turn the question of guilt away from Raymond. This time Bates's attempt to prove innocence by means of an insanity defense looked promising—Raymond's chance of acquittal was also improving. But soon a young physician came forward who claimed to have been a lodger at the City Hotel on the night of the murder, and once again the case seemed to turn away from Bates's favor. According to an account written by Theophil Papin, no one knew the physician. He was from the East but "seemed intent on giving unprejudiced testimony." This unbiased account wasn't what Bates wanted the jury to hear. Nonetheless, prosecutor Lackland asked the doctor to tell the jury what he saw. Papin wrote that the doctor was "both clear and emphatic in denouncing Raymond as the homicide who held the gun."

After the doctor finished telling the jury what he had seen, it was the defense's turn for cross-examination. Bates approached the stand, and Papin recorded his questioning as follows:

"Doctor, you say that this young gentlemen (motioning to the accused Raymond who sat at his table) held the gun and fired the fatal shots? But the porch was very dark. How did you distinguish him from his brother?"

The doctor replied, "[He was standing] probably not as far as I now sit from you. The light from the window shone direct on them. I saw both the men distinctly."

"But they are brothers," stated Bates. "Their faces are covered with beards fashioned the same. Their features, where visible, are not unlike, soeven, their complexions in the shadowy lamplight. Are there, or were there, any distinguishing marks upon the brothers respectively to make you so emphatic in this incriminating evidence, which, my God forbid it, send some innocent man to death!"

The doctor said, "I know the accused Raymond first by his face and features. Then he wore an unforgettable garment which I noticed particularly."

"What was the garment?" Bates asked. "Describe it fully, if you can."

"Oh yes I can very well. He was enveloped in a sort of morning gown of grey material, buttoned well up to the throat. The buttons, I observed, were uncommonly large and I think, cloth covered. The gown evidently had been tailor-made—it fitted him snugly and well at every part."

"Now, doctor, you look to me like a man of good, gentle nature, who might, and doubtless would, go considerably out of your way to do a needed kindness," continued Bates. "Evidently, too, you are a well-informed, intelligent man. Such being the case, will you please explain to the jury how it happens that in all this appalling catastrophe—when the blood of innocent men was being shed so cruelly about you, and the unwary souls sent unshriven to be judged by their maker—you could, amid the overwhelming horrors of such a drama, occupy yourself with the study of a coat—its fit and cut—with the very size of the buttons that held it together?"

The witness answered, "Well, I don't know. I was surely horrified by the murders, but the garment was an uncommon one, and it made a strong impression, I suppose."

"Very good," Bates said. "It served you as a mark of identification. The coat, you observed, Raymond had fastened up to his throat, now how far did it fall?"

"Some inches below the knee," the physician responded.

Bates continued his line of questions about the fit of the coat. He wanted the jury to hear the doctor's detailed description. Then Bates called for the coat to be brought into the courtroom. He asked the doctor whether this was indeed the coat in question. The witness confirmed it was. Then Bates pulled a tactic reminiscent of the famous glove episode in the O. J. Simpson trial conducted nearly 150 years later: He asked Raymond to try on the coat. When Raymond stood and slipped on the coat, Papin reported that those present in the courtroom audibly gasped. He observed that, "It might have been his grandfather's overall. It hung on him like a loose sack. It was Gonsalve's robe."

With this new evidence, the witness was suddenly confused: "I am as much astounded, at least as you are. I thought I had seen clearly that night—but this new evidence—I may have been mistaken. Probably I was."[41]

This was the break Bates had hoped for. It seemed like the end had come, but after four weeks of testimony that seemed to show no doubt of Raymond's innocence, Bates was deflated when on June 29, 1850, "another hung jury has made all that labor useless."[42]

Resolution at Last

Hoping to avoid yet another trial, Bates and his fellow defense attorneys decided to change strategies. If a jury couldn't decide, then perhaps they could convince Missouri governor Austin King to grant pardons for the brothers. Bates's co-counsel, Charles Gibson, traveled to Jefferson City to meet with the governor; he returned with a signed pardon for Gonsalve. King had been convinced of Gonsalve's insanity, but Raymond's case was a bit more complicated. The governor gave Gibson a conditional pardon that would exonerate Raymond only if the circuit attorney agreed to dismiss the case. This seemed like a good compromise to Bates, but Raymond wasn't as pleased because receiving a pardon implied guilt, and he was innocent.[43]

On October 12, 1850, nearly a full year after the events of that tragic night at the City Hotel, Gonsalve de Montesquiou boarded a steamboat escorted by St. Louis County marshal John Long and Vice-Consul Borg. The three men were bound for the Port of New York. When they reached it, Long put the young Frenchman in Borg's custody; Borg then proceeded on to France with Gonsalve. The fam-

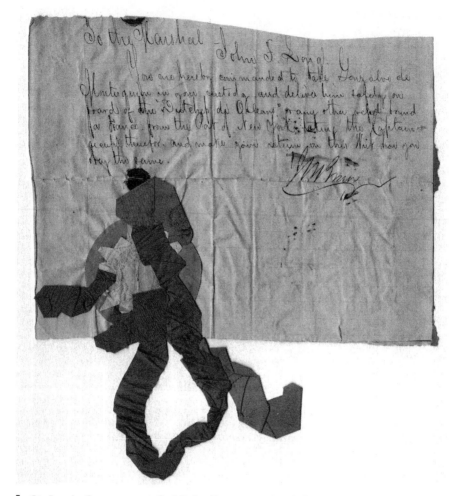

St. Louis County marshal John Long received this order instructing him to transport Gonsalve de Montesquiou to New York City so he could board a ship bound for France. John Long Papers, Missouri Historical Society Collections.

ily had him committed to a Paris asylum immediately but seemed to hope for a recovery that never materialized. The Montesquious' brother-in-law, Gerard de Cessac, wrote to the Chouteaus in 1851 and mentioned that Gonsalve was still in a sanitarium and seemed to have worsened. He was, wrote Cessac, "very suspicious of everyone. His

Aunt Perron went to see him and he placed a table between them and did not wish to kiss her." Count Gonsalve de Montesquiou lived for forty-three years in a sanitarium near Paris and died there in 1893. He most likely suffered the effects of paranoid schizophrenia, an illness that nineteenth-century medicine was unable to treat.[44]

Back in St. Louis, Raymond's fate was yet to be decided. After the conditional pardon that had at least released him from the confines of the calaboose, Raymond had taken up residence in the Planter's House Hotel with Cessac to await his next hearing. The proceedings were eventually set for the court's November term. During what became his last day in court, Bates "exhibited the pardon," and the prosecutor agreed to dismiss the charges. The long nightmare was finally over. Unlike his brother, Raymond needed no escort—he was simply free to go. It must have been a truly liberating experience to see St. Louis disappear around the bend of the river as his steamboat chugged south toward New Orleans. Raymond returned home to France before moving to Madrid to serve as an attaché in the French diplomatic corp. He reportedly died young.[45]

Edward Bates may have had an exhausting year, but his notoriety continued to spread, giving him little time to rest. Ten years after the Montesquiou trial, Bates was standing on the floor of the Republican National Convention in Chicago, put forward as a candidate for the party's presidential nomination. Instead, Springfield, Illinois, attorney Abraham Lincoln took the nomination and won the presidency in November 1860, but he didn't leave Bates behind. Bates served as attorney general of the United States for most of Lincoln's presidency, despite the fact that he and the president differed on many issues. When a seat on the U.S. Supreme Court opened in 1864, Bates eagerly wanted Lincoln to nominate him for the position, but the president chose Salmon Chase instead. Bates then resigned as attorney general and came home to St. Louis. He died in 1869 and is buried in Bellefontaine Cemetery.[46]

On the west side of St. Louis's Forest Park, at the intersection of Lagoon and Fine Arts drives, stands a statue of Edward Bates. It was erected in 1876 by those who sought to pay homage to his loyalty to the Union and service to his country. For Bates, that loyalty and dedication was grounded in his belief in the sanctity of the law and his faith in the American justice system. It was those unwavering convictions that allowed the Montesquios, the enslaved Lucy Delaney, and even Nathaniel Childs Jr. to receive a fair trial despite those who attempted to manipulate the law for the sake of expediency or vigilante justice.

CHAPTER EIGHT: THE LASTING LEGACIES OF 1849

Almost 170 years have passed since the events of 1849, yet reminders of that fateful year still linger today. Some are obvious, such as the plaque in St. Francis Xavier College Church praising God for protecting the residents of Saint Louis University from the ravages of cholera, or the stone crucifix that marks the mass grave of cholera victims reinterred in Calvary Cemetery. Others are less recognizable but worth noting.

Commuter Suburbs

St. Louis's older suburban communities are a direct result of the aftermath of the 1849 cholera epidemic and the Great Fire. After these events, those with the means sought to remove themselves from the city to healthier climates during the warmest months of the year, and the construction of the new Pacific Railroad provided just the opportunity to create a country refuge. Real-estate promoters Hiram Leffingwell and Richard Elliot established their firm in the spring of 1849, just as the year's calamities were beginning to unfold. The city's disasters eventually proved profitable for the young real-estate agents: By the end of 1849 they had found a ready market and an easy way to promote their interests.

Within the next three years, the city's merchants and manufacturers began purchasing land along the rail line with the aim of building summer and weekend estates. The Kirkwood Association was formed as a way of plotting a village and encouraging buyers. With the beauty of its rolling hills, easy recreational access to the nearby Meramec River, the convenience of jumping on the train to head back into the city, and the possibility of the continued progress of the railroad heading west, the site was an ideal location. By 1863 the Kirkwood Association had sold all of its original property, and Kirkwood, Missouri, became the first commuter suburb west of the Mississippi River. It was soon joined by Webster Groves and other communities whose populations consisted of those with many of the same backgrounds and intentions.[1]

New and Moved Cemeteries

Besides building new towns along the city's periphery, the cholera epidemic accelerated the desire and need to construct new resting places for the dearly departed. Bellefontaine Cemetery was already in the planning stages by the spring of 1849. Its design was rooted in the Victorian movement to landscape cemeteries that would double as beautiful final resting places for the deceased and city parks.

This combination, known as the rural cemetery movement, was an answer to the growing problem of finding suitable burial space for America's booming cities with the added benefit of preserving the natural splendor of many of these areas. It wasn't unusual for families to gather in these parks to picnic near the graves of their beloved relatives or even hunt within the confines of the cemetery. By the mid-nineteenth century, any American, British, or French city worthy of praise had laid out a parklike memorial garden, often with lakes, rolling pathways, and forested hills. Many of these cemeteries are now monuments in themselves, such as Mount Auburn in Boston, Green-Wood in Brooklyn, Forest Lawn in Buffalo, Graceland in Chicago, and Oak Hill in Washington, DC.[2]

In March 1849 the Missouri General Assembly approved the incorporation of the Rural Cemetery Association. This act created Bellefontaine Cemetery on St. Louis's northern border. It opened the following year and grew quickly as the decades passed.[3]

Meanwhile, as the city's population continued to expand and construction grew along with it, developers emptied out a number of city graveyards so they could sell the land. One such site was Rock Springs Cemetery. As the city limits moved west, encroaching on Rock Springs, a decision was made to reinter the graves in the new cemetery purchased by the Roman Catholic Church under the leadership of Archbishop Peter Richard Kenrick. Calvary Cemetery opened to burials in 1853 and later became home to many of the graves of the 1849 cholera victims who were moved from their original resting places.[4]

Another former cemetery, City Cemetery, was located on the east corner of Jefferson and Arsenal. A large portion of present-day Benton Park is situated upon this spot, which was one of St. Louis's largest graveyards until the Civil War years. In 1864 the land around City Cemetery was marked for residential redevelopment, and men were hired to dig up the plots for reinterment in the new cemeteries. These workmen were surprised (and probably more than delighted) to find that the graves often contained treasures. In 1849 the need to bury the dead was a rushed affair. Fear of contracting cholera from the bodies and the sheer number of deaths made for quick and dirty burials. Because many of the dead were simply passing through St. Louis and had no local relatives, they were buried together with any possessions they'd had in the pockets of their jackets and pants. As the gravediggers moved their bodies fifteen years later, they found gold and silver coins, jewelry, and other valuables. With no one to claim the property, it was free for the taking.[5]

Improved Infrastructure and Building Codes

With the horrors of the year fresh in mind, a new emphasis was placed on updating the city's infrastructure as it spread outward. Sewer and street improvements had been previously planned, but the cholera epidemic and the Great Fire made these projects a much higher priority. The Biddle Street sewer was a major step toward improving waste disposal and runoff. Work began on the project, a forty-foot trench, during the summer of 1849 as a way of draining the putrid waters of Kayser's Lake. This formed the basis of the sewer system still in place in St. Louis today.

The filthy waters of Chouteau's Pond also became history as the old lake was drained by the construction of the Mill Creek sewer basin, which became the city's largest sewer in the nineteenth century. The city's public water system received a much-needed overhaul too, and building codes were rewritten to ensure that the threat of fire was diminished through the use of fireproof materials such as brick and iron frames. St. Louis's brick façades are therefore just as much a result of the Great Fire as the vast clay deposits that made the city a brick-manufacturing center.[6]

Today's advancements in technology, engineering, sanitation, and medical science have made our lives safer and more comfortable than St. Louisans' in 1849. The city has come a long way, but we should forever learn from our ancestors' example of determination and resilience and continue striving toward a better, cleaner, and more just community.

ACKNOWLEDGMENTS

Several extraordinary individuals deserve a multitude of thanks for assisting me with this project. First, the Missouri Historical Society's Library and Collections Division contributed greatly toward making this book a reality. Dennis Northcott, reference archivist, graciously gave me many interesting leads and brought a number of items to my attention that I probably would have overlooked otherwise. Digitized archival sources and photo images were provided courtesy of Jaime Bourassa, associate archivist, who always does a superb job. Emily Jaycox and her library staff offered me valuable support throughout this effort as well, and I appreciate everything they do on a daily basis. Finally, Jeff Meyer, collections manager, pointed me toward several great artifacts from our objects collections that offered excellent illustration material.

I am grateful for the support I received from Katherine Van Allen, managing director of museum services at MHS, and the encouragement of Dr. Frances Levine, MHS president. I also want to thank Lauren Mitchell, director of publications, and her excellent staff for their good work. A special thanks is also due to Lauren's predecessor, Victoria Monks, who was instrumental in getting the ball rolling on this project.

Furthermore, I cannot fail to mention the assistance I received from Molly Kodner, MHS's head archivist. Molly not only provided me with great reference leads but also endured listening to my many stories and reading my first drafts. I thank her for her support and her numerous valuable suggestions.

Many good stories in this book were strengthened by the reference assistance of Mike Everman, archivist for the St. Louis branch of the Missouri State Archives. Mike chased down many clues for me, and we should all be grateful to him for going above and beyond for the benefit of archival research in St. Louis. A further thank-you goes to Lori Cox-Paul, director of archival operations at the Central Plains branch of the National Archives and Records Administration in Kansas City, Missouri, who managed to find exactly what I was looking for.

Finally, a tremendous amount of credit goes to my family for their constant support. I dedicate this book to them for encouraging me to pursue my interests and joining me in my journey.

253

NOTES

Chapter One

1. Edward Bates to R. B. Frayser, June 1849, Bates Family Papers, Missouri Historical Society (hereafter cited as MHS).

2. John Snow, *On the Mode of Communication of Cholera* (London: Wilson & Ogilvy, 1849), 11.

3. Dhiman Barua and William B. Greenough III, ed., *Cholera* (New York: Plenum Medical Book, 1992), 130; Frank Snowden, "Epidemics in Western Society Since 1600" (online lecture 13.2013, Yale University, accessed July 15, 2016).

4. *Daily Missouri Republican* (St. Louis), September 4, 1832.

5. Ibid., September 11, 1832.

6. Ibid.

7. Ann Biddle to Dr. Dennis Delany, 5 November 1832, Mullanphy Family Papers, MHS.

8. *Republican*, November 13, 1832.

9. James Neal Primm, *Lion of the Valley: St. Louis, Missouri, 1764–1980*, 3rd ed. (St. Louis: Missouri Historical Society Press, 1998), 154–155.

10. Primm, *Lion of the Valley*, 154–155; Rob Wilson, "The Disease of Fear and the Fear of Disease: Cholera and Yellow Fever in the Mississippi Valley" (dissertation, Saint Louis University, 2007), 61–63.

11. *General Catalogue of the Medical Graduates of the University of Pennsylvania*, 3rd ed. (Philadelphia: Lydia R. Bailey, 1845); Robert McNamara, "Charles Carroll of Belle Vue Co-founder of Rochester," *Rochester History* XLII, no. 4 (October 1980).

12. Biddle to Delany, 5 November 1832, MHS.

13. James Green, *Green's St. Louis Directory for 1845* (St. Louis: James Green, 1845).

14. *Republican*, August 14, 1846.

15. William McPheeters, "History of Epidemic Cholera in St. Louis in 1849," *The St. Louis Medical and Surgical Journal* VII, no. 2 (March 1850).

16. Ibid.

17. Necrology scrapbook 2C, MHS, 203.

18. *Republican*, January 11, 1849; *St. Louis Daily Union*, January 15, 1849.

19. Wilson, "The Disease of Fear and the Fear of Disease," 68–69; *Daily Union*, January 15, 1849.

20. *Weekly Reveille* (St. Louis), January 11, 1849.

21. Candace O'Connor, *A Surgical Department of Distinction: 100 Years of Surgery at Washington University School of Medicine* (St. Louis: Washington University in St. Louis, 2014), 14–15.

22. *Reveille*, January 4, 1849.

23. Ibid.

24. Ibid., January 1, 1849; Ibid., January 15, 1849.

25. Emory M. Thomas, *Robert E. Lee: A Biography* (New York: W. W. Norton, 1995), 88; *Daily Union*, March 27, 1849.

26. Reverend Charles Peabody diary, 6 November 1846, MHS.

27. *The Mayor's Message with Accompanying Documents, to the City Council of the City of St. Louis, at Its May Session* (St. Louis: St. Louis Times, May 1848).

28. Charles van Ravenswaay, *Saint Louis: An Informal History of the City and Its People, 1764–1865* (St. Louis: Missouri Historical Society Press, 1991), 388.

29. *Republican*, December 27, 1848.

30. *Reveille*, January 14, 1849.

31. *St. Louis Daily New Era*, March 6, 1849; Van Ravenswaay, *Saint Louis: An Informal History*, 388.

32. Primm, *Lion of the Valley*, 146.

33. *Republican*, March 28, 1849.

34. *Daily Union*, April 6, 1849.

35. Danny Blair and W. F. Rannie, "Wading to Pembina: 1849 Spring and Summer Weather in the Valley of the Red River of the North and Some Climatic Implications," *Great Plains Research: A Journal of Natural and Social Sciences* 4, no. 1 (February 1994): 4.

36. Jefferson Barracks weather report, January–December 1849, National Archives Microfilm Publication T907, Roll 284.

37. *New Era*, May 15, 1849.

38. Ibid., May 16, 1849.

39. William S. Potts, *God in the Pestilence and the Fire* (St. Louis: Second Presbyterian Church, 1849); I. H. Headlee to S. H. Headlee, 13 June 1849, MHS.

40. Adam Jortner, "Cholera, Christ, and Jackson: The Epidemic of 1832 and the Origins of Christian Politics in Antebellum America," *Journal of the Early Republic* 27, no. 2 (Summer 2007): 233–264; *Republican*, August 27, 1848.

41. McPheeters, "History of Epidemic Cholera," 103.

42. Joseph Mersman diary, 13 May 1849, MHS.

43. John Fletcher Darby, *Personal Recollections of Many Prominent People Whom I Have Known. . . .* (St. Louis: G. I. Jones, 1880).

44. Ibid., 271.

45. Minutes of the Committee of Public Health, 27 June 1849, MHS.

46. Ibid.

47. "St. Louis News," *MHS Bulletin* VI, no. 1 (October 1949): 79.

48. Minutes, 29 June 1849, MHS.

49. Ibid.

50. Jefferson Barracks weather report, National Archives.

51. *Republican*, June 4, 1849.

52. Minutes, 2 July 1849, MHS.

53. Ibid., 3 July 1849, MHS.

54. Ibid., June 29, 1849, MHS.

55. *Republican*, March 20, 1849.

56. Barua and Greenough, *Cholera*, 149.

57. Ibid.

58. Eliza Keesacker Howard to Comfort McJilton, 4 July 1849, MHS.

59. Census Collection, MHS; "U.S. French Catholic Church Records (Druin Collection), 1695–1954," Ancestry.com, http://search.ancestry.com/search/db.aspx?dbid=1111; McPheeters, "History of Epidemic Cholera," 109.

60. *Republican*, July 7, 1849.

61. Ibid., July 10, 1849.

62. *North Wales Chronicle* (Bangor, Wales), July 24, 1849.

63. *The North Star* (Rochester, New York), July 13, 1849.

64. "St. Louis News," *Bulletin*, 78.

65. Albertina Glyckherr Loring, *Albertina: Biography of a Loyal American* (St. Louis, 1907).

66. Michael McEnnis, *Cholera–1849*, Cemeteries Collection, MHS.

67. St. Louis City Registrar's Records, MHS.

68. *Reveille*, July 9, 1849.

69. Minutes, 3 July 1849, MHS.

70. Family Bible, Hardage Lane Collection, MHS.

71. *Republican*, July 13, 1849.

72. Ibid.

73. Ibid., June 30, 1849.

74. *Republican*, July 4, 1849; Minutes, 2 July 1849, MHS.

75. Minutes, 3 July 1849, MHS.

76. Ibid., 5 July 1849.

77. Ibid.

78. Frank J. Lutz, ed., *The Autobiography and Reminiscences of S. Pollak, M.D.* (St. Louis: St. Louis Medical Review, 1904), 58–59.

79. Minutes, 8 July 1849, MHS; *Republican*, July 12, 1849.

80. Minutes, 14 July 1849, MHS.

81. Minutes, 7 July 1849, MHS.

82. *Republican*, July 10, 1849.

83. Ibid.; Minutes, 8 July 1849, MHS.

84. Minutes, 11 July 1849, MHS.

85. "Autobiography of John Martin," Mormon Migration, accessed May 23, 2017, https://mormonmigration.lib.byu.edu/mii/account/117.

86. *Republican*, July 22, 1849; McPheeters, "History of Epidemic Cholera," 103.

87. *Republican*, July 22, 1849.

88. Ibid., July 18, 1849.

89. Ibid., July 22, 1849; Ibid., July 25, 1849.

90. Ibid., July 22, 1849.

91. Ibid., July 28, 1849.

92. *Reveille*, August 5, 1849; *Republican*, July 31, 1849.

93. *Republican*, August 2, 1849.

94. McPheeters, "History of Epidemic Cholera," 106.

95. Ibid., 105.

Chapter Two

1. *Daily Missouri Republican* (St. Louis), November 11, 1848; *Republican*, December 3, 1848.

2. Reverend Charles Peabody diary, 15 December 1848, Missouri Historical Society (hereafter cited as MHS).

3. *Weekly Reveille* (St. Louis), January 1, 1849.

4. *Republican*, January 20, 1849.

5. *Reveille*, April 2, 1849.

6. *St. Louis Daily New Era*, March 5, 1849.

7. *Republican*, March 1, 1849; *Republican*, March 11, 1849.

8. *New Era*, January 5, 1849.

9. *Republican*, April 4, 1849.

10. Ibid., April 5, 1849.

11. *Reveille*, April 23, 1849; Willoughby M. Babcock, "Steamboat Travel on the Upper Mississippi in 1849," *Minnesota History Magazine* 7 (March 1926): 54–61.

12. *Reveille*, March 19, 1849.

13. J. Goldsborough Bruff, *Gold Rush: The Journals, Drawings, and Other Papers of J. Goldsborough Bruff, Captain, Washington City and California Mining Association, April 2, 1849–July 20, 1851*, eds. Georgia Willis Read, Ruth Gaines, and Frederick Webb Hodge (New York: Columbia University Press, 1944), 436–438; *Republican*, April 16, 1849.

14. Bruff, *Gold Rush*, 438.

15. Ibid.

16. *Republican*, March 11, 1849.

17. Edward McGowan, *The Strange Eventful History of Parker H. French* (Los Angeles: Glen Dawson, 1958); William Miles, *Journal of the Sufferings and Hardships of Capt. Parker H. French's Overland Expedition to California in 1850* (Chambersburg, PA: Valley Spirit Office, 1851).

18. *Republican*, May 17, 1849; *New Era*, May 28, 1849; J. H. Sloss, *1848 City Directory*, (St. Louis: Charles and Hammond, 1848), 87.

19. Miles, *Journal of the Sufferings and Hardships*, 5.

20. Sloss, *1848 City Directory*, 80, 229; *Republican*, February 21, 1849; *New Era*, March 8, 1849.

21. *New Era*, March 21, 1849.

22. *Republican*, February 21, 1849.

23. Ibid., May 17, 1849.

24. Ibid., May 4, 1849.

25. *Reveille*, May 7, 1849.

26. *New Era*, July 19, 1849; *New Era*, July 21, 1849.

27. *The Daily Crescent* (New Orleans), September 19, 1849; *The New York Herald*, January 20, 1850; Charles van Ravenswaay Papers, MHS; Charles van Ravenswaay, *Saint Louis: An Informal History of the City and Its People, 1764–1865* (St. Louis: Missouri Historical Society Press, 1991), 380; James P. Delgado, *Gold Rush Port: The Maritime Archaeology of San Francisco's Waterfront* (Berkeley: University of California Press, 2009).

28. Miles, *Journal of the Sufferings and Hardships*, 5–26.

29. E. G. Simmons to Simeon Leland, 9 May 1849, St. Louis History Collection, MHS.

30. Walter B. Stevens, *Missouri's Centennial* (Columbia: State Historical Society of Missouri, 1917), 264, 284; *Reveille*, August 27, 1849.

31. *New Era*, November 27, 1849.

Chapter Three

1. Sally Smith Flagg journal, St. Louis Volunteer Firemen Collection, Missouri Historical Society (hereafter cited as MHS).

2. Frederick A. Hodes, *Rising on the River: St. Louis 1822 to 1850, Explosive Growth from Town to City* (Tooele, UT: Patrice Press, 2009); "St. Louis in Patches," *Glimpses of the Past* 6 (1939): 18.

3. "St. Louis in Patches," 19; *The People's Organ* (St. Louis), May 21, 1849.

4. James Neal Primm, *Lion of the Valley: St. Louis, Missouri, 1764–1980*, 3rd ed. (St. Louis: Missouri Historical Society Press, 1998), 159–160; "St. Louis in Patches," 19–20.

5. Frederick M. Colburn account, St. Louis Volunteer Firemen Collection, MHS.

6. Reverend Charles Peabody diary, 29 October 1846, MHS; Peabody diary, 18 April 1848, MHS.

7. Peabody diary, 6 November 1846, MHS.

8. *St. Louis Daily New Era*, November 26, 1849.

9. Ibid., November 27, 1849.

10. *Daily Missouri Republican* (St. Louis), May 2, 1849.

11. Tom Lynch, *The Volunteer Fire Department of St. Louis, 1819–1859* (St. Louis: R. & T. A. Ennis, 1880), 98; Walter B. Stevens, *St. Louis: The Fourth City, 1764–1909* (St. Louis: S. J. Clarke, 1909), 1,070.

12. Lynch, *The Volunteer Fire Department*, 79, 22, 85.

13. Ibid., 86.

14. *Republican*, May 2, 1849; Mrs. John L. Carver account, St. Louis Volunteer Firemen Collection, MHS; Edward F. Mochel, comp., *1804–1859, A–K*, vol. 1, bk. 1, *Index to St. Louis, Missouri, Marriages* (St. Louis: St. Louis Genealogical Society, 1999), 124.

15. *Republican*, June 3, 1849.

16. John S. Beggs account, St. Louis Volunteer Firemen Collection, MHS.

17. Ibid.

18. *St. Louis Globe-Democrat*, December 28, 1890.

19. James T. Lloyd, *Lloyd's Steamboat Directory and Disasters on the Western Water. . . .* (Cincinnati: James T. Lloyd, 1856), 263.

20. Colburn account, MHS; Michael Fitzpatrick account, St. Louis Volunteer Firemen Collection, MHS.

21. Colburn account, MHS; Edward Edwards, *History of the Volunteer Fire Department of St. Louis* (St. Louis: Veteran Volunteer Firemen's Historical Society, 1906), 51; Hodes, *Rising on the River*, 399; *Globe-Democrat*, December 28, 1890.

22. James Leroy Carver account, St. Louis Volunteer Firemen Collection, MHS; J. H. Sloss, *1848 St. Louis City Directory* (St. Louis: Charles and Hammond, 1848), 49; George Kyler account, St. Louis Volunteer Firemen Collection, MHS.

23. Edwards, *History of the Volunteer Fire Department*, 56.

24. Ibid., 57.

25. Clarence Nelson Roberts, "The History of the Brick and Tile Industry in Missouri" (thesis, University of Missouri, 1950), 9.

26. James Carlisle account, St. Louis Volunteer Firemen Collection, MHS; Volunteer Firemen's Minutes, St. Louis Volunteer Firemen Collection, MHS.

27. Frances Sublette to Solomon Sublette, 21 May 1849, Sublette Papers, MHS; Firemen's Minutes, MHS.

28. Firemen's Minutes, MHS; Frank J. Lutz, ed., *The Autobiography and Reminiscences of S. Pollak, M.D.* (St. Louis: St. Louis Medical Review, 1904), 56.

29. Lutz, *Pollak*, 57.

30. *New Era*, May 22, 1849; Carlisle account, MHS.

31. *Republican*, May 23, 1849.

32. Edwards, *History of the Volunteer Fire Department*, 60.

33. Ibid., 63.

34. Fitzpatrick account, MHS.

35. *Republican*, April 23, 1874.

36. Carlisle account, MHS.

37. Edwards, *History of the Volunteer Fire Department*, 62–65; Joseph Boyce, "Thomas B. Targee and the Great St. Louis Fire," *Boston Courier* (reprint), May 31, 1849.

38. Fitzpatrick account, MHS.

39. Carver account, MHS.

40. Boyce, "Thomas B. Targee," May 31, 1849.

41. *Republican*, April 23, 1874.

42. Federal Reserve Bank of Minneapolis, accessed November 17, 2015, https://www.minneapolisfed.org/community/teaching-aids/cpi-calculator-information/consumer-price-index-1800.

43. *The Weekly Herald* (New York), May 26, 1849.

44. *Globe-Democrat*, December 28, 1890.

45. *Reveille*, May 20, 1849; Edwards, *History of the Volunteer Fire Department*, 34.

46. Kyler account, MHS.

47. *Republican*, June 3, 1849.

48. Lloyd, *Lloyd's Steamboat Directory*, 264; William Lass, *Navigating the Missouri: Steamboating on Nature's Highway, 1819–1935* (Norman, OK: Arthur H. Clark, 2008).

49. *Republican*, June 3, 1849.

50. Ibid., June 6, 1849.

51. Ibid.

52. Ibid.

53. *New Era*, June 9, 1849.

Chapter Four

1. *St. Louis Daily Union*, January 6, 1849.

2. *Daily Missouri Republican* (St. Louis), January 9, 1849; *Republican*, October 18, 1849; *Republican*, October 19, 1849.

3. *Weekly Reveille* (St. Louis), March 25, 1849.

4. Ibid., April 7, 1849.

5. *Republican*, March 30, 1849.

6. Ibid., March 25, 1849.

7. Ivan Reichard Maximilan, "Origins of Urban Police: Freedom and Order in Antebellum St. Louis" (Ph.D. dissertation, Washington University in St. Louis, 1978); *Mayor's Message to the City Council of St. Louis*, May 1849.

8. *Daily Union*, January 22, 1849.

9. Ibid., March 27, 1849.

10. *Republican*, April 7, 1849; *St. Louis Daily New Era*, April 6, 1849.

11. *Reveille*, April 10, 1849.

12. Ibid., April 7, 1849.

13. William A. Robards, *Reports of Cases Argued and Decided in the Supreme Court of the State of Missouri* vol. 12 (Jefferson City: James Luck, 1849); State v. Francis Conley, Criminal Record Book 6, Office of the Circuit Clerk–St. Louis, St. Louis Circuit Court Historical Records Project; "Francis Conley," Missouri State Penitentiary Database, http://s1.sos.mo.gov/records/archives/archivesdb/msp/Detail.aspx?id=68; "George Barnett," Missouri State Penitentiary Database, http://s1.sos.mo.gov/records/archives/archivesdb/msp/Detail.aspx?id=31; "William B. Thompson," Missouri State Penitentiary Database, http://s1.sos.mo.gov/records/archives/archivesdb/msp/Detail.aspx?id=32; *Annual Report of the Inspectors of Penitentiary to the General Assembly of the State of Missouri* (Jefferson City: James Luck, 1853).

14. *Republican*, May 5, 1849.

15. Ibid., May 6, 1849.

16. Ibid., April 6, 1849.

17. *Reveille*, April 12, 1849.

18. W. J. Rorabaugh, *The Alcoholic Republic: An American Tradition* (New York: Oxford University Press, 1979), 10.

19. *Reveille*, November 26, 1849.

20. *Republican*, July 15, 1849.

21. *Reveille*, July 23, 1849.

22. Ibid., January 1, 1849.

23. *Republican*, February 10, 1849; *Republican*, November 20, 1849; *Republican*, July 5, 1849.

24. "1850 United States Federal Census," Ancestry.com, accessed July 23, 2016, http://search.ancestry.com/search/db.aspx?dbid=8054&o_iid=61792&o_lid=61792&o_sch=Web+Property; J. H. Sloss, *1848 St. Louis City Directory* (St. Louis: Charles and Hammond, 1848), 129; *Republican*, August 26, 1849.

25. *Reveille*, May 28, 1849.

26. *Republican*, August 26, 1849.

27. Ibid.

28. *Reveille*, September 3, 1849.

29. Ibid.

30. *Republican*, August 26, 1849; *Republican*, August 29, 1849; *Republican*, August 30, 1849; *Republican*, September 1, 1849; *Deutsche Tribune*, September 30, 1849.

31. *Republican*, January 17, 1849.

32. Ibid., August 19, 1849; Ibid., October 30, 1849; Ibid., November 5, 1849.

Chapter Five

1. Donnie D. Bellamy, "The Education of Blacks in Missouri Prior to 1861," *The Journal of Negro History* 59, no. 2 (April 1974): 143–157.

2. *Missouri Courier* (Hannibal), October 25, 1849; William Wells Brown, *The Narrative of William W. Brown, An American Slave, Written by Himself* (London: Charles Gilpin, reprint 1849); Harrison Anthony Trexler, *Slavery in Missouri, 1804–1865* (Baltimore, MD: John Hopkins University Press, 1914), 226.

3. *St. Louis Daily New Era*, August 20, 1849.

4. Cyprian Clamorgan, *The Colored Aristocracy of St. Louis*, ed. Julie Winch (Columbia: University of Missouri Press, 1999), 45.

5. *The Revised Statutes of the State of Missouri. . . .* (St. Louis: Chambers & Knapp, 1845), 392.

6. Ira Berlin, *Slaves Without Masters: The Free Negro in the Antebellum South* (New York: New Press, 2007).

7. Donnie D. Bellamy, "Free Blacks in Antebellum Missouri, 1820–1860," *Missouri Historical Review* 67, no. 2 (January 1973): 198–226.

8. Louis P. Masur, *1831: Year of Eclipse* (New York: Hill and Wang, 2001), 9–62; Bellamy, "Free Blacks in Antebellum Missouri," 205.

9. St. Louis County Court Register, Book 5, 342 St. Louis County–Missouri Court Proceedings, MHS.

10. John Fletcher Darby, *Personal Recollections of Many Prominent People Whom I Have Known. . . .* (St. Louis: G. I. Jones, 1880), 241.

11. *The Revised Ordinances of the City of St. Louis, Revised and Digested by the Fifth City Council* (St. Louis: Chambers and Knapp, 1843), 312; *Weekly Reveille* (St. Louis), October 22, 1849.

12. *Revised Ordinances*, 311–313; *Daily Missouri Republican* (St. Louis), August 1, 1849.

13. *New Era*, November 23, 1849.

14. Ibid., December 12, 1849.

15. Trexler, *Slavery in Missouri*, 226.

16. Census Collection, MHS; *Republican*, December 28, 1849.

17. *Revised Ordinances*, 293.

18. *Republican*, December 23, 1846; *Republican*, December 11, 1846.

19. *The Revised Ordinances of the City of St. Louis, Revised and Digested by the City Council* (St. Louis: Chambers and Knapp, 1850), 394; *Republican*, July 4, 1849.

20. St. Louis County Minutes, Book 5, 346, Missouri State Archives; *Republican*, October 7, 1849.

21. *Reveille*, June 25, 1849.

22. *The New York Herald*, June 26, 1849.

23. *Republican*, June 18, 1849.

24. *New Era*, June 16, 1849.

25. Office of the Secretary of State, Missouri State Archives–St. Louis; Circuit Court Case Files, 1804–1875, Office of the Circuit Clerk–St. Louis, St. Louis Circuit Court Historical Records Project.

26. "U.S. French Catholic Church Records (Druin Collection) 1695–1954," Ancestry.com, http://search.ancestry.com/search/db.aspx?dbid=1111; *St. Louis Post-Dispatch*, November 19, 1895; *Republican*, June 14, 1849.

27. Marshall D. Hier, "Blood on the Barroom Floor, The 1855 O'Blenis Murder Trial," *St. Louis Bar Journal* 29, no. 4 (Spring 1993).

28. John A. Wright, *Discovering African-American St. Louis: A Guide to Historic Sites* (St. Louis: Missouri Historical Society Press, 1991), 3.

29. "1850 United States Federal Census," Ancestry.com, http://search.ancestry.com/search/db.aspx?dbid=8054&o_iid=61792&o_lid=61792&o_sch=Web+Property; Clamorgan, *The Colored Aristocracy*, 79.

30. Dexter Tiffany Collection, MHS; "1880 United States Federal Census," Ancestry.com, http://search.ancestry.com/search/db.aspx?dbid=6742; Thomas Pearson, ed., *Free Men and Women of Color in St Louis, 1821–1860* (St. Louis: St. Louis Public Library, 1997).

31. *New Era*, November 6, 1849; Joseph and Owen Lovejoy, *Memoir of the Rev. Elijah P. Lovejoy Who Was Murdered in the Defense of Liberty of the Press at Alton, Illinois, Nov. 7, 1837*, Richard C. Holt, ed. (St. Louis: Lovejoy Press, 2002); Brown, *Narrative*, 46.

32. *Republican*, November 13, 1846.

33. Brown, *Narrative*, 21, 41.

34. *Republican*, November 13, 1846.

35. Lea VanderVelde, *Mrs. Dred Scott: A Life on Slavery's Frontier* (New York: Oxford University Press, 2009), 268.

36. *Republican*, November 19, 1849.

37. *New Era*, November 5, 1849.

38. *St. Louis Daily Union*, January 3, 1849; *Republican*, January 8, 1849; Harriet Frazier, *Runaway and Freed Missouri Slaves and Those That Helped Them, 1763–1865* (Jefferson, NC: McFarland, 2004), 128.

39. *Republican*, October 10, 1849.

40. *Reveille*, September 13, 1849.

41. *Republican*, June 25, 1850.

42. Ibid., April 18, 1849.

43. Ibid., August 12, 1849.

44. William L. Andrews, *Six Women's Slave Narratives* (New York: Oxford University Press, 1988).

45. *Republican*, April 18, 1849; *Republican*, January 16, 1849.

46. Ibid., April 18, 1849.

47. *The North Star* (Rochester, NY), reprinted in the *Daily Wisconsin*, June 27, 1850.

48. *The National Era* (Washington, DC), September 24, 1849, reprinted in *The North Star* (Rochester, NY) November 5, 1849.

49. *North Star*, June 16, 1850.

50. Allan E. Yarema, *The American Colonization Society: An Avenue to Freedom?* (Lanham, MD: University Press of America, 2006), 36–42.

51. William Hyde and Howard L. Conard, eds., *Encyclopedia of the History*

of St. Louis: A Compendium of History and Biography for Ready Reference, vol. 2 (n.p.: Southern History, 1899), 869; *Republican*, March 17, 1849.

52. *Republican*, March 17, 1849.

53. Elizabeth Keckley, *Behind the Scenes; or, Thirty Years a Slave, and Four Years in the White House* (n.p.: G. W. Carleton, 1868), 44; VanderVelde, *Mrs. Dred Scott*, 274.

54. Keckley, *Thirty Years a Slave*, 56.

55. VanderVelde, *Mrs. Dred Scott*, 275.

56. Richard Edwards, *Edward's Great West and Her Commercial Metropolis and a Complete History of St. Louis* (St. Louis, 1860), 511.

57. "1840 United States Federal Census," Ancestry.com, http://search.ancestry.com/search/db.aspx?dbid=8057.

Chapter Six

1. Jeffrey S. Adler, *Yankee Merchants and the Making of the Urban West: The Rise and Fall of Antebellum St. Louis* (New York: Cambridge University Press, 1991).

2. James Neal Primm, *Lion of the Valley: St. Louis, Missouri, 1764–1980*, 3rd ed. (St. Louis: Missouri Historical Society Press, 1998), 106; John Ray Cable, *The Bank of the State of Missouri* (New York: Columbia University Press, 1923), 26.

3. Primm, *Lion of the Valley*, 182.

4. Ibid.

5. Edward Bates to Elihu Shepard, 24 July 1866, Elihu Shepard Papers, Missouri Historical Society (hereafter cited as MHS); Primm, *Lion of the Valley*, 116.

6. Lucy Ann Delaney, *From the Darkness Cometh the Light; or, Struggles for Freedom* (St. Louis: Publishing House of J. T. Smith, 1892), 36.

7. Edward J. Giddings, comp., *American Christian Rulers; or, Religion and Men of Government* (New York: Bromfield, 1890), 39; Edward Bates diary, Bates Family Papers, MHS.

8. Bates diary, MHS.

9. *The Trial of Nathaniel Childs, Jr., in the Criminal Court of St. Louis County on an Indictment Charging Him with the Embezzlement of Money Belonging to the Bank of the State of Missouri* (St. Louis: Chambers & Knapp, 1850), 5.

10. *St. Louis Daily New Era*, November 20, 1849; *Daily Commercial Bulletin and Missouri Literary Register*, December 9, 1836.

11. Mr. and Mrs. Francis Williams, comps., *Centenary Methodist Church of*

St. Louis: The First Hundred Years, 1839–1939 (St. Louis: Mound City Press, 1939).

12. *The Trial of Nathaniel Childs, Jr.*, 3.

13. Cable, *Bank of the State of Missouri*, 27.

14. *Daily Missouri Republican* (St. Louis), May 17, 1838; *Missouri Argus* (St. Louis), May 24, 1838.

15. *Journal of the Senate of the State of Missouri at the 11th Session of the Missouri General Assembly* (Jefferson City: James Luck, 1840), 576–578.

16. *The Trial of Nathaniel Childs, Jr.*, 15; "1850 United States Federal Census," Ancestry.com, http://search.ancestry.com/search/db.aspx?d-bid=8054&0_iid=61792&0_lid=61792&0_sch=Web+Property; Williams, *Centenary Methodist Church*, 64.

17. *The Trial of Nathaniel Childs, Jr.*, 17–19.

18. Ibid., 46.

19. Ibid., 5; Ibid. 3.

20. *New Era*, November 16, 1849; John D. Lawson, ed., *American State Trials: A Collection of the Important and Interesting Criminal Trials. . . .* (St. Louis: F. H. Thomas Law Book, 1914), 262.

21. *The Trial of Nathanial Childs, Jr.*, 22.

22. *New Era*, November 8, 1849.

23. *Republican*, August 19, 1849; *Weekly Missouri Statesman* (Columbia, MO), August 17, 1849.

24. *Statesman*, August 17, 1849.

25. *New Era*, March 8, 1849.

26. *The Trial of Nathanial Childs, Jr.*, 10, 20.

27. Ibid., 10.

28. Ibid., 69.

29. Lawson, ed., *American State Trials*, 277–278.

30. Bates diary, MHS.

31. Primm, *Lion of the Valley*, 279.

32. *The Trial of Nathaniel Childs, Jr.*, 1; Christopher Gordon, "Murder, Mayhem, and Modernity: St. Louis in 1849" (paper presented at the Annual Meeting of the Society for Historians of the Early American Republic, St. Louis, July 2013); *Republican*, November 9, 1849.

33. Lawson, ed., *American State Trials*, 208; "1850 United States Federal Census," Ancestry.com, http://search.ancestry.com/search/db.aspx-?dbid=8054&0_iid=61792&0_lid=61792&0_sch=Web+Property; "1870 United States Federal Census," Ancestry.com, http://search.ancestry.com/search/db.aspx?dbid=7163; "1880 United States Federal Census," Ancestry.com, http://search.ancestry.com/search/db.aspx?dbid=6742.

34. *The Trial of Nathaniel Childs, Jr.*, 12, 40–41; Lawson, ed., *American State Trials*, 263–264.

35. *The Trial of Nathanial Childs, Jr.*, 40–41.

36. Ibid., 14–15.

37. Lawson, ed., *American State Trials*, 289–290.

38. Ibid., 278–279.

39. *Republican*, November 11, 1849; *Republican*, November 18, 1849.

40. Bates diary, MHS.

41. *Argument in the Case of State of Missouri vs. N. Childs, Jr., Upon a Charge of Embezzling the Funds of the Bank of Missouri* (St. Louis, 1850), 15.

42. Ibid., 49.

43. *Daily Alta California* (San Francisco, CA), November 18, 1859; *Glasgow Weekly Times* (Glasgow, MO), July 14, 1859.

44. *Weekly Times*, July 14, 1859

45. *Daily Alta*, November 18, 1859.

46. "United States Census, 1880," FamilySearch.org, https://familysearch.org/search/collection/1417683.

Chapter Seven

1. *The Baltimore Sun*, May 26, 2006; Walter B. Stevens, "The Missouri Tavern," *Missouri Historical Review* 68, no. 1 (October 1973).

2. Charles Gibson autobiography, Missouri Historical Society (hereafter cited as MHS).

3. J. Thomas Scharf, *History of St. Louis City and County*, vol. 2 (St. Louis, 1883), 1,467.

4. *Daily Missouri Republican* (St. Louis), April 28, 1878; *Republican*, May 3, 1878.

5. *Weekly Reveille* (St. Louis), November 5, 1849.

6. *St. Louis Daily New Era*, October 31, 1849.

7. Ibid., October 30, 1849.

8. Ibid.

9. Ibid., October 31, 1849.

10. Ibid.

11. *Republican*, November 13, 1849.

12. Scharf, *History*, 1,467; *Republican*, November 4, 1849.

13. *Republican,* November 4, 1849.

14. Charles van Ravenswaay Papers, MHS; A. J. D. Stewart, ed., *The History of the Bench and Bar of Missouri* (n.p.: Legal Publishing, 1898), 94.

15. Van Ravenswaay Papers, MHS; Stewart, *Bench and Bar*, 94.

16. *New Era*, October 31, 1849.

17. *Daily Reveille*, November 5, 1849.

18. Scharf, *History*, 1,466–1,467.

19. *Republican*, November 8, 1849.

20. *New Era*, November 17, 1849.

21. Comtesse Alfred de Montesquiou to Charles P. Chouteau, 22 December 1849, Chouteau Family Papers, MHS.

22. Edward Bates diary, Bates Family Papers, MHS.

23. Ibid.

24. Ibid.

25. Scharf, *History*, 1,467.

26. Bates diary, MHS.

27. Ibid.

28. Janet A. Tighe, "Francis Wharton and the Nineteenth-Century Insanity Defense: The Origins of a Reform Tradition" *The American Journal of Legal History* 27, no. 3 (July 1983): 229.

29. Bates diary, MHS.

30. State v. Montesquiou, Court Records, Missouri State Archives.

31. Bates diary, MHS.

32. Missouri Circuit Court records, January 1850, Missouri State Archives; Charles Gibson autobiography, MHS.

33. Bates diary, MHS.

34. *United States Law Magazine*, 103.

35. Bates diary, MHS.

36. Ibid.

37. Ibid.

38. Ibid.

39. State v. Montesquiou, Missouri State Archives.

40. Ibid.

41. William Hyde and Howard L. Conard, eds., *Encyclopedia of the History of St. Louis: A Compendium of History and Biography for Ready Reference*, vol. 2 (n.p.: Southern History, 1899), 649–650.

42. Bates diary, MHS.

43. Ibid.

44. Gerard de Cessac to Charles P. Chouteau, 7 May 1851, Chouteau Family Papers, MHS; The *New York Times*, April 25, 1893.

45. Cessac to Chouteau, 20 July 1851, MHS; *St. Louis Post-Dispatch*, April 23, 1893.

46. John Fletcher Darby, *Personal Recollections of Many Prominent People Whom I Have Known. . . .* (St. Louis: G. I. Jones, 1880), 253.

Chapter Eight

1. June Wilkinson Dahl, *A History of Kirkwood, Missouri, 1851–1965* (Kirkwood, MO: Kirkwood Historical Society, 1965), 5–24.

2. Keith Eggener, *Cemeteries* (New York: W. W. Norton, 2010), 9–35.

3. Bellefontaine Cemetery, Bellefontaine Cemetery Association, 1863.

4. "Calvary Cemetery," Catholic Cemeteries of the Archdiocese of St. Louis, accessed January 27, 2017, http://archstl.org/cemeteries/index.php?option=com_content&task=view&id=91&Itemid=233.

5. Map of the City of St. Louis and vicinity, City of Carondelet, MHS; *Columbia Statesman* (Columbia, MO), July 14, 1864.

6. George Homan, ed., *A Sanitary Survey of St. Louis: Being a Series of Short Papers on Leading Public Health Topics Contributed by City Officials and Local Sanitarians* (Concord, NH: Republican Press Association, 1885), 16–17.

BIBLIOGRAPHY

Adler, Jeffrey S. *Yankee Merchants and the Making of the Urban West: The Rise and Fall of Antebellum St. Louis.* New York: Cambridge University Press, 1991.

Bakken, Gordon Morris and Alexandra Kindell, eds. *Encyclopedia of Immigration and Migration in the American West, Vol. 2 M–Z.* 2 vols. Thousand Oaks, CA: Sage Publications, 2006.

Barua, Dhiman, and William B. Greenough III, eds. *Cholera.* New York: Plenum Medical Book, 1992.

Bellamy, Donnie D. "Free Blacks in Antebellum Missouri, 1820–1860." *Missouri Historical Review* 67, no. 2 (January 1973): 198–226.

Bieber, Ralph P. "The Southwestern Trails to California in 1849." *Mississippi Valley Historical Review* 12, no. 3 (December 1925): 343–375.

Blair, Danny, and W. F. Rannie. "Wading to Pembina: 1849 Spring and Summer Weather in the Valley of the Red River of the North and Some Climatic Implications." *Great Plains Research: A Journal of Natural and Social Sciences* 4, no. 1 (February 1994): 3–26.

Brown, William Wells. *From Fugitive Slave to Free Man: The Autobiographies of William Wells Brown.* Edited by William L. Andrews. Columbia: University of Missouri Press, 2003.

Bruce, H. C. *The New Man: Twenty-Nine Years a Slave, Twenty-Nine Years a Free Man.* York, PA: P. Andstadt, 1895.

Cable, John Ray. *The Bank of the State of Missouri.* New York: Columbia University Press, 1923.

Chambers, William Nesbit. *Old Bullion Benton: Senator from the New West.* Boston: Little Brown, 1956.

Daily Missouri Republican. Multiple articles. 1849.

Darby, John Fletcher. *Personal Recollections: Many Prominent People Whom I Have Known. . . .* St. Louis: G. I. Jones, 1880.

Delgado, James P. *Gold Rush Port: The Maritime Archaeology of San Francisco's Waterfront.* Berkeley: University of California Press, 2009.

Edwards, Edward. *History of the Volunteer Fire Department of St. Louis.* St. Louis: Veteran Volunteer Firemen's Historical Society, 1906.

Gould, Emerson W. *Fifty Years on the Mississippi; or, Gould's History of River Navigation.* St. Louis: Nixon-Jones, 1889.

Green, James. *Green's St. Louis Directory for 1845.* St. Louis: James Green, 1845.

Greenspan, Ezra. *William Wells Brown: An African American Life*. New York: W. W. Norton, 2014.

Hodes, Frederick A. *Rising on the River: St. Louis 1822 to 1850, Explosive Growth from Town to City*. Tooele, UT: Patrice Press, 2009.

Lass, William. *Navigating the Missouri: Steamboating on Nature's Highway, 1819–1935*. Norman, OK: Arthur H. Clark, 2008.

Lutz, Frank J., ed. *The Autobiography and Reminiscences of S. Pollack, M.D.* St. Louis: St. Louis Medical Review, 1904.

Masur, Louis P. *1831: Year of Eclipse*. New York: Hill and Wang, 2001.

McAllister, Paul E. "Missouri Voters, 1840–1856: An Analysis of Antebellum Voting Behavior and Political Parties." Diss., University of Missouri–Columbia, August 1976.

McGowan, Edward. *The Strange Eventful History of Parker H. French*. Los Angeles: Glen Dawson, 1958.

Miles, William. *Journal of the Sufferings and Hardships of Capt. Parker H. French's Overland Expedition to California in 1850*. Chambersburg, PA: Valley Spirit Office, 1851.

Mochel, Edward F., comp. *Index to St. Louis, Missouri, Marriages, 1804–1859, A–K*. Vol. 1, book 1. St. Louis: St. Louis Genealogical Society, 1999.

O'Connor, Candace. *A Surgical Department of Distinction: 100 Years of Surgery at Washington University School of Medicine*. St. Louis: Washington University in St. Louis, 2014.

Primm, James Neal. *Economic Policy in the Development of a Western State, Missouri, 1820–1860*. Cambridge, MA: Harvard University Press, 1954.

———. *Lion of the Valley: St. Louis, Missouri, 1764–1980*. 3rd ed. St. Louis: Missouri Historical Society Press, 1998.

Bruff, J. Goldsborough. *Gold Rush: The Journals, Drawings, and Other Papers of J. Goldsborough Bruff, Captain, Washington City and California Mining Assocaition, April 2, 1849–July 20, 1851*. Edited by Ruth Gaines and Georgia Willis Read. New York: Columbia University Press, 1944.

Rorabaugh, W. J. *The Alcoholic Republic: An American Tradition*. New York: Oxford University Press, 1979.

Sloss, J. H. *St. Louis City Directory for 1848*. St. Louis: Charles and Hammond, 1848.

Stevens, Walter B. *Missouri's Centennial*. Columbia: State Historical Society of Missouri, 1917.

Thomas, Emory M. *Robert E. Lee: A Biography*. New York: W. W. Norton, 1995.

Van Ravenswaay, Charles. *Saint Louis: An Informal History of the City and its People, 1764–1865*. St. Louis: Missouri Historical Society Press, 1991.

VanderVelde, Lea. *Mrs. Dred Scott: A Life on Slavery's Frontier*. New York: Oxford University Press, 2009.

Williams, Mr. and Mrs. Francis, comps. *Centenary Methodist Church of St. Louis: The First Hundred Years, 1839–1939*. St. Louis: Mound City Press, 1939.

Wilson, Rob. "The Disease of Fear and the Fear of Disease: Cholera and Yellow Fever in the Mississippi Valley." Diss. Saint Louis University, 2007.

Yarema, Allan E. *The American Colonization Society: An Avenue to Freedom?* Lanham, MD: University Press of America, 2006.

INDEX

abolitionism, 10, 154, 168, 182
Acadia boat, 105
African American community, 10,
  153–190
Alexander Hamilton boat, 105
Alice boat, 105
Alvarez, Joe, 165
American Colonization Society, 196
American Eagle boat, 105
Apollo Hall boat, 115
Arsenal Island. *See* Quarantine
  Island

Bank of the State of Missouri, 194,
  197, 201, 220
Barnett, George, 128
Barnum, Kirby, 225, 233, 236
Barnum, Theron, 223, 226, 237
Barry, Mayor James, 34, 35, 47, 59,
  112, 120
Bates, Edward, 13, 44, 104, 170, 185,
  195–221, *196*, 223–246
Battle Row, 109
Beggs, John S., 103
*Behind the Scenes; or, Thirty Years a
  Slave, and Four Years in the White
  House*, 187
Bellefontaine Cemetery, 147, 250
Belle Isle boat, 105
Benton, Thomas Hart, 10, 182, *183*, 208
Biddle, Ann, 17, 20
Blennerhasset, R. S., 207
Blount, Charles, 122–124
Boreas Number Three boat, 105
Boyce, Joseph, 114
Brown, William Wells, 154, 168
Bruff, J. Gainsborough, 77
Burnt District, 119, 124

Calvary Cemetery, 249, 250
Carlisle, Captain James S., 108–113
Centenary Methodist Church, 200

Central Fire Company No. 1, 107
Cessac, Gerard de, 233
Childs Jr., Nathaniel, 199–221
cholera, 13–67; ban on produce,
  54–56; burials, 60–61; causes,
  14–17, 37–38; earlier pandemics,
  13–19; end, 66; hospitals, 48–51;
  number of victims, 67; orphans,
  47; pollution, 17, 26–30, 38–40,
  54; public morale, 44; quarantine
  boat, 51
Chouteau, Charles, 233
Chouteau's Pond, 29, 251
City Cemetery, 141, 250
City Hotel, 223
Clamorgan, Cyprian, 156, 166
Clamorgan, Jacques, 166
Clark, Thaddeus, 128
Clementine, Madame, 143–147, 165
Colburn, Frederick, 105, 106
colonization, 184
*Colored Aristocracy of St. Louis,
  The*, 156
Colt, James B., 238
Committee of Public Health, 36, 40,
  44, 48, 51
Couley, Francis, 129–131, 138, 139
Couzins, J. E. D., 131–139, *135*
crime, 10, 79, 127–150

Delaney, Lucy Ann, 170, 196
DeSmet, Father Pierre Jean, 236
Donovan, Michael, 148

Eliza Stewart boat, 105
Elliot, Richard, 249
Esther, 166
Eudora boat, 106, 108, 122, 123
Excelsior Stove Works, 8, *9*

Fayette Clique, 182
Field, Roswell Martin, 207

Index

Filley, Giles Franklin, 8–9
Fitzpatrick, Michael, 113, 116, 117
Forbes, Isaac, 204, 210–213
Foster, David, 135
Franklin Fire Company, 103, 107, 108, 121
free blacks, 155–167
freedom suits, 170
Free-Soilism, 183
French, Parker H., 79–85
Frolic boat, 105

Garland, Hugh, 185–188
General Brooke boat, 105
German community, 8, 33, 39, 55, 143
Geyer, Henry, 208, 213, 218, 219, 238
Gibson, Charles, 238, 243
gold fever, 10, 69–87; crime, 79; Matilda, 81–85; Parker H. French, 79–85; travel, 75
Gorman, Patrick, 100, 112–113
Great Fire, 88–124; aftermath, 117; begins, 101; cause, 120; damage and death toll, 118; ends, 116; firebreak, 114; looters, 111; property destruction, 110; spreads to levee, 106; spreads to steamboats, 104; Captain Thomas Targee, 114–116, 119

Happy Hollow neighborhood, 158
Hawken, Samuel, 101
Hawks, Cicero S., 231
Henderson, H. M., 226
Hubbell, Captain William, 226
Hughes, James, 205
Hurschburg, L. C., 198, 203, 216

Irish community, 8, 39, 40, 62, 64–66, 109, 143

Jackson, Claiborne Fox, 182
Jackson, Mattie J., 177, 190
Jones, Albert, 165, 226, 229, 236
Jones, Collin, 163
Julia boat, 105

Keckley, Elizabeth, 187–188
Kennett, Luther, 55
Kirkwood Association, 249
Kit Carson boat, 105
Kitzmiller, William W., 123
Krum, Mayor John, 106, 133, 161

LaBeaume, Theodore, 230–234
Lackland, James, 238
Lambert, George, 148
Lambert, Sarah, 148
Lane, Dr. Hardage, 19, 20, 49, 50
Lee, Robert E., 26
Leffingwell, Hiram, 249
Liberty Fire Company, 103, 106, 107, 113, 117
Locofocos, 194, 206
Long, John, 243
Lovejoy, Elijah P., 161, 168
Lynch, Bernard M., 177, 178
Lyon, Charles, 161

Macomber, John, 225, 226
Madame Clementine's brothel, 143
Mameluke boat, 105
Mandan boat, 105
Martha boat, 105, 111, 112, 119
Matilda boat, 81–85
McDowell, Dr. Joseph Nash, 8, 24, 207
McPheeters, Dr. William, 21, 34, 42, 61, 66, 67
Mexican War, 9, 10
Meyercourt, Henry, 143–147
Michau, Saugrain, 138
Missouri Fire Company, 103, 107, 114, 115
Missouri Compromise, 155
M'Naghten Rules, 235
Montauk boat, 105
Montesquiou, Arthur de, 233–234
Montesquiou, Gonsalve de, 223–246
Montesquiou, Raymond, 223–246
Moran, John, 128
Mound Fire Company, 107, 117
Mount Olive Cemetery, 189
Mower, Lyman, 165

Nisbet case, 128–132, 134–139

O'Blenis, Robert Mac, 165, 229, 231
O'Fallon, John, 169
Old Cathedral, 113, 117
Old Courthouse, 180
Oliffe, Charles, 233

Pentland, Arthur, 123
police force, 132–134
Polk, Trusten, 207
Pollak, Dr. Simon, 55–56, 110
population, 6, 17
Potts, Reverend William Stephen, 32
Prairie State boat, 105
Price, Enoch, 155, 169
Price, Governor Sterling, 139
Primm, Wilson, 238
prostitution, 10

Quarantine Island, 52–54, *53*, 57–59, 63

racism, 153
Red Wing boat, 105
Rock Springs Cemetery, 45, 250
Rural Cemetery Association, 250
Ryland, John, 210–213

Saint Peters boat, 105
Sarah boat, 105, 121
Scott, Dred, 188
Shurlds, Henry, 198, 202, 204, 205, 213–215
slavery, 8, 10, 153–155; colonization, 184; escape, 170–178; slave sales, 178–182
Snow, Dr. John, 14, 67
Sons of Temperance, 141
South Market building, 108, 112, 117
State of Missouri v. Nathaniel Childs, Jr., 209
St. Louis, alcoholism, 140; crime, 10, 79, 127–150; infrastructure, 17; mob violence, 143; police force, 132; pollution, 17, 26–30, 38–40, 54; population, 6, 17; prostitution,

10; religious tension, 8; riots, 143; slavery, 8, 10, 153–155, 170–182, 184; volunteer fire companies, 98–116
St. Louis Anti-Abolitionist Society, 168, 170
St. Louis Arsenal, 114
St. Louis Greys, 66
St. Louis steamboat, 51, 52, 54, 57
Sturgeon, Isaac, 112, 116, 119, 229
Sublette, Frances, 110
Sutter, John, 10

Taglioni boat, 105, 121
Targee, Captain Thomas, 114–116, *115*, 119
temperance societies, 140
Thompson, William B., 128
Timour boat, 105

Union Fire Company, *99*, *100*, 101, 107, 112, 113

Veteran Volunteer Firemen's Historical Society of St. Louis, 114
volunteer fire companies, 98–116

Washington City and California Mining Association, 77
Wegman, Peter, 47
White Cloud steamboat, 102, 104, 119–123
Whitlock, Margaret, 210–213, 217, 220
Wilkinson, Joseph, 165
Williams, Willis, 208, 210–213, 218, 220
Withnell, John, 189
Wm. Nisbet & Co., 128–139
Wright, Anna Jarette. *See* Clementine, Madame
Wright, Uriah, 207, 219

Yeatman, James, 210–213, *211*

ABOUT THE AUTHOR

Christopher Gordon has been the director of library and collections for the Missouri Historical Society since 2007. He frequently writes, teaches, and lectures on Missouri and American history.